Lecture Notes in Artificial Intelligence 2938

Edited by J. G. Carbonell and J. Siekmann

Subseries of Lecture Notes in Computer Science

Springer
Berlin
Heidelberg
New York
Hong Kong
London
Milan
Paris
Tokyo

Zili Zhang Chengqi Zhang

Agent-Based Hybrid Intelligent Systems

An Agent-Based Framework for Complex Problem Solving

Series Editors

Jaime G. Carbonell, Carnegie Mellon University, Pittsburgh, PA, USA
Jörg Siekmann, University of Saarland, Saarbrücken, Germany

Authors

Zili Zhang
Southwest China Normal University
Faculty of Computer and Information Science
Chongqing 400715, China
E-mail: zhangzl@swnu.edu.cn

Chengqi Zhang
Deakin University
School of Information Technology
Geelong, VIC 3217, Australia
E-mail: zzhang@deakin.edu.au

Cataloging-in-Publication Data applied for

A catalog record for this book is available from the Library of Congress.

Bibliographic information published by Die Deutsche Bibliothek
Die Deutsche Bibliothek lists this publication in the Deutsche Nationalbibliografie; detailed bibliographic data is available in the Internet at <http://dnb.ddb.de>.

CR Subject Classification (1998): I.2, D.2, H.2.8, J.1, F.1

ISSN 0302-9743
ISBN 3-540-20908-5 Springer-Verlag Berlin Heidelberg New York

Springer-Verlag is a part of Springer Science+Business Media

springeronline.com

Printed in Germany

Typesetting: Camera-ready by author, data conversion by Olgun Computergrafik
Printed on acid-free paper SPIN: 10981160 06/3142 5 4 3 2 1 0

Preface

Many complex problems, such as financial investment planning, involve many different components or sub-tasks, each of which requires different types of processing. To solve such complex problems, a great diversity of intelligent techniques, including traditional hard computing techniques (e.g., expert systems) and soft computing techniques (e.g., fuzzy logic, neural networks, and genetic algorithms), are required. These techniques are complementary rather than competitive, and thus must be used in combination and not exclusively. This results in systems called *hybrid intelligent systems*. In other words, hybrid solutions are crucial for complex problem solving and decision-making. However, the design and development of hybrid intelligent systems is difficult because they have a large number of parts or components that have many interactions. Existing software development techniques cannot manage these complex interactions efficiently as these interactions may occur at unpredictable times, for unpredictable reasons, and between unpredictable components.

An *agent* is an encapsulated computer system that is situated in a certain environment and that is capable of flexible, autonomous action in that environment in order to meet its design objectives. A multi-agent system (MAS) can be defined as a loosely coupled network of entities that work together to make decisions or solve problems that are beyond the individual capabilities or knowledge of each entity. These entities, or agents, are autonomous and may be heterogeneous in nature. Thus, from a multi-agent perspective, agents in MASs are autonomous and can engage in flexible, high-level interactions. The flexible nature of interactions means that agents can make decisions about the nature and scope of interactions at run-time rather than design time. Such agents are good at dealing with complex, dynamic interactions. They offer a new and often more appropriate route to the development of complex systems, especially in open and dynamic environments. It is now widely recognized that *interaction* is probably the single most important characteristic of complex software. It is evident that hybrid intelligent systems are typical complex systems, as they have a large number of parts or components with many interactions. Thus agent perspectives are well suited to hybrid intelligent system construction, especially where loosely coupled hybrid intelligent systems are concerned.

This book presents an agent-based framework that can greatly facilitate the building of hybrid intelligent systems, as well as two agent-based hybrid intelligent systems based on that framework. These two systems, one for financial investment planning and one for data mining, are based on real-life applications and are used here to demonstrate how to analyze, design and implement such systems from the viewpoints of agents.

This book strongly advocates the construction of hybrid intelligent systems from an agent's point of view. Each intelligent technique/model is treated as one building block of a hybrid intelligent system in the form of an agent. Different intelligent techniques can easily be integrated into one loosely coupled hybrid intelligent system under a unifying agent framework. Because of this, many complex problems can be solved within a shorter timeframe. Also, due to a variety of complementary problem-solving techniques/approaches being combined together, higher-quality solutions can be produced with such systems.

The book consists of nine chapters, which are divided into four major parts.

Part I comprises an introduction. Chapter 1 discusses the importance of hybrid intelligent systems for complex problem solving and decision-making, and explains why agent perspectives are suitable for modeling, designing and constructing hybrid intelligent systems.

Chapter 2 briefly presents some basic concepts and existing knowledge on hybrid intelligent systems. The advantages and disadvantages of different intelligent techniques are summarized. The drawbacks in the current practice of hybrid intelligent system development are identified. In Chap. 3, the fundamentals of agents and multi-agent systems are introduced. The distinctions between agents and objects, as well as agents and expert systems, are presented. A brief survey of typical agent-based hybrid intelligent systems and some approaches to incorporating intelligent techniques into agents are provided. Typical approaches to converting legacy intelligent-technique software packages into agents are also given. State-of-the-art agent-based hybrid intelligent systems are summarized.

Part II presents the methodologies and framework for hybrid intelligent system construction from an agent perspective. Chapter 4 first discusses some typical agent-oriented methodologies. A methodology suitable for analysis and design of agent-based hybrid intelligent systems is then extracted and tailored from the current practice of agent-oriented software engineering, which is mainly based on the *Gaia* methodology.

In Chap. 5, a unifying agent-based framework for building hybrid intelligent systems is proposed. The ontology issue, which is important for application system development, is addressed. Chapter 6 discusses matchmaking in middle agents, which is crucial for the success of agent-based hybrid intelligent systems. This chapter also addresses some improvements to matchmaking algorithms which are currently used.

Part III presents two agent-based hybrid intelligent systems, one for financial investment planning, the other for data mining. Both are built based upon the framework proposed in Chap. 5. Chapter 7 discusses the analysis, design and implementation of an agent-based hybrid intelligent system for financial investment planning. This system consists of 13 different agents. Many techniques/packages, including fuzzy logic, neural networks, genetic algorithms, expert systems, an operations research software package, a matrix operation software package, portfolio selection models based on standard probability theory, fuzzy probability theory, and possibility distribution theory, are integrated under the unifying agent framework.

Chapter 8 presents another application system–agent-based hybrid intelligent system for data mining. The *Weka* system is reimplemented from agent perspectives. Different data mining techniques/algorithms can be easily integrated into a data mining system in the form of agents for a specific mining task.

Part IV contains concluding remarks, in which Chap. 9 summarizes this book. The future work of the proposed agent-based framework is pointed out.

Many thanks go to the Faculty of Computer and Information Science at Southwest China Normal University, the School of Information Technology at Deakin University, and the Faculty of Information Technology at the University of Technology, Sydney, which provided support for us to complete this book. Special thanks to Alfred Hofmann at Springer-Verlag.

Chongqing, Geelong and Sydney
November 2003

Zili Zhang
Chengqi Zhang

Contents

Part I Fundamentals of Hybrid Intelligent Systems and Agents

1 **Introduction** ... 3
  1.1 Hybrid Intelligent Systems Are Essential for Solving Complex Problems ... 4
  1.2 Hybrids Are Complex ... 5
  1.3 Agent Perspectives Are Suitable for Hybrids ... 7
  1.4 Motivation and Targets ... 11

2 **Basics of Hybrid Intelligent Systems** ... 13
  2.1 Typical Intelligent Techniques ... 14
    2.1.1 Expert Systems ... 14
    2.1.2 Fuzzy Sets and Fuzzy Logic ... 15
    2.1.3 Neural Networks ... 16
    2.1.4 Genetic Algorithms ... 19
  2.2 Advantages and Disadvantages of Typical Intelligent Techniques ... 21
    2.2.1 Knowledge Acquisition ... 21
    2.2.2 Brittleness ... 21
    2.2.3 Explanation ... 22
  2.3 Classification of Hybrid Intelligent Systems ... 23
    2.3.1 Medsker's Classification Scheme ... 23
    2.3.2 Goonatilake's Classification Scheme ... 26
  2.4 Current Practice in Typical Hybrid Intelligent System Development ... 27

3 **Basics of Agents and Multi-agent Systems** ... 29
  3.1 Concepts of Agents and Multi-agent Systems ... 29
  3.2 Agents as a Paradigm for Software Engineering ... 30
  3.3 Agents and Objects ... 31
  3.4 Agents and Expert Systems ... 33

3.5 Approaches to Agentification ... 33
3.5.1 Implementing a Transducer ... 34
3.5.2 Implementing a Wrapper ... 34
3.5.3 Rewriting ... 34
3.5.4 Steps for Implementing a Wrapper ... 34
3.6 Approaches to Incorporating Intelligent Techniques into Agents ... 35
3.7 Agent-Based Hybrid Systems: State of the Art ... 35
3.7.1 The MIX Multi-agent Platform ... 35
3.7.2 The PREDICTOR System ... 36
3.7.3 Intelligent Multi-agent Hybrid Distributed Architecture ... 37
3.7.4 Multi-agent Architecture for Fuzzy Modeling ... 38
3.7.5 Generic Architecture for Hybrid Intelligent Systems ... 38
3.7.6 Summary ... 38

Part II Methodology and Framework

4 Agent-Oriented Methodologies ... 43
4.1 Traditional Methodologies ... 43
4.2 Gaia Methodology ... 44
4.3 Coordination-Oriented Methodology ... 45
4.4 Prometheus Methodology ... 45
4.5 Methodology for Analysis and Design of Agent-Based Hybrids ... 46
4.5.1 Outline of the Methodology ... 46
4.5.2 Role Model ... 49
4.5.3 Interaction Model ... 51
4.5.4 Organizational Rules ... 52
4.5.5 Agent Model ... 53
4.5.6 Skill Model ... 53
4.5.7 Knowledge Model ... 54
4.5.8 Organizational Structures and Patterns ... 54
4.6 Summary ... 55

5 Agent-Based Framework for Hybrid Intelligent Systems ... 57
5.1 A Unifying Agent Framework for Hybrid Intelligent Systems ... 57
5.2 Issues on Ontologies ... 59
5.2.1 Why Ontologies? ... 60
5.2.2 Ontologies in Finance ... 60
5.2.3 Construction of Financial Ontology ... 61
5.3 Summary ... 63

6 Matchmaking in Middle Agents 65
6.1 Description of the Problem 66
6.2 Related Work of Matchmaking in Middle Agents 67
6.3 Improvements to Matchmaking Algorithms in Middle Agents 73
6.3.1 Representation of Track Records 73
6.3.2 Accumulation of Track Records 74
6.3.3 Generation of Initial Values 74
6.3.4 Use of Track Records 85
6.3.5 Impact of Track Records on Matchmaking 88
6.4 Discussion 90

Part III Application Systems

7 Agent-Based Hybrid Intelligent System for Financial Investment Planning 93
7.1 Introduction to Some Models Integrated in the System 94
7.1.1 Financial Risk Tolerance Model 94
7.1.2 Asset Allocation Model 95
7.1.3 Portfolio Selection Models 96
7.1.4 Interest Prediction Models 99
7.1.5 Ordered Weighted Averaging Operation 100
7.2 Analysis of the System 104
7.3 Design of the System 108
7.4 Architecture of the System 111
7.5 Implementation of the System 112
7.5.1 Internal Structures of Agents 113
7.5.2 Practical Architecture of the System 115
7.6 Case Study 116
7.6.1 A Typical Scenario for Investment 117
7.6.2 Example 117
7.6.3 Running the System 121
7.6.4 Empirical Evaluation of the Aggregated Results 122

8 Agent-Based Hybrid Intelligent System for Data Mining 127
8.1 Typical Data Mining Techniques 128
8.1.1 Classification 128
8.1.2 Clustering 130
8.1.3 Association Rules 131
8.2 Data Mining Requires Hybrid Solutions 133
8.3 Requirements of the Agent-Based Hybrid Systems for Data Mining 134
8.4 Analysis and Design of the System 135
8.5 Implementation of the System 138
8.6 Case Study 140

Part IV Concluding Remarks

9 The Less the More 145
- 9.1 Flexibility and Robustness Testing 145
- 9.2 Future Work 146

Appendix: Sample Source Codes of the Agent-Based Financial Planning System 149
- A Source Codes for Data Supply Agent (StockData) 150
- B Source Codes of Planning Agent for Portfolio Selection (Stock) 153
- C Source Codes for Portfolio Selection Agent Based on Markowitz's Model (Moki) 159
- D Source Codes for Portfolio Selection Agent Based on Fuzzy Logic Model (Fuzz) 162
- E Source Codes for Portfolio Selection Agent Based on Possibility Distribution Model (Poss) 165
- F Source Codes for Decision Aggregation Agent Based on Ordered Weighted Averaging Operators (Aggr) 168
- G Source Codes for Planning Agent of Investment Decision-Making (Invpolicy) 170
- H Source Codes for Investment Decision-Making Agent (Invppt) . 173
- I Source Codes for Interest Prediction Agent Based on Fuzzy Logic and Genetic Algorithms (Flga) 176
- J Source Codes for Interest Prediction Agent Based on Neural Networks (Ffin) 179

References 183

Index 193

List of Figures

1.1 View of a Canonical Complex System 9
1.2 Canonical View of a Multi-Agent System 9

2.1 Basic Structure of an Expert System 15
2.2 An Example of a Two-Dimensional FAM Matrix 17
2.3 Three-Layer Feedforward Neural Network Architecture 18
2.4 Models for Integrating Intelligent Systems 24
2.5 Hybrid Intelligent System Development Cycle 27

3.1 Architecture of PREDICTOR 36
3.2 Agent Building Blocks of IMAHDA 37

4.1 Relationships between Models 48
4.2 Template for Role Schemata 50
4.3 Schema for Role PRICEWATCHER 51
4.4 The GetPrice Protocol Definition 52

5.1 General Framework of Agent-Based Hybrid Intelligent Systems. 58
5.2 Financial Ontology Conceptual Structure (Example) 62

6.1 Curves of Benchmark Values, SC_Agent_NN, and SC_Agent_FLGA 80
6.2 Distances with Benchmark Values 80

7.1 Decision Table for Output *savings* 96
7.2 Decision Table for Output *income* 96
7.3 Decision Table for Output *growth* 96
7.4 Block Diagram for the Interest Rate Model 100
7.5 Schema for Role USERHANDLER 105
7.6 Schema for Role WORKPLANNER 105
7.7 Schema for Role CAPABILITYRECORDER 106
7.8 Schema for Role CAPABILITYMATCHER 106

7.9 Schema for Role DecisionMaker ... 107
7.10 Schema for Role HelpProvider ... 107
7.11 Schema for Role DecisionAggregator ... 108
7.12 Schema for Role User ... 108
7.13 Definition of Protocols Associated with the DecisionMaker Role: (**a**) ReceiveTask, (**b**) GetInformation, (**c**) AskforHelp, and (**d**) InformDecisionAggregator ... 109
7.14 Agent Model of the Financial Planning System ... 110
7.15 Architecture of Agent-Based Financial Investment Planning System ... 111
7.16 Decision Making Agent Structure ... 113
7.17 Serving Agent Structure ... 113
7.18 Intelligent Technique Agent Structure ... 114
7.19 Aggregation Agent Structure ... 114
7.20 Planning Agent Structure ... 114
7.21 Interface Agent Structure ... 114
7.22 Practical Architecture of Financial Investment Planning System ... 116
7.23 User Interface of Financial Investment Planning System ... 116
7.24 Example Asset Allocation Results ... 121
7.25 Example Explanations of Financial Planning System ... 122
7.26 Comparison of the Portfolios ... 123

8.1 Classification of Clustering Algorithms ... 131
8.2 Schema for the Role AttributeSelector ... 136
8.3 Schema for Role AssociationRuleMiner ... 136
8.4 Schema for Role ResultAccuracyAnalyzer ... 137
8.5 Definition of Protocols Associated with the AssociationRuleMiner Role: (a) ReceiveTask, (b) AccessItemsets, and (c) SendMinedResults. ... 137
8.6 Agent Model for the Data Mining System ... 138
8.7 Architecture of Agent-Based Data Mining System ... 139
8.8 Planning Agent Structure ... 140
8.9 User Interface of the System ... 141
8.10 Output from the M5 Agent for Numeric Prediction ... 142

List of Tables

2.1 Property Assessment of Typical Intelligent Techniques 23

4.1 Operators for Liveness Expressions 51

6.1 Description of Benchmark (BM) Problems 76
6.2 Mapping Results between Distance and Satisfactory Degree 76
6.3 Change in Consumer Price Index 77
6.4 Change in Gross National Product in 1982 US Dollars (Billions) 78
6.5 Change in M2 Money Supply in 1982 US Dollars (Billions) 78
6.6 Personal Wealth in 1982 US Dollars (Billions) 78
6.7 Two-Quarter Moving Average Change in T-Bill Discount Rate . 79
6.8 Predicting Results on Benchmark Problems 79
6.9 Agents' Solutions to One Benchmark Problem 84
6.10 Partial Benchmark Values for Benchmark Problems 84
6.11 Distances between Agents' Solutions and Benchmark Values ... 85
6.12 Track Records with n = 40 89
6.13 Agents' Scores with Different Track Records 89

7.1 Services in Skill Model 110
7.2 Returns on Nine Securities 120
7.3 Portfolios and Variances Based on 12 Years Return Data 123
7.4 Realized Average Returns of the Portfolios (%) 124
7.5 Returns on Twelve Securities from ASX 124
7.6 Portfolios and Variances Based on ASX 8 Years Return Data .. 124
7.7 Realized Average Returns of the Portfolios Based on ASX Data (%) 125

1 Introduction

Solving complex problems, such as financial investment planning, foreign exchange trading, and knowledge discovery from large/multiple databases, involves many different components or sub-tasks, each of which requires different types of processing. To solve such complex problems, a great diversity of intelligent techniques, including traditional hard computing techniques (e.g., expert systems) and soft computing techniques (e.g., fuzzy logic, neural networks, and genetic algorithms), are required. For example, in financial investment planning, neural networks can be used as a pattern watcher for the stock market; genetic algorithms can be used to predict interest rates; and approximate reasoning based on fuzzy logic can be used to evaluate financial risk tolerance ability of clients. These techniques (referred to here as *intelligent techniques*) are complementary rather than competitive, and thus must be used in combination and not exclusively [12]. This results in systems called *hybrid intelligent systems* [65]. Hybrid solutions are crucial for complex problem solving and decision making. However, the design and development of hybrid intelligent systems is difficult, because they have a large number of parts or components with many interactions. Existing software development techniques cannot manage these complex interactions efficiently, as these interactions may occur at unpredictable times, for unpredictable reasons, and between unpredictable components [81].

Multi-agent systems are systems composed of multiple interacting computing elements, known as *agents*. Agents are computer systems with two important capabilities. First, they are at least to some extent capable of *autonomous action* – of deciding *for themselves* what they need to do in order to satisfy their design objectives. Second, they are capable of interacting with other agents – not simply by exchanging data, but by engaging in analogue of the kind of social activity that we all engage in every day of our lives: cooperation, coordination, negotiation, and the like [4].

Some researchers in the agent research community have produced a qualitative analysis to provide the intellectual justification of precisely why agent-based systems are well suited to engineering complex software systems [2, 71].

Z. Zhang, C. Zhang: Agent-Based Hybrid Intelligent Systems, LNAI 2938, pp. 3–11, 2004.

On the other hand, hybrid intelligent systems are complex software systems because they have a large number of parts or components that have many interactions. Thus a multi-agent perspective is suitable for the modeling, design, and construction of hybrid intelligent systems [126]. Furthermore, the flexible nature of agent interactions means that agents can make decisions about the nature and scope of interactions at run-time rather than design time. This can overcome the shortcomings in the current practices of hybrid intelligent system development [65].

In the rest of this chapter, it will be argued that hybrid intelligent systems are required for dealing with complex problems, hybrid intelligent systems are complicated systems, and that agent perspectives are suitable for these complex systems.

1.1 Hybrid Intelligent Systems Are Essential for Solving Complex Problems

In complex problem solving and decision making many different components or sub-tasks are involved, each of which requires different types of processing. Because of this, many techniques have been developed for complex problem solving and decision making. These techniques can be divided into two categories:

- traditional hard computing techniques, including operations research, system science/engineering, expert systems, and
- soft computing techniques, including fuzzy logic, neural networks, and genetic algorithms.

The techniques in both categories are referred to here as *intelligent techniques*.

While there is now an array of different types of intelligent techniques, each technique has particular strengths and limitations, and cannot be successfully applied to every type of problem (refer to Sect. 2.2). For example, in a decision making task that requires explicit explanations, neural networks are less applicable than a rule induction approach. Similarly, for tasks that require constant adaptation and learning from the operating environment, a static expert system is far less useful than an adaptive technique such as a neural network. As we have said, these techniques and methodologies are complementary rather than competitive, and thus must be used in combination and not exclusively. This allows us to take advantage of their respective component strengths and compensate for individual weaknesses.

Within soft computing, each of the constituent techniques has a set of capabilities to offer. In the case of fuzzy logic, there is a body of concepts and techniques for dealing with imprecision, information granularity, approximate reasoning and, most importantly, computing with words. In the case of neural networks, there is the capability of learning, adaptation and identification. In the case of genetic algorithms, the capability to employ systematized random search and achieve optimal performance, and so on.

Hybrid intelligent systems (*hybrids* for short) are computational systems that integrate different intelligent techniques in these two categories. These systems are presently being used to support problem solving and decision making in a wide variety of tasks [93, 122]. Hybrid intelligent systems allow the representation and manipulation of different types and forms of data and knowledge which may come from various sources. Refined system knowledge is used during reasoning and decision making processes, producing more effective results.

To solve a problem, or make a decision, the problem solvers or decision makers (agents) must have great skills to utilize the knowledge related to a particular problem, and process the relevant information. This includes the capability to deal with imprecise, uncertain or vague information. Dealing with real-world uncertainty is an important part of decision making. In order to make good decisions, agents must have the ability to deal with imprecision information, achieve optimal performance, and be adaptive. That is, they should have a high MIQ (machine intelligence quotient [12]). In Zadeh's view [12], most high MIQ systems are hybrid intelligent systems that use for example, soft computing techniques such as fuzzy logic, neural networks, and genetic algorithms, in some combination.

From this discussion, it is concluded that hybrid intelligent systems are required for complex problem solving and decision making.

However, the design and development of *hybrid intelligent systems* is difficult because they have a large number of parts, or components, that have many interactions. This makes hybrids very complicated. Existing software development techniques cannot manage these complex interactions efficiently, because, as we have said, interactions may occur at unpredictable times, for unpredictable reasons, and between unpredictable components.

1.2 Hybrids Are Complex

As different individual intelligent techniques have their own advantages and disadvantages, they cannot be applied universally to every problem. Whereas, many complex problems have many different component problems, each of which require different types of processing. Thus it is necessary to combine different intelligent techniques so as to overcome the limitations of individual techniques in complex problem solving and decision making. Moreover, hybrid intelligent systems represent, not only a combination of different intelligent techniques, but also the integration of intelligent techniques with legacy computing systems or programs. All this contributes to making hybrid intelligent systems complicated. Decisions need to be made about:

- which techniques are suitable for certain kinds of problems;
- which messages are to be exchanged among different processing components (using different intelligent techniques) in the systems as they must communicate with each other, as well as legacy programs, to achieve synergism;
- how to allow the easy exchange or addition of new processing techniques;
- how to know exactly where components reside on the network in complex problem solving and decision making, and how to make them work together across a heterogeneous network of computers.

Although complex, the complexity of hybrid intelligent systems exhibits a number of important regularities [84]:

- Complexity frequently takes the form of a hierarchy. That is, the system is composed of inter-related subsystems, each of which is in turn hierarchical in structure. The precise nature of these organizational relationships varies between subsystems. However some generic forms (such as client-server, peer, team, etc.) can be identified. These relationships are not static, however, they often vary over time.
- The choice of which components in the system are primitive is relatively arbitrary and is defined by the observer's aims and objectives.
- Hierarchical systems evolve more quickly than non-hierarchical ones of comparable size. In other words, complex systems will evolve from simple systems more rapidly if there are stable intermediate forms, than if there are not.
- It is possible to distinguish between the interactions among subsystems and the interactions within subsystems. The latter are both more frequent and more predictable than the former. This gives rise to the view that complex systems are nearly decomposable: That is,subsystems can be treated almost as if they are independent of one another, but not quite, since there are some interactions between them. Moreover, although many of these interactions can be predicted at design time, some cannot.

Drawing these insights together, it is possible to define a canonical view of a complex system. (Refer to Fig. 1.1, which is adapted from [85].)

Given these observations, software engineers have devised a number of powerful tools in order to tackle this complexity. The principal mechanisms, as described in [85], include:

- *Decomposition*: The most basic technique for tackling any large complex problem is to divide it into smaller, more manageable chunks, each of which can then be dealt with in relative isolation. Decomposition helps tackle complexity because it limits the designer's scope.
- *Abstraction*: Abstraction is the process of defining a simplified model of a system that emphasizes some of the details or properties, while suppressing others. Again, this works, because it limits the designer's scope of interest at a given time.

- *Organization*: Organization is the process of identifying and managing interrelationships between various problem solving components. The ability to specify and enact organizational relationships helps designers tackle complexity in two ways:
  - by enabling a number of basic components to be grouped together and treated as a higher-level unit of analysis; and
  - by providing a means of describing high-level relationships between various units.

Any approach to building hybrid intelligent systems should support these three mechanisms – decomposition, abstraction, and organization.

1.3 Agent Perspectives Are Suitable for Hybrids

Agent techniques represent an exciting new means of analyzing, designing and building complex software systems. They have the potential to significantly improve current practice in software engineering and to extend the range of applications that can feasibly be tackled [70].

Although a precise definition of an intelligent agent is still forthcoming, an increasing number of researchers find the following characterization useful [1, 2]:

> An agent is an encapsulated computer system that is situated in some environment and that is capable of flexible, autonomous action in that environment in order to meet its design objectives.

When adopting an agent-oriented view of the world, it soon becomes apparent that most problems require, or involve, multiple agents; to represent the decentralized nature of the problem, the multiple loci of control, the multiple perspectives, or the competing interests. Moreover, the agents will need to interact with one another, either to achieve their individual objectives or to manage the dependencies that ensue from being situated in a common environment. A multi-agent system can be defined as a loosely coupled network of entities that work together to make decisions, or solve problems that are beyond the individual capabilities or knowledge of each entity [16]. These entities (agents) are autonomous and may be heterogeneous in nature. The characteristics of multi-agent systems are as described in [8]:

- each agent has incomplete information, or capabilities, for making a decision or solving a particular problem, thus each agent has a limited viewpoint;
- there is no global system control;
- data is decentralized; and
- computation is asynchronous.

In this book, the terms 'agents' or 'software agents' are used to indicate 'intelligent agents that can interact'. 'Intelligent' indicates that the agents pursue their goals and execute their tasks such that they optimize some given performance measures ([10], pp. 2-3). To say that agents are intelligent does not mean that they are omniscient or omnipotent, nor does it mean that they never fail. Rather, it means that they operate flexibly and rationally in a variety of environmental circumstances, given the information they have and their perceptual and effectual capabilities.

From a multi-agent perspective, agents in multi-agent systems are autonomous and can engage in flexible, high-level interactions. Here, autonomy means that the agents have their own persistent thread of control (i.e., they are active) and that they can decide for themselves which actions they should perform at what time. The fact that agents are active means they know for themselves when they should be acting and when they should update their state. The flexible nature of interactions means that agents can make decisions about the nature and scope of interactions at run-time rather than design time.

Multi-agent systems are ideally suited to representing problems that have multiple problem solving methods, multiple perspectives and/or multiple problem solving entities. Such systems have the traditional advantage of distributed and concurrent problem solving, but have the additional advantage of sophisticated patterns of interactions. Examples of common types of interaction include cooperation, coordination, and negotiation. It is the flexibility and high-level nature of these interactions which distinguishes multi-agent systems from other forms of software, and which provides the underlying power of the paradigm.

Furthermore, N. Jennings defined the canonical views of a complex system and a multi-agent system [71]. In the canonical view of a complex system (see Fig. 1.1), the system's hierarchical nature is expressed through the 'related to' links, where components within a subsystem are connected through 'frequent interaction' links, and interactions between components are expressed through 'infrequent interaction' links.

In the canonical view of a multi-agent system (see Fig. 1.2), it can be seen that adopting an agent-oriented approach to software engineering means decomposing the problem into multiple, autonomous components that can act and interact in flexible ways to achieve their set objectives. The key abstraction models that define the agent-oriented mind-set are agents, interactions, and organizations. Finally, explicit structures and mechanisms are often used to describe and manage the complex and changing web of organizational relationships that exist between the agents.

From the canonical view of a multi-agent system (Fig. 1.2), it can be seen that adopting an agent-oriented approach to software engineering means decomposing the problem into multiple, interacting, autonomous components (agents) that have particular objectives to achieve. The key abstraction models that define the 'agent-oriented mind-set' are agents, interactions and or-

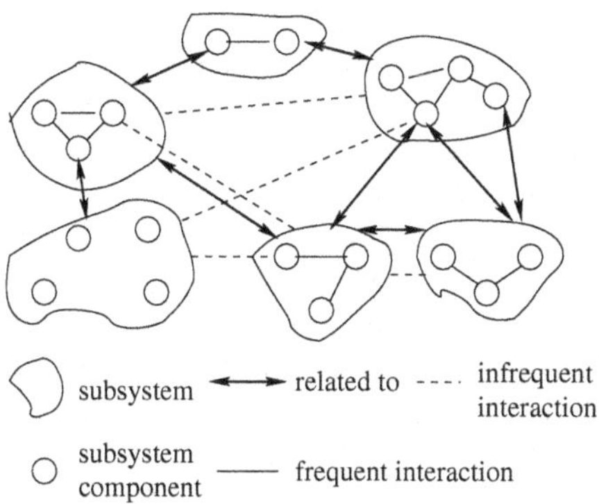

Fig. 1.1. View of a Canonical Complex System

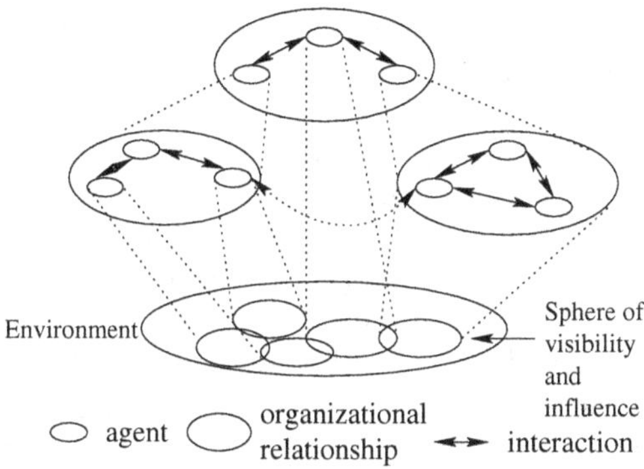

Fig. 1.2. Canonical View of a Multi-Agent System

ganizations. Finally, explicit structures and mechanisms are often available for describing and managing the complex and changing web of organizational relationships that exist between the agents.

Some researchers in this field have given a qualitative analysis to provide the intellectual justification of precisely why agent-based systems are well suited to engineering complex software systems [2, 70, 71, 73, 74]. They have also provided a detailed analysis of the merits of agent-oriented decomposition, the appropriateness of agent-oriented abstractions, and the need for flexible management of changing organizational structures in the process of building complex software systems. On the other hand, it is evident that hybrid intelligent systems are complex software systems and have all the features of other industrial-strength software systems. Thus, agent-oriented approaches can significantly enhance our ability to model, design and build hybrid intelligent systems for the following reasons:

- *Merits of agent-oriented decomposition.* Hybrid intelligent systems consist of a number of related subsystems organized in a hierarchical fashion. At any given level, subsystems work together to achieve the functionality of their parent system. Moreover, within a subsystem, the constituent components work together to deliver overall functionality. Thus, the same basic model of interacting components, working together to achieve particular objectives, occurs throughout the system. The agent-oriented approach advocates decomposing problems in terms of autonomous agents that can engage in flexible, high-level interactions. The fact that agents are active means they know for themselves when they should be acting and when they should update their state (cf. passive objects that need to be invoked by some external entity to do either). Such self-awareness reduces control complexity since the system's control know-how is taken from a centralized repository and localized inside each individual problem solving component. The fact that agents make decisions about the nature and scope of interactions at run-time makes the engineering of hybrid intelligent systems easier for two main reasons. Firstly, the system's inherent complexity means it is impossible to know *a priori* about all potential links. Interactions will occur at unpredictable times, for unpredictable reasons, and between unpredictable components. For this reason, it is futile to try and predict, or analyze, all the possibilities at design-time. Rather, it is more realistic to endow the components with the ability to make decisions about the nature and scope of their interactions at run-time. Thus agents are specifically designed to deal with unanticipated requests, and they can spontaneously generate requests for assistance whenever appropriate. Secondly, the problem of managing control relationships between the software components is significantly reduced.
- *Suitability of agent-oriented abstractions.* A significant part of the design process is finding the right models for viewing the problem. In general, there will be multiple candidates, and the difficult task is to pick out the most appropriate one. When designing software, the most powerful abstractions are those that minimize the semantic gap between the units of analysis that are intuitively used to conceptualize the problem and the constructs present in the solution paradigm. In the case of complex hybrid intelligent systems, the problem to be characterized consists of subsystems, subsystem components, interactions and organizational relationships. Taking each in turn: subsystems naturally correspond to agent organizations; the appropriateness of viewing subsystem components as agents has been made above; the interplay between the subsystems and between their constituent components is most naturally viewed in terms of high-level social interactions; and complex hybrid intelligent systems involve changing webs of relationships between their various components. They also require collections of components to be treated as a single conceptual unit when viewed from a different level of abstraction. Here again the agent-oriented mind-set provides suitable abstractions.

- *The need for flexible management of changing organizational structures.* Organizational constructs are first-class entities in agent systems. Thus, explicit representations are made of organizational relationships and structures. Moreover, agent-based systems have the concomitant computational mechanisms for flexibly forming, maintaining and disbanding organizations. This representational power enables agent-oriented systems to exploit two facets of complex hybrid intelligent systems. Firstly, the notion of a primitive component can be varied according to the needs of the observer. Thus at one level, entire subsystems can be viewed as a singleton, a collection of agents can be viewed as primitive components, and so on, until the system eventually bottoms out. Secondly, such structures provide a variety of stable intermediate forms. These forms are essential for rapid development of complex hybrid intelligent systems. Their availability means that individual agents or organizational groupings can be developed in relative isolation, and then added into the system in an incremental manner. This, in turn, ensures there is a smooth growth in functionality.

From this discussion, it is apparent that multi-agent perspectives are well suited for modeling hybrid intelligent systems when solving complex problems.

In this book, the term *agent-based systems* is also used to refer to systems that are both designed and implemented as several interacting agents, i.e., multi-agent systems. When discussing agent techniques from a software engineering point of view and comparing them with object-oriented techniques, *agent-oriented* is used. In Chap. 3, the distinctions between agents and objects, agents and expert systems will be detailed.

1.4 Motivation and Targets

As described in the previous sections, hybrid solutions are crucial for many real-world applications, and they are difficult to build. Whereas agent technology is suitable for constructing such systems. This motivated us to combine these two and construct agent-based hybrid intelligent systems.

When building hybrid intelligent systems from agent perspectives, there are many ways to follow. One can build such systems from scratch. Obviously this is inconvenient and inefficient. What we plan to do here is propose a unifying agent framework that can greatly facilitate the construction of hybrid intelligent systems. Such a unifying agent framework is presented, and two agent-based hybrid intelligent systems are provided, which are built on the proposed framework. The ultimate goal is to deploy an industrial strength toolkit for the construction of hybrid intelligent systems.

For the convenience of readers from the agent research community, some basic concepts and knowledge of hybrid intelligent systems are provided in Chap. 2. For the sake of readers from the hybrid intelligent system community, Chapter 3 presents some fundamentals concerning agent and multi-agent systems.

2

Basics of Hybrid Intelligent Systems

In the past decade, the amount of research and development involving hybrid intelligent systems has increased rapidly. Initial work addressed the integration of neural networks and expert systems, or the use of fuzzy logic with expert systems. Research on hybrid symbolic and subsymbolic systems has provided an excellent foundation for models and techniques that are now used in applications and development tools. The existing systems demonstrate their feasibility and advantages, and many are in use in practical situations. More recently, genetic algorithms and case-based reasoning techniques have become more accessible through convenient development tools and environments, and they are appearing individually in growing numbers of applications. A natural step is to integrate all of these intelligent technologies to produce more powerful and effective systems [66].

A fundamental stimulus to investigations into hybrid intelligent systems is the awareness in the research and development communities that combined approaches will be necessary if the remaining tough problems in artificial intelligence are to be solved. The successes in integrating expert systems and neural networks, and the advances in theoretical research on hybrid systems, point to similar opportunities for when other intelligent technologies are included in the mix. From a knowledge of their strengths and weaknesses, we can construct hybrid systems to mitigate the limitations and take advantage of the opportunities to produce systems that are more powerful than those that could be built with single technologies. The intelligent technologies and their hybrid systems represent a range of building blocks that may eventually allow us to simulate human-like intelligence.

In the hybrid intelligent system community, research work mainly falls into areas like micro-level integration of fuzzy logic and expert systems, fuzzy systems and neural networks, genetic algorithms and neural networks, genetic algorithms and fuzzy systems, genetic algorithms and expert systems.

Our work here advocates integrating different intelligent techniques from an agent's point of view. An agent-based framework is proposed to construct hybrid intelligent systems. Different intelligent techniques can easily be in-

Z. Zhang, C. Zhang: Agent-Based Hybrid Intelligent Systems, LNAI 2938, pp. 13–28, 2004.

tegrated into one system under a unifying agent framework. From an agent perspective, each intelligent technique is treated as one building block of hybrid intelligent systems in the form of an agent.

For the convenience of readers, and to make this book self-contained, some basic concepts and information about hybrid intelligent systems are given in this chapter.

2.1 Typical Intelligent Techniques

As pointed out in Chap. 1, to solve complex problems in real-world, a great diversity of intelligent techniques including traditional hard computing techniques (e.g., expert systems) and soft computing techniques (e.g., fuzzy logic, neural networks, and genetic algorithms) are required. These intelligent techniques are complementary rather than competitive and thus must be used in combination and not exclusively [12]. These typical intelligent techniques are briefly introduced in this section.

2.1.1 Expert Systems

One of the most successful applications of artificial intelligence reasoning techniques using facts and rules has been in building *expert systems* that embody knowledge about a specialized field of human endeavor, such as medicine, engineering, or business [143]. The following definition is given in [142]:

> Artificial Intelligence programs that achieve expert-level competence in solving problems by bringing to bear a body of knowledge are called knowledge-based systems or expert systems. often, the term expert systems is reserved for programs whose knowledge base contains the knowledge used by human experts, in contrast to knowledge gathered from textbooks or non-experts. more often than not, the two terms – expert system and knowledge-based system – are used synonymously.

The basic structure of an expert system is shown in Fig. 2.1 (adapted from [142]). The major parts of the system are the *knowledge base* and the *inference engine*. The knowledge base consists of facts and rules about the subject at hand. The inference engine consists of all processes that manipulate the knowledge base to deduce information requested by the user – resolution or forward or backward chaining, for example. The *user interface* might consist of some kind of natural language processing system that allows the user to interact with the system in a limited form of natural language. Graphical user interfaces with menus are also used. The *explanation subsystem* analyzes the structure of the reasoning performed by the system and explains it to user.

These four parts of the system are the parts that constitute the system as it is used in an application. In the construction of an expert system, a '*knowledge engineer*' (usually a computer scientist with artificial intelligence training) works with an expert (or experts) in the field of application in order

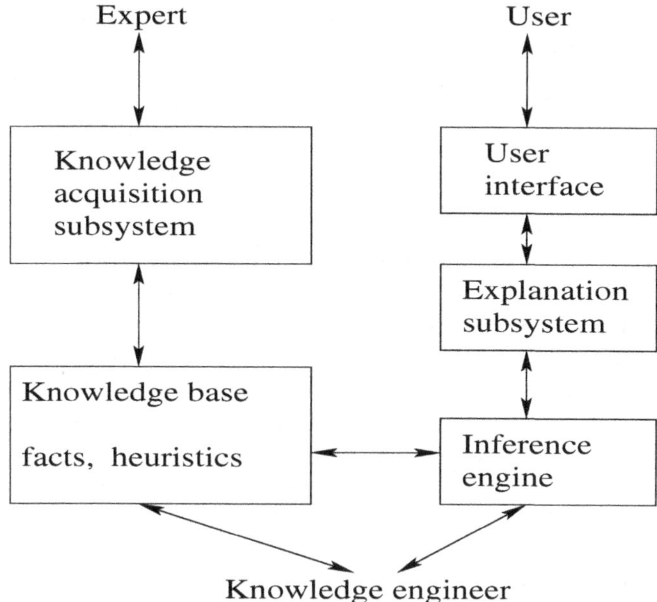

Fig. 2.1. Basic Structure of an Expert System

to represent the relevant knowledge of the expert in a form that can be entered into the knowledge base. This process is often aided by a *knowledge acquisition subsystem* that, among other things, checks the growing knowledge base for possible inconsistencies and incomplete information. These are then presented to the expert for resolution.

The process of building the system usually iterates through many cycles. At each step of the cycle, a prototype system is tested by the knowledge engineer and the expert to see if it makes the same kinds of inferences that the expert would make on typical problems that might be posed by a user. If the system responds differently than the expert would, the *explanation subsystem* is used to help the development team decide which information and inferences are responsible for the discrepany. It may be that the expert needs to articulate certain information in more detail or provide additional information to cover the case at hand. This process continues until the development team is satisfied that the system operates appropriately [143].

2.1.2 Fuzzy Sets and Fuzzy Logic

A *set* is normally thought of as a collection of objects. An ordinary (classical) set divides the universe into those items that are completely in the set and those items that are completely outside of the set. We can describe this phenomenon by assigning the value 1 to all those items which are members of the set and the value 0 to all items which are not members of the set. For ordinary sets, only these two values are possible. The function which assigns these values is called *characteristic function* of the set.

Consider a classical set A of the universe U. A *fuzzy set* $\mathcal{A}$ is defined by a set or ordered pairs, a binary relation,

$$\mathcal{A} = \{(x, \mu_{\mathcal{A}}(x))|x \in A, \mu_{\mathcal{A}} \in [0, 1]\} \tag{2.1}$$

where $\mu_{\mathcal{A}}(x)$ is a function called *membership function*; $\mu_{\mathcal{A}}(x)$ specifies the *grade* or *degree* to which any element x in A belongs to the fuzzy set $\mathcal{A}$. Definition 2.1.2 associates with each element x in A a real number $\mu_{\mathcal{A}}(x)$ in the interval $[0, 1]$ which is assigned to x. Larger values of $\mu_{\mathcal{A}}(x)$ indicate higher degrees of membership.

In fuzzy sets, an element x is said to belong to $\mathcal{A}$ with probability $\mu_{\mathcal{A}}(x)$ and simultaneously to be in $\neg\mathcal{A}$ with probability $1 - \mu_{\mathcal{A}}(x)$. In actuality, this is not a true probability, but rather the degree of truth associated with the statement that x is in the set. To show the difference, let us look at a fuzzy set operation. Suppose the membership value for Mary being tall is 0.7 and the value for her being thin is 0.4. The membership value for her being both is 0.4, the minimum of the two values. if these were really probabilities, we would look at the product of the two values.

There is not a unique system of knowledge called *fuzzy logic* but a variety of methodologies proposing logical consideration of imperfect and vague knowledge. It is an active area of research with some topics still under discussion and debate. Fuzzy logic focuses on linguistic variables in natural language and aims to provide foundations for approximate reasoning with imprecise propositions. It reflects both the rightness and vagueness of natural language in common-sense reasoning.

Fuzzy rules combine two or more input fuzzy sets, called the *antecedent* sets, and associate with them an output, or *consequent*, set. The antecedent sets are combined by means of operators that are analogous to the usual logical conjunctives "and," "or," etc. One method of storing and representing fuzzy rules is through the use of a fuzzy associative memory (FAM) matrix [49]. FAM is a very simple and useful way to process fuzzy rules. Figure 2.2 shows an example of a FAM matrix that represents the nine rules described in Sect. 7.1.1. For example, the shadowed entry in Fig. 2.2 represents rule 8 (refer to Sect. 7.1.1).

2.1.3 Neural Networks

Neural networks, often referred to as *artificial neural networks* to distinguish them from biological neural networks, are modeled after the workings of the human brain. The neural network is actually an information processing system that consists of a graph representing the processing system as well as various algorithms that access the graph. As with the human brain, the neural network consists of many connected processing elements. The neural network, then, is

		X		
		L	M	H
	L	L	L	MO
Y	M	L	MO	H
	H	MO	H	H

Fig. 2.2. An Example of a Two-Dimensional FAM Matrix

structured as directed graph with many nodes (processing elements) and arcs (interconnections) between them. The nodes in the graph are like individual neurons, while the arcs are their interconnections. Each of these processing elements functions independently from the others and uses only local data (input and output to the node) to direct its processing. This features facilitates the use of neural networks in a distributed and/or parallel environment.

The neural network can be viewed as a directed graph with source (*input*), sink (*output*), and internal (*hidden*) nodes. The input nodes exist in an *input layer*, while the output nodes exist in an *output layer*. The hidden nodes exist over one or more *hidden layers*.

Neural networks can be classified based on the type of connectivity and learning. The basic type of connectivity is *feedforward*, where connections are only to layers later in the structure. Alternatively, a neural network may be *feedback* where some links are back to earlier layers. Figure 2.3 (adapted from [49]) shows the classic three-layer feedforward neural network architecture.

Figure 2.3 actually represents a function acting on a vector, or list of numbers. The notation $\mathbf{R}^d$ is used to denote the d-dimensional space of all vectors of the form $(x_1, \ldots, x_d)$, where each x_i is a real number and $d \geq 1$ is an integer. $\mathbf{R}^1$, for example, is a line, and $\mathbf{R}^2$ is a two-dimensional plane. The neural network function sends the vector $(x_1, \ldots, x_N)$ in $\mathbf{R}^N$ to the vector $\mathbf{R}^M$. Thus, the feedforward network can be represented as:

$$y = F(x)$$

where $\mathbf{x} = (x_1, \ldots, x_N)$ and $\mathbf{y} = (y_1, \ldots, y_M)$. The action of this function is determined in a specific way. For a network with N input nodes, H hidden nodes, and M output nodes, the values y_k are given by:

$$y_k = g(\sum_{j=1}^{H} w_{jk}^o h_j), k = 1, \ldots, M \tag{2.2}$$

Here, w_{jk}^o is the output 'weight' from hidden node j to output node k, and g is a function mapping $\mathbf{R}^1$ to $\mathbf{R}^1$. The values of the hidden layer nodes $h_j, j = 1, \ldots, H$ are given by:

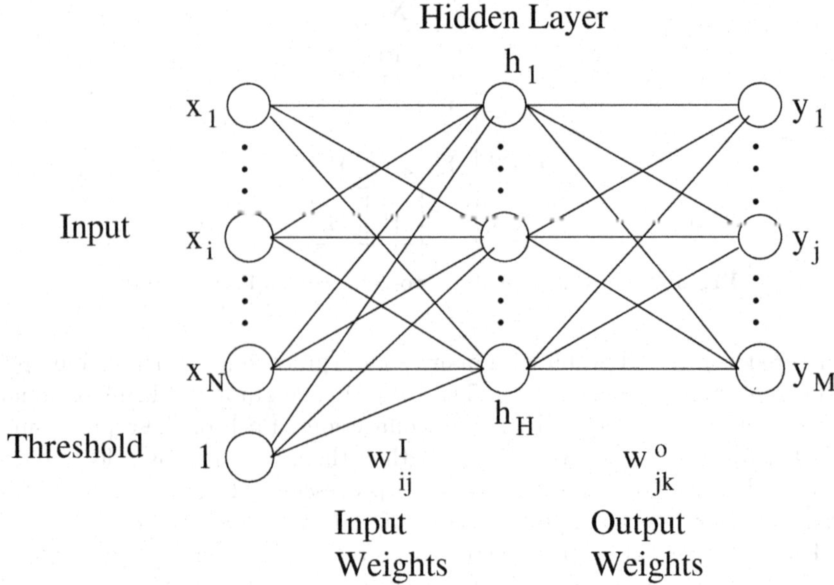

Fig. 2.3. Three-Layer Feedforward Neural Network Architecture

$$h_j = \sigma(\sum_{i=1}^{N} w_{ij}^I x_i + w_j^T), j = 1, \ldots, H \tag{2.3}$$

Here, w_{ij}^I is the output 'weight' from input node i to hidden node j, w_j^T is a threshold 'weight' from an input node which has the constant value 1 to hidden node j, x_i is the value at input node i, and σ is so-called 'sigmoid' function given by

$$\sigma(x) = \frac{1}{1 + e^{-x}} \tag{2.4}$$

The function σ in (2.3) is called the *activation function* of the neural network. The function g in (2.2) may be the same as the activation function or may be a different function.

The action of the feedforward network is determined by two things: the architecture, that is, how many input, hidden, and output nodes it has; and the values of the weights. The numbers of input and output nodes are determined by the application and so are, in effect, fixed. The number of hidden nodes is a variable that can be adjusted by the user. To date, this adjustment has remained pretty much of an 'art,' although various methods for setting the number of hidden nodes, or 'pruning' away unnecessary nodes, have been proposed in the literature.

With the architecture set, it is then the weight values that determine how the network performs. The process of adjusting these weight values in order to obtain a desired network performance is known as 'training' the network. The network is said to 'learn' as the weight values are being modified to achieve the training goal. The weights are nothing more than a set of parameters, like the coefficients in a polynomial, which determine the behavior of a particular function. While terms like 'training' and 'learning' recall the biological inspiration for these networks, the neural network practitioners would do well to keep in mind that, from a mathematical and computing point of view, these terms refer to nothing more than the adaptation of a function parameter set.

2.1.4 Genetic Algorithms

Genetic algorithms are a biologically inspired class of algorithms that can be applied to, among other things, the optimization of nonlinear multimodal (many local maxima and minima) functions. This class of algorithms solves problems in the same way that nature solves the problem of adapting living organisms to the harsh realities of life in a hostile world: evolution. Genetic algorithms are examples of *evolutionary computing* methods. Given a population of potential problem solutions (individuals), evolutionary computing expands this population with new and potentially better solutions. The basic for evolutionary computing algorithms is biological evolution, where over time evolution produces the best or 'fittest' individuals. Chromosomes, which are DNA strings, provide the abstract model for a living organism. Subsections of the chromosomes, which are called *genes*, are used to define different traits of the individual. During reproduction, genes from parents are combined to produce the genes for child.

When using genetic algorithms to solve a problem, the first thing, and perhaps the most difficult task, which must be determined is how to model the problem as a set of individuals. Given an alphabet A, an *individual* or *chromosome* is a string $I = I_1, I_2, \ldots, I_n$ where $I_j \in A$. Each character in the string, I_j, is called a *gene*. The values that each character can have are called the *alleles*. A *population*, P, is a set of individuals.

Although individuals are often represented as bit strings, any encoding is possible. An array with nonbinary characters could be used, as could more complicated data structures including trees and arrays. The only real restriction is that the genetic operators (mutation, crossover) must be defined.

In genetic algorithms, reproduction is defined by precise algorithms that indicate how to combine the given set of individuals to produce new ones. These are called *crossover* algorithms. Given two individuals (parents) from the population, the crossover technique generates new individuals (offspring or children) by switching subsequences of the strings. There are many variations of the crossover approach. A crossover probability is used to determine how many new offspring are created via crossover. In addition, the actual crossover point may vary within one algorithm.

As in nature, however, mutations sometimes appear, and these also may be present in genetic algorithms. The mutation operation randomly changes characters in the offspring. A very small probability of mutation is set to determine whether a character should change.

Since genetic algorithms attempt to model nature, only the strong survive. When new individuals are created, a choice must be made about which individuals will survive. This may be the new individuals, the old ones, or more likely a combination of the two. The third major component of genetic algorithms, then, is the part that determines the best (or fittest) individuals to survive.

One of the most important components of a genetic algorithm is determining how to select individuals. A fitness function, f, is used to determine the best individuals in a population. This is then used in the selection process to choose parents. Given an objective by which the population can be measured, the fitness function indicates how well the goodness objective is being met by an individual.

Now a more formal definition for genetic algorithms can be given as follows: A *genetic algorithm* is a computational model consisting of five parts:

- Starting set of individuals, P.
- Crossover technique.
- Mutation algorithm.
- Fitness function.
- Algorithm that applies the crossover and mutation techniques to P iteratively using the fitness function to determine the best individuals in P to keep. The algorithm replaces a predefined number of individuals from the population with each iteration and terminates when some threshold is met.

The main steps of genetic algorithms are them described below, which are heavily borrowed from [144]:

- Initialize the algorithm. Randomly initialize each individual chromosome in the population of size N (N must be even), and compute each individual's fitness.
- Select $N/2$ pairs of individuals for crossover. The probability that an individual will be selected for crossover is proportional to its fitness.
- Perform crossover operation on $N/2$ pairs selected in the second step. Randomly mutate bits with a small probability during this operation.
- Compute fitness of all individuals in new population.
- Optional: Select N fittest individuals from combined population of size $2N$ consisting of old and new populations pooled together.
- Rescale fitness of population.
- Determine maximum fitness of individuals in population. If $|max\,fitness - optimum\,fitness| < tolerance$ then STOP. Otherwise, go to the second step.

2.2 Advantages and Disadvantages of Typical Intelligent Techniques

There is an array of intelligent techniques, which can be divided into two main categories – traditional hard computing techniques and soft computing techniques. One typical hard computing technique is expert systems, while the principal members of soft computing techniques are fuzzy logic, neural networks, and genetic algorithms. In this section, the four typical intelligent techniques are compared and contrasted on three key information processing capabilities – knowledge acquisition, brittleness and explanation. This section is mainly based on the discussions in [65] (pp.3-5). Similar discussion can also be found in [39, 66].

2.2.1 Knowledge Acquisition

Knowledge acquisition is a crucial stage in the development of intelligent systems. As a process, it involves eliciting, interpreting and representing the knowledge from a given domain. Knowledge acquisition for expert systems (from domain experts) is time consuming, expensive and potentially unreliable. Furthermore, expert systems do not have mechanisms to deal with any changes in their decision making environment – they cannot adapt and learn from changes in their operating environment. Thus, the maintenance of knowledge in expert systems is also time consuming and expensive.

Due to these problems, intelligent techniques, such as neural networks and genetic algorithms, which can learn from domain data, have certain advantages. Also in expert systems, the decision boundaries – the bounds used to make particular decisions – are specified by a domain expert, while in neural networks and genetic algorithms these decision boundaries are learned. Changes in the operating environment cause the decision boundaries to be shifted or changed. Systems that learn, can detect and adapt to these changes.

2.2.2 Brittleness

Although there are notable successes in the use of expert systems, many of these systems operate in very narrow domains under limited operational conditions. This phenomenon in expert systems is referred as *brittleness*. The systems are brittle in the sense that they respond appropriately only in narrow domains and require substantial human intervention to compensate for even slight shifts in domain.

An operational view of the brittleness problem can be seen as the inability of an intelligent system to cope with inexact, incomplete or inconsistent knowledge. Causes of this brittleness problem are twofold – inadequate representation structures and inadequate reasoning mechanisms. In expert systems, knowledge is represented as discrete symbols, and reasoning consists of logical operations on these constructs.

In contrast, reasoning in neural networks involves the numeric aggregation of representation over the whole network. This distributed representation and reasoning allows these systems to deal with incomplete and inconsistent data, and also allows the systems to gracefully degrade. That is, even if some parts of a neural network are made non-operational, the rest of the neural network will function and attempt to give an answer. This type of inherent fault tolerance contrasts strongly with expert systems, which usually fail to function even if one single processing part is non-operational.

Fuzzy logic deals with the problem of brittleness by adopting novel knowledge representation and reasoning methods. Fuzzy sets, the form in which knowledge is represented, diffuse the boundaries between concepts. There are no sharp divisions where one concept ends and the next begins. This fuzzy data representation, in conjunction with fuzzy (approximate) reasoning mechanisms, allows the processing of data which are inexact or partially correct.

Genetic algorithms are able to cope with brittleness. It is the maintenance of a population of solutions which makes genetic algorithms and classifier systems non-brittle. Each rule in the classifier system population contains a relationship describing the system being modeled. The system's flexibility arises from the rules representing a wide range of competing, conflicting hypotheses. The selection of the appropriate rule to fire is dependent on its past performance – a statistical aggregation of its correct performance. Similar to neural networks, it is this statistical reasoning property, based on the past performance that gives genetic algorithms their ability to cope with brittleness.

2.2.3 Explanation

The ability to provide users with explanations of the reasoning process is important for complex decision making. Explanation facilities are required, both for user acceptance of the decisions made by a system, and for the purpose of understanding whether the reasoning procedure is sound. Good examples of this requirement can be found in medical diagnosis, loan granting, and legal reasoning. There have been fairly successful solutions to the explanation problem in expert systems, symbolic machine learning, and case-based reasoning systems. In expert systems, explanations are typically provided by tracing the chain of inference during the reasoning process.

In a fuzzy logic system the final decision is generated by aggregating the decisions of all the different rules contained in the fuzzy rule base. In these systems a chain of inference cannot be easily obtained, but the rules are in a simple-to-understand 'IF-THEN' format which users can easily inspect.

Genetic algorithms, especially in the form of classifier systems, can build reasoning models in the form of rules. As in the case of expert systems, it is possible to trace a chain of inference and provide some degree of explanation of the reasoning process.

In contrast, in neural networks it is difficult to provide adequate explanation facilities. This is due to neural networks not having explicit, declarative knowledge representation structures, but instead having knowledge encoded as weights distributed over the whole network. It is therefore more difficult to find a chain of inference which can be used for producing explanations.

Table 2.1. Property Assessment of Typical Intelligent Techniques

Techniques	Properties		
	Automated Knowledge Acquisition	Coping with Brittleness	Explanation
Expert Systems	†	†	†††††
Fuzzy Logic	†	†††††	††††
Neural Networks	†††††	†††††	†
Genetic Algorithms	†††††	†††	†††

(†– weak, †††††– strong)

Table 2.1 summarizes the above computational properties with respect to the four typical intelligent techniques. It is clear that these intelligent techniques are complementary and should be used in combinations for complex problem solving and decision making.

2.3 Classification of Hybrid Intelligent Systems

Hybrid intelligent systems can be classified into different categories based on different criteria. Here, two typical classification schemes are provided.

2.3.1 Medsker's Classification Scheme

In [137], Medsker and Bailey discuss the integration of expert systems and neural networks. Five different hybrid development strategies have been identified: stand-alone, transformations, loose coupling, tight coupling, and full integration. (See Fig. 2.4.) The benefits and limitations of these strategies are briefly outlined below. Refer to [66] and [137] for details. Although this classification scheme is only for the integration of expert systems and neural networks, and some of the descriptions do not hold now, it is helpful for us to discuss the advantages that agent technology can bring in hybrid intelligent system construction.

Stand-Alone Models

Stand-alone models of combined intelligent system applications consist of independent software components. These components do not interact in any way.

One of the benefits of a stand-alone model is the simplicity and ease of development using commercially-available software packages. On the other hand, the development efforts in expert systems or neural networks are not transferable, neither can they support the weakness of each other, and the maintenance requirements are doubled. Both must be updated simultaneously to avoid confusion, and updates to one cannot help the other.

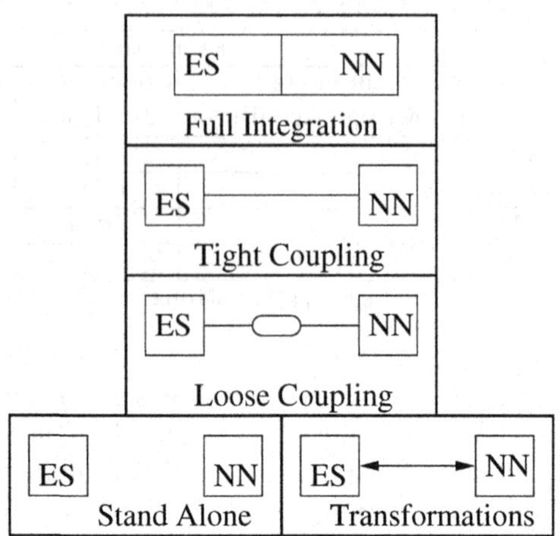

Fig. 2.4. Models for Integrating Intelligent Systems

Transformational Models

Transformational models are similar to stand-alone models in that the end result of development is an independent model that does not interact with others. What distinguishes the two types of models is that transformational systems begin as one type of system and end up as the other.

Transformational models offer several benefits to developers. They are often quick to develop, and ultimately require maintenance on only one system. Development occurs in the most appropriate environment. Similarly, the delivery technique offers operational benefits suitable to its environment.

Limitations to transformational models are significant. First, a fully automated means of transforming an expert system to a neural network, or vice versa, is still needed. Also, significant modifications to the system may require a new development effort, which leads to another transformation. In addition to maintenance issues, the finished transformational system is limited operationally to the capabilities of the target technique.

Loosely-Coupled Models

Loosely-coupled models comprise the first true form of integrated intelligent systems. Compared to the more integrated intelligent system applications, loosely-coupled models are easy to develop. They are amenable to the use of commercially available intelligent systems software, which reduces the programming burden on developers. Both the system design and implementation processes are simplified with loosely-coupled models. Finally, maintenance time is reduced because of the simplicity of the data file interface mechanism.

Some limitations are associated with loosely-coupled models. Because of the file-transfer interface, communication costs are high and operating time is longer. The development of separate intelligent system components leads to redundancy of effort. Both must be capable of solving subproblems in order to perform their unique computations. But, because they lack direct access to each other's internal processing, they must develop independent capabilities. This may also lead to overlap in data input environments and internal processing.

Tightly-Coupled Models

The categories of loose and tight coupling have significant overlap. Both utilize independent expert system and neural network components. However, tightly-coupled systems pass information via memory resident data structures rather than external data files. This improves the interactive capabilities of tightly-coupled models, in addition to enhancing their performance.

Tight coupling has the benefits of reduced communication overheads and improved runtime performance, compared to loose coupling. Several commercial packages are suitable for developing tightly-coupled models, and maintaining the modularity of the expert system and neural network components. Overall, tight coupling offers design flexibility and robust integration.

Tightly-coupled systems have three principal limitations. First, development and maintenance complexity increases due to the internal data interface. Second, tight coupling suffers from redundant data gathering and processing, as does loose coupling. Once again, this is due to the independence of the intelligent system components. Finally, the verification and validation process is more difficult particularly for embedded applications.

Fully-Integrated Models

Fully-integrated systems share data structures and knowledge representations. Communication between the different components is accomplished via the dual nature (for example, symbolic and neural) of the structures. Reasoning is accomplished either cooperatively or through a component designated as the controller.

The benefits of full integration include robustness, improved performance, and increased problem solving capabilities. Robustness and performance improvements stem from the dual nature of the knowledge representations and data structures. In addition, little or no redundancy occurs in the development process. Finally, fully integrated models can provide a full range of capabilities – such as adaptation, generalization, noise tolerance, justification, and logical deduction – not found in non-integrated models.

Full integration has limitations caused by the increased complexity of the inter-module interactions. Specifying, designing, and building fully-integrated models is complex, tools that facilitate full integration are distinctly lacking on the market, and verifying, validating, and maintaining fully-integrated systems are issues for further research and development.

2.3.2 Goonatilake's Classification Scheme

Goonatilake and Khebbal [65] point out that there are three main reasons for creating hybrid systems: *technique enhancement*, the *multiplicity of application tasks* and *realizing multi-functionality*. Based on the three factors, they have divided hybrid systems into three classes: *function-replacing*, *intercommunicating* and *polymorphic*.

Function-Replacing Hybrids

Function-replacing hybrids address the functional composition of a single intelligent technique. In this hybrid class, a principal function of the given technique is replaced by another intelligent processing technique. The motivation for these hybrid systems is the technique enhancement factor discussed above.

Intercommunicating Hybrids

Inter-communicating hybrids are independent, self-contained, intelligent processing modules that exchange information and perform separate functions to generate solutions. If a problem can be subdivided into distinct processing tasks, then different independent intelligent modules can be used to solve the parts of the problem at which they are best suited. These independent modules, which collectively solve the given task, are coordinated by a control mechanism.

Polymorphic Hybrids

Polymorphic hybrids are systems that use a single processing architecture to achieve the functionality of different intelligent processing techniques. The broad motivation for these hybrid systems is realizing multi-functionality within particular computational architectures. These systems can functionally mimic, or emulate, different processing techniques.

2.4 Current Practice in Typical Hybrid Intelligent System Development

As pointed out previously, hybrid intelligent systems are very important for complex problem solving and decision making. At the same time, they are difficult to build.

Many hybrid intelligent systems used in different application fields appeared in the past ten years [39, 65, 66, 67, 68, 69]. All these systems fall into the three classes in Goonatilake's scheme. A typical development cycle in the implementation of these hybrid intelligent systems is shown in Fig. 2.5. This is based on object-oriented techniques. There are six stages in the construction of hybrid intelligent systems: problem analysis, property matching, hybrid category selection, implementation, validation, and maintenance [65]. Most current hybrid intelligent systems are built either from scratch or following this development process.

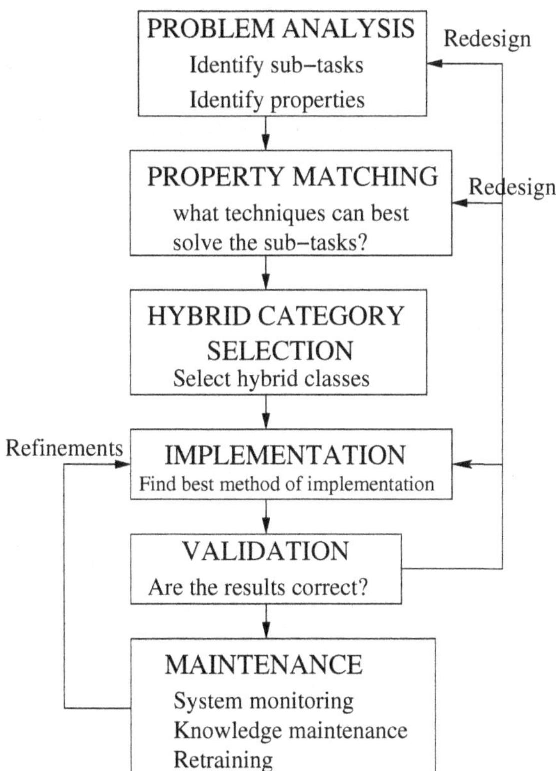

Fig. 2.5. Hybrid Intelligent System Development Cycle

There are some shortcomings of the hybrid intelligent systems involved in following this development process. The most obvious one is that the organization of such a hybrid system is not adaptive. Once the techniques are selected in the property matching stage, it is difficult to change or replace them even though a better one might be found later on.

Another difficulty lies in the hybrid category selection phase. At this stage, developers must choose the type of hybrid system required (function-replacing, inter-communicating, or polymorphic) for solving the specific problem. This is not easy. The inherent complexity of the hybrid intelligent systems means it is impossible to know *a priori* about all potential links or relationships among components that comprise a system. Interactions will occur at unpredictable times, for unpredictable reasons, and between unpredictable components. For this reason, it is futile to try and predict, or analyze, all the possibilities at design-time. On the other hand, the flexible nature of agent interactions means that agents can make decisions about the nature and scope of interactions at run-time rather than design-time.

We also note that there are some limitations in different models based on Medsker's classification scheme. By employing agent technology and building hybrid systems from agent perspectives, most of the limitations can be eliminated, and the shortcomings can be overcome. In this book, all hybrid intelligent systems are classified into two categories – loosely-coupled and tightly-coupled.

3

Basics of Agents and Multi-agent Systems

Agents (adaptive or intelligent agents and multi-agent systems) constitute one of the most prominent and attractive technologies in Computer Science at the beginning of this new century. Agent and multi-agent system technologies, methods, and theories are currently contributing to many diverse domains. These include information retrieval, user interface design, robotics, electronic commerce, computer mediated collaboration, computer games, education and training, smart environments, ubiquitous computers, and social simulation.

This is not only a very promising technology, it is emerging as a new way of thinking, a conceptual paradigm for analyzing problems and for designing systems, for dealing with complexity, distribution and interactivity, and perhaps a new perspective on computing and intelligence.

As was discussed in Chap. 1, agent technology is also suitable for the analysis, design, and construction of hybrid intelligent systems. For the convenience of readers in the hybrid intelligent system area, a brief introduction to agents and multi-agent systems is provided in this chapter. Wooldridge [4] is a good introductory text for agent and multi-agent systems. For a more comprehensive discussion on these topics, refer to [10]. For a road map of agent and multi-agent system research, refer to [8] and [9].

3.1 Concepts of Agents and Multi-agent Systems

There is no universally accepted definition of the term 'agent'. One definition, which is adapted from [7], is attracting more and more attention. This states that: an agent is a computer system that is situated in some environment, and that is capable of autonomous action in this environment in order to meet its design objectives. Multi-agent systems are systems composed of multiple interacting agents.

The following paragraph from the "executive Summary" of [9] gives a clear picture of the role agent technologies can play.

Z. Zhang, C. Zhang: Agent-Based Hybrid Intelligent Systems, LNAI 2938, pp. 29–39, 2004.

Agent technologies are a natural extension of current component-based approaches, and have the potential to greatly impact the lives and work of all of us and, accordingly, this area is one of the most dynamic and exciting in computer science today. Some application domains where agent technologies will play a crucial role include: *Ambient Intelligence*, the seamless delivery of ubiquitous computing, continuous communications and intelligent user interfaces to consumer and industrial devices; *Grid Computing*, where multi-agent system approaches will enable efficient use of the resources of high-performance computing infrastructure in science, engineering, medical and commercial applications; *Electronic Business*, where agent-based approaches are already supporting the automation and semi-automation of information-gathering activities and purchase transactions over the Internet; the *Semantic Web*, where agents are needed both to provide services, and to make best use of the resources available, often in cooperation with others; *Bioinformatics and Computational Biology*, where intelligent agents may support the coherent exploration of data revolution occurring in biology; and other including monitoring and control, resource management, and space, military and manufacturing applications, for example.

3.2 Agents as a Paradigm for Software Engineering

When building hybrid intelligent systems from agent perspectives, each intelligent technique is a construction module in the form of an agent. That is, agents are building blocks in agent-based hybrid intelligent systems. This is one of the views of agents – agents as a paradigm for software engineering [4].

Software engineers have derived a progressively better understanding of the characteristics of complexity in software. It is now widely recognized that *interaction* is probably the most important single characteristic of complex software. Software architecture that contains many dynamically interacting components, each with their own thread of control, and engaging in complex, coordinated protocols, typically have orders of magnitude more complex to engineer correctly and efficiently than those that simply compute a function of some input through a single thread of control. Unfortunately, it turns out that many (if not most) real-world applications have precisely these characteristics. As a consequence, a major research topic in computer science over at least the past two decades has been the development of tools and techniques to model, understand and implement systems in which interaction is the norm. Indeed, many researchers now believe that in the future, computation itself will be understood chiefly as a process of interaction. Just as we can understand many systems as being composed of essentially passive objects, which have a state, and upon which we can perform operations, so we can understand many others as being made up of interacting, semi-autonomous agents. This recognition has led to the growth of interest in agents as a new paradigm for software engineering.

3.3 Agents and Objects

Programmers familiar with object-oriented languages such as Java, C++, or Smalltalk sometimes fail to see anything novel in the idea of agents. When one stops to consider the relative properties of agents and objects, this is perhaps not surprising. Objects are defined as computational entities that *encapsulate* some state, are able to perform actions, or *methods* on this state, and communicate by message passing. Here, the difference between agents and objects are summarized. More details can be found in [4, 8, 10].

While there are obvious similarities, there are also significant differences between agents and objects. The first is in the degree to which agents and objects are autonomous. Recall that the defining characteristic of object-oriented programming is the principle of encapsulation–the idea that objects can have control over their own internal state. In programming languages like Java, we can declare instance variables (and methods) to be *private*, meaning they are only accessible from within the object. We can of course also declare them *public*, meaning that they can be accessed from anywhere, and indeed we must do this for methods so that they can be used by other objects. But the use of *public* instance variable is generally considered poor programming style. In this way, an object can be thought of as exhibiting autonomy over its state: it has control over it. But an object does not exhibit control over its *behaviour*. That is, if a method m is made available for other objects to invoke, then they can do so whenever they wish; the object has no control over whether or not that method is executed. Of course, an object must make methods available to other objects, or else we would be unable to build a system out of them. This is not normally an issue, because if we build a system, then we design the objects that go in it, and they can thus be assumed to share a "common goal". But, in many types of multi-agent systems, (in particular, those that contain agents built by different organizations or individuals), no such common goal can be assumed. It cannot be taken for granted that an agent i will execute an action (method) a just because another agent j wants it to – a may not be in the best interest of i. We thus do not think of agents as invoking methods upon one-another, but rather as *requesting* actions to be performed. If j requests i to perform a, then i may perform the action or it may not. The locus of control with respect to the decision about whether to execute an action is thus different in agent and object systems. In the object-oriented case, the decision lies with the object that invokes the method. In the agent case, the decision lies with the agent that receives the request.

Note that there is nothing to stop us implementing agents using object-oriented techniques. For example, we can build some kind of decision making about whether to execute a method into the method itself, and in this way achieve a stronger kind of autonomy for our objects. However, the point is that autonomy of this kind is not a component of the basic object-oriented model.

The second important distinction between object and agent systems is with respect to the notion of flexible (reactive, pro-active, social) autonomous behaviour. The standard object model has nothing whatsoever to say about how to build systems that integrate these types of behaviour. Again, one could argue that we can build object-oriented programs that do integrate these types of behaviour. But this argument misses the point, which is that the standard object-oriented programming model has nothing to do with these types of behaviour.

The third important distinction between the standard object model and the view of agent systems is that agents are each considered to have their own thread of control – in the standard object model, there is a single thread of control in the system. Of course, a lot of work has recently been devoted to *concurrency* in object-oriented programming. For example, the Java language provides built-in constructs for multi-thread programming. There are also many programming languages available (most of them admittedly prototypes) that were specifically designed to allow concurrent object-oriented programming. But such languages do not capture the idea we have of agents as *autonomous* entities. Note, however, that *active objects* come quite close to the concept of autonomous agents – though they are not agents capable of flexible autonomous behaviour.

In addition to the above mentioned distinctions, there are two points that qualitatively differentiate agent interactions from those that occur in other software engineering paradigms such as the object-oriented paradigm. Firstly, agent-oriented interactions generally occur through a high-level agent communication language. Consequently, interactions are usually conducted at the knowledge level; in terms of which goals should be followed, at what time, and by whom. Secondly, as agents are flexible problem solvers, operating in an environment over which they have only partial control and observability, interactions need to be handled in a similarly flexible manner. Thus, agents need the computational apparatus to make context-dependent decisions about the nature and scope of their interactions and to initiate (and respond to) interactions that were not necessarily foreseen at design time.

To summarize, the traditional view of an object and our view of an agent have at least three distinctions:

- Agents embody a stronger notion of autonomy than objects, and in particular, they decide for themselves whether or not to perform an action on request from other agents;
- Agents are capable of flexible (reactive, pro-active, social) behavior, and the standard object model has nothing to say about such types of behavior; and
- A multi-agent system is inherently multi-threaded, in that each agent is assumed to have at least one thread of control.

3.4 Agents and Expert Systems

There are also some differences between agents and expert systems [4, 10].

Expert systems were the most important artificial intelligence technology of the 1980s. An expert system is one that is capable of solving problems or giving advice in some knowledge-rich domain. (Refer to Sect. 2.1.1.) A classic example of an expert system is MYCIN, which was intended to assist physicians in the treatment of blood infections in humans. MYCIN worked by a process of interacting with a user in order to present the system with a number of (symbolically represented) facts, which the system then used to derive some conclusion. MYCIN acted very much as a consultant: it did not operate directly on humans, or indeed any other environment. Thus perhaps the most important distinction between agents and expert systems is that expert systems like MYCIN are inherently *disembodied*. By this, we mean that they do not interact directly with any environment: they get their information not via sensors, but through a user acting as middle man. In the same way, they do not act on any environment, but rather give feedback, or advice, to a third party. In addition, expert systems are not generally capable of cooperating with other agents.

In summary, the main differences between agents and expert systems are as follows:

- classic expert systems are disembodied – they are not coupled to any environment in which they act, but rather act through a user as a "middleman";
- expert systems are not generally capable of reactive, proactive behaviour; and
- expert systems are not generally equipped with social ability, in the sense of cooperation, coordination, and negotiation.

Despite these differences, some expert systems (particularly those that perform real-time control tasks) look very much like agents. A good example is the ARCHON system [127].

3.5 Approaches to Agentification

There are many legacy software packages of intelligent techniques available for different applications. When constructing hybrid intelligent systems, it is of paramount importance to utilize these software packages. On the other hand, for hybrid intelligent systems to be fully accepted in real-world applications, they must be able to integrate and communicate with legacy computing systems. When constructing hybrid intelligent systems from an agent-oriented viewpoint, this implies that some techniques should be available for converting such legacy programs into agents. In work thus far, a number of different approaches have been taken – implementing a *transducer*, implementing a *wrapper*, and *rewriting* the original program [42].

3.5.1 Implementing a Transducer

One approach is to implement a *transducer* that mediates between an existing program and other agents. The transducer accepts messages from other agents, translates them into the program's native communication protocol, and passes those messages to the program. It accepts the program's responses, translates into agent communication language (ACL) such as Knowledge Query and Manipulation Language (KQML) [44, 46], and sends the resulting messages on to other agents. This approach has the advantage of requiring no knowledge of the program other than its communication behavior. It is, therefore, especially useful for situations in which the code for the program is unavailable or too delicate to modify. This approach also works for other types of resources, such as files and people. It is a simple matter to write a program to read or modify an existing file with a specialized format, thereby providing access to that file via ACL. Similarly, it is possible to provide a graphical user interface for a person, allowing one to interact with the system in a specialized graphical language, which is then converted into ACL, and vice versa.

3.5.2 Implementing a Wrapper

A second approach to dealing with legacy software is to implement a *wrapper*, i.e., inject code into a program to allow it to communicate in ACL. The wrapper can directly examine the data structures of the program and can modify those data structures. Furthermore, it may be possible to inject calls out of the program so it can take advantage of externally available information and services. This approach has the advantage of greater efficiency than the transduction approach, since there is less serial communication. It also works for cases having no interprocess communication ability in the original program. However, this requires the code for the program to be available.

3.5.3 Rewriting

Of course, the third and most drastic approach to dealing with legacy software is to rewrite the original program. The advantage of this approach is that it may be possible to enhance its efficiency or capability beyond what would be possible in either the transduction or wrapping approaches.

3.5.4 Steps for Implementing a Wrapper

In the implementation of agent-based hybrid intelligent systems that will be described in Chaps. 7 and 8, the second approach – implementing a wrapper – was adopted to wrap the legacy programs by using Java Native Interface [50].

In order to access a native method (typically written in C/C++) from a Java program, a class was created for the native method, and the native method invoked using normal Java method invocation syntax. Native methods are created using the following steps:

- Create a Java class for the native method and include code to load the native method's shared library (under Unix) or dynamically linked library (under Microsoft Windows);
- Use *javah* to create C language header files for the native method;
- Implement the native method as a C function;
- Compile and link the C code to create the shared library or dynamically linked library.

These are the steps we use when implementing the two systems.

3.6 Approaches to Incorporating Intelligent Techniques into Agents

There are many ways one can incorporate different intelligent techniques such as fuzzy logic, neural networks, and genetic algorithms into agents. The applicability of any method depends heavily on one's selection of the agent development language and delivery platforms, as well as on one's overall agent architecture and, to a lesser extent, the infrastructure over or within which the agent system exists. All these approaches can be divided into two categories: loosely coupled and tightly coupled, which correspond to the two categories of hybrid intelligent systems.

There are three principal methods for incorporating intelligent techniques into individual agents from the implementation point of view [29]:

- Via .DLL (Dynamically Linked Libraries) or other callable APIs (Application Programming Interface);
- Through specific interface agents and stand-alone intelligent systems;
- Intelligent technique components as Object-Oriented classes [35].

The first two methods are usually used in loose-coupling models, whereas the third one is usually used in tight-coupling models.

3.7 Agent-Based Hybrid Systems: State of the Art

Each intelligent technique has particular strengths and weaknesses, and they cannot be applied universally to every problem. Furthermore, a collection of agents are needed for complex decision making. Hence integrating two or more intelligent techniques with multiple agents is very important. There has been some research work involving in this topic.

3.7.1 The MIX Multi-agent Platform

One of such attempts is the MIX multi-agent platform [37, 83]. The focus of MIX is to develop strategies and tools for integrating neural and symbolic technologies. This test-bed consists of a distributed system of multiple cooperating heterogeneous agents. The system includes a multi-agent toolkit with generic agent structures, services, and communication protocols. Specific agents have been developed for different types of neural networks and for other functions such as fuzzy inference and case-based reasoning.

3.7.2 The PREDICTOR System

Another such attempt is the PREDICTOR system. In [38] Scherer and Schlageter detail the use of distributed artificial intelligence approaches for combining neural networks and expert systems. The approach is based on a blackboard architecture and is demonstrated in the domain of economic forecasting. The authors have implemented a system called PREDICTOR using this approach to solve prediction tasks in economics. The architecture of the PREDICTOR system is shown in Fig. 3.1.

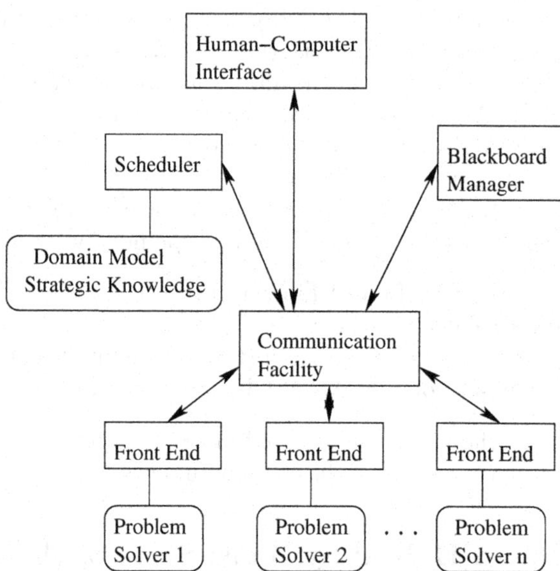

Fig. 3.1. Architecture of PREDICTOR

In this architecture, each problem solver has specific knowledge about the domain and has the ability to react to messages that are distributed via the communication facility. To handle the communication aspects of this system, each problem solver has a front end processor which is responsible for managing its co-operative aspects. The communication facility distributes messages all over the system (scheduler, problem solvers). The blackboard manager provides other nodes with blackboard operations like *search*, *read*, *write*, and *update*. The scheduler is responsible for the task analysis, task allocation and task synthesis. Domain dependent knowledge, specific analysis and allocation strategies are stored at a meta level within a knowledge base. This meta knowledge controls the problem solving abilities of the scheduler.

3.7.3 Intelligent Multi-agent Hybrid Distributed Architecture

In [39], Khosla and Dillon introduce a computational architecture called IMAHDA (Intelligent Multi-Agent Hybrid Distributed Architecture). The role and knowledge content of IMAHDA consists of four layers. They are: object, software agent, intelligent agent, and problem solving agent respectively. The IMAHDA can be seen as being constructed from generic software agents (distributed processing, distributed communication, belief base, and relational software agents), generic intelligent agents (expert/knowledge based system, supervised neural network, unsupervised neural network, fuzzy logic, genetic algorithm intelligent agents), and problem solving agents (global preprocessing, decomposition, control, decision, and post processing agents) as shown in Fig. 3.2.

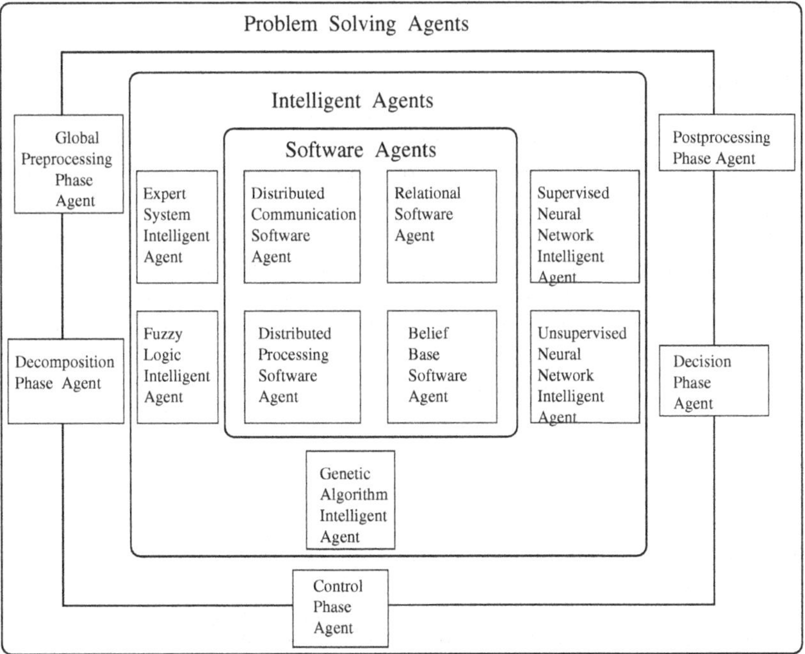

Fig. 3.2. Agent Building Blocks of IMAHDA

3.7.4 Multi-agent Architecture for Fuzzy Modeling

A more recent attempt is the multi-agent architecture for fuzzy modeling [40]. Delgado et al. have proposed a hybrid learning system that combines different fuzzy modeling techniques by means of a multi-agent architecture. The proposed multi-agent architecture, involving agents which embody the different problem solving methods, is a flexible tool to be used in the fuzzy modeling process. The system consists of four kinds of agents: a service agent or facilitator acting as a Yellow Page to other agents, task agents (including clustering, rule generation, tuning, and evaluator agents), resource agents, and control agents (containing planner, decisor, and error control agents).

3.7.5 Generic Architecture for Hybrid Intelligent Systems

In [121], Jacobsen has proposed a generic architecture for hybrid intelligent systems, which is based on the conceptual learning agent architecture according to Russell and Norvig [3]. They presented two instantiations of the architecture – reinforcement-driven fuzzy-relation-adaptation architecture and an expert-guided hybrid neuro-fuzzy system, and have experimentally validated their designs.

3.7.6 Summary

Among the above five agent-based hybrid systems, the MIX, PREDICTOR, and architecture for fuzzy modeling only integrated very limited soft computing techniques. Both the MIX and PREDICTOR systems are focused on the integration of neural networks and symbolic technologies such as expert systems. The multi-agent architecture of Delgado et al. concentrated on the integration of different fuzzy modeling techniques such as fuzzy clustering, fuzzy rule generation, and fuzzy rule tuning techniques. In MIX and PREDICTOR systems, the way for integrating intelligent techniques into multi-agent systems is to embed the intelligent techniques in each individual agent. The MIX and IMAHDA architectures are inflexible as no middle agent [41] was used. The work in [121] is focused on the micro (intra-agent) level of agents, i.e., the integration and interaction of different components within one agent. The macro (inter-agent) level integration and interaction are ignored.

In summarizing, the approaches used in the above systems have the following limitations.

- It is impossible to embed many intelligent techniques within a single agent. Otherwise, the agents will be overloaded. In many applications, the agents in multi-agent systems should be kept simple for ease of maintenance, initialization, and customization.

- It is not flexible to add more intelligent techniques to, or delete some unwanted one from, the multi-agent systems. For example, one software agent may be equipped with fuzzy logic, the other with a neural network etc. In such a case, one agent can only have one soft computing capability. If we want the agent to possess two or more soft computing or hard computing capabilities, the implementations must be modified.
- The agents in these systems are difficult to inter-operate as they do not use a common type of or standard agent communication language.

In addition to the above limitations, all these systems do not follow any agent-oriented analysis and design methodology. (In IMAHDA, object-oriented analysis and design approaches were adopted.) Therefore it is essential to find a new way to integrate intelligent techniques with multi-agent systems that can overcome the drawbacks of currently used approaches. Moreover, it is vital to tailor an agent-oriented methodology for agent based hybrid intelligent system construction which is based on currently available agent-oriented approaches.

4 Agent-Oriented Methodologies

Developing applications in terms of autonomous software agents that exhibit proactive and intelligent behavior, and that interact with one another in terms of high-level protocols and languages, leads to a new programming paradigm. By dint of being a new programming paradigm, the development of agent-based applications implies new programming abstractions and techniques, as well as new methodologies.

Agent-based systems for complex problem solving and decision making, like hybrid intelligent systems, usually have a large number of parts or components that have many interactions. These interactions may occur at unpredictable times, for unpredictable reasons, between unpredictable components. Existing software development techniques (typically, object-oriented) are inadequate for modeling agent-based systems, as they cannot manage these complex interactions efficiently. Existing approaches fail to adequately capture an agent's flexible, autonomous problem-solving behavior, the richness of an agent's interactions, and the complexity of an agent system's organizational structures [81]. For these reasons, agent-oriented methodologies are required to build agent-based systems for different applications.

This chapter first provides a brief overview of the present state of the art in the area of software engineering methodologies for agent-based systems. An agent-oriented methodology for the analysis and design of agent-based hybrid intelligent systems is then extracted, which is mainly based on the Gaia methodology [81].

4.1 Traditional Methodologies

A number of different methodologies have been proposed in recent years for modeling and engineering agents and multi-agent systems [75, 76, 86, 88]. However, traditional methodologies for analysis and design are poorly suited to multi-agent systems because of the fundamental mismatch between the respective levels of abstraction. Despite this mismatch, several proposals do take

Z. Zhang, C. Zhang: Agent-Based Hybrid Intelligent Systems, LNAI 2938, pp. 43–55, 2004.

object-oriented modeling techniques or methodologies as their basis. On the one hand, some proposals directly extend the applicability of object-oriented methodologies and techniques to the design of agent systems. However, these proposals fail to capture the autonomous and proactive behavior of agents, as well as the richness of their interactions. On the other hand, some proposals seek to extend and adapt object-oriented models and techniques to define a methodology for use in multi-agent systems. This can lead, for example, to extended models suitable for representing agent behavior and their interactions [77, 90], as well as to agent-tuned extensions of UML (Unified Modeling Language) [77]. However, although these proposals can sometimes achieve a good modeling of the autonomous behavior of agents and of their interactions, they lack the conceptual mechanisms for adequately dealing with organizations and agent societies.

A different set of proposals build upon, and extend, methodologies and modeling techniques from knowledge engineering [78]. These techniques provide formal and compositional modeling languages for the verification of system structure and function. These approaches are well-suited to modeling knowledge- and information- oriented agents. However, since these approaches usually assume a centralized view of knowledge-based systems, they fail to provide adequate models and support for the societal view of multi-agent systems.

Other models and approaches attempt to model and implement multi-agent systems from an "organization-oriented" point of view [79]. These help pave the way for agent-oriented methodologies by explicitly conceiving multi-agent systems as organizations or as societies. However, these proposals define an organization merely as a collection of interacting roles, thus failing, again, to deal with the key issue of social tasks.

4.2 Gaia Methodology

The Gaia methodology [80, 81] represents one of the few attempts specifically tailored to the analysis and design of multi-agent systems, and which deals with both the micro (intra-agent) level and the macro (inter-agent) level of analysis and design. Gaia makes explicit use of an organizational point of view. In this methodology, analysis and design are well-separated phases. The analysis aims to develop an understanding of the system and its structure, in terms of the roles that have to be played in agent organization and interaction, without any reference to implementation details. The design phase aims to define the actual structure of the agent system of the services to be provided by each agent, and of the acquaintances' structure. However, Gaia, as it presently stands, is not a general methodology for all kinds of multi-agent systems. Rather, it is intended to support the development of distributed problem solvers in which the system's constituent components are known at design time (i.e., it is a closed system) and in which all agents are expected to cooperate toward the achievement of a global goal. For these reasons, Gaia is not suitable for modeling open systems, and for controlling the behavior of self-interested agents.

Similar shortcomings also affect most of the recently proposed organization-oriented methodologies. For example, the MASE (Multi-Agent Systems Engineering) methodology [89, 86, 88] provides clean guidelines for developing multi-agent systems, based on a well-defined seven-step process (capturing goals, applying use cases, refining roles, creating agent classes, constructing conversations, assembling agent classes, and system design). This process drives developers from analysis to implementation. However, once again, the design process fails to identify any organizational abstraction other than the role model.

4.3 Coordination-Oriented Methodology

In [75], the authors broaden the scope of Gaia, and indicate that insights from the area of coordination models can be incorporated in order to make it more suitable for developing Internet-based applications. The adoption of a coordination model as the conceptual abstraction to be exploited in the analysis and design of multi-agent systems for the Internet enables open systems, self-interested agents, and social laws, to find suitable accommodation. On this basis, the methodological concepts introduced by Gaia can be effectively complemented by the concepts of social laws and coordination media, leading to the definition of a coordination-oriented methodology suitable for multi-agent Internet systems. Yet, to date, the coordination-oriented methodology is far from being well-defined.

To date, the organizational concepts of agent roles and role models have become an important research area in the field of agent-based systems. In [87], Zambonelli, Jennings, and Wooldridge introduced three further organizational abstractions: organizational rules, organizational structures, and organizational patterns. They sketched some general guidelines for a new methodology for the analysis and design of multi-agent systems that is centered around organizational abstractions.

4.4 Prometheus Methodology

Another agent-oriented methodology that has proven effective in assisting developers to design, document, and build agent systems is the *Prometheus* methodology [139]. This methodology supports, in particular, the development of BDI-like agents.

The *Prometheus* methodology consists of three phases. The *system specification phase* focuses on identifying the basic functionalities of the system, along with inputs (percepts), outputs (actions) and any important shared data sources. The *architectural design phase* uses outputs from the previous phase to determine which agents the system will contain and how they will interact. The *detailed design phase* looks at the internals of each agent and how it will accomplish its tasks within the overall system.

4.5 Methodology for Analysis and Design of Agent-Based Hybrids

From the discussions so far, it is clear that hybrid intelligent systems are crucial for complex problem solving and decision making. It is also apparent that agent abstraction can be used by software developers to more naturally and easily understand, model, and develop hybrid intelligent systems. Agent-based hybrid intelligent systems have the following main characteristics:

- agents are heterogeneous, in that different agents may be implemented using different programming languages, architectures, and techniques;
- the organizational structure of the system is dynamic, and agents can dynamically leave and enter the system;
- agents exhibit social behavior, in that they interact with one another to cooperate to achieve a common objective;
- there are no self-interested agents in the systems; and
- integration and interaction of different techniques is crucial.

An agent-oriented methodology that has been specifically tailored to the analysis and design of agent-based hybrid intelligent systems is required. Dozens of agent-oriented methodologies have been proposed [76]. Although there is no one methodology that can fully meet the requirements of the analysis and design of agent-based hybrid intelligent systems, the Gaia methodology is the most suitable, after comparing many of the methodologies. The methodology used in the development of the systems in Chaps. 7 and 8 is outlined below. It is mainly based on the *Gaia methodology* [81], the *coordination-oriented methodology* [75], and the *organization abstraction* [87], but is extended with the *knowledge* and *skills* models as *rich knowledge* and *adequate information* as well as *proficient skills* to use the knowledge and information are key factors in complex problem solving and decision making.

4.5.1 Outline of the Methodology

In any agent-based hybrid intelligent system for real-world applications, the dynamic arrival of unknown agents needs to be taken into account, but with no self-interested behavior in the course of the interactions. The Gaia methodology is ill suited to handling the dynamic arrival of new agents into the system, whereas coordination-oriented methodology is focused on the processing of self-interested agents. Thus both methodologies cannot be applied to the analysis and design of hybrid intelligent systems directly.

In Gaia methodology, analysis and design are well-separated phases. The analysis phase aims to identify what the actual organization of the multiple agents should look like. It does this by decomposing the system into abstract "loci of control", i.e., the *roles* to be played in the organization, and the way in which they interact accordingly to specific *protocols*. This defines the *role model* and *interaction model*. The design phase starts from the models defined during the analysis phase and aims to define the actual agent system in such a way that it can easily be implemented. To this end, the design phase has to decide which classes of agents, and how many, have to play the roles identified during the analysis phase (*agent model*); which services agents must provide to fulfill their role (*service model*); and what is the actual topology of the interactions that flows from interaction and the agent models (*acquaintance model*).

The concept of *coordination models* can be exploited in the context of designing multi-agent systems for use on the Internet, where openness and self-interest are key factors. A coordination model can be thought of as consisting of three elements [75]. They are:

- the *coordinables*: the entities whose mutual interaction is ruled by the model, e.g., the agents in a multi-agent system;
- the *coordination media*: the abstractions enabling agent interactions, as well as the core around which the components of a coordinated system are organized. Examples are semaphores, monitors, channels, or more complex media like tuple spaces, blackboards;
- the *coordination laws*: define the behavior of the coordination media in response to interaction events. The laws can be defined in terms of a communication language (a syntax used to express and exchange data structures) and a coordination language (a set of interaction primitives and their semantics).

The architecture of a multi-agent system can naturally be viewed as a computational organization. For the complete specification of computational organizations, three additional organizational concepts – organizational rules, organizational structures, and organizational patterns are introduced [87]. Zambonelli, Jennings, and Wooldridge [87] argue that these concepts are of fundamental importance in multi-agent systems, and they should play a central role in any methodology.

Furthermore, in complex problem solving and decision making, the rapport of information, knowledge, and skills to use the information and knowledge is of paramount importance. When working on a methodology for such agent-based systems, one should pay attention to the *knowledge* and *skills* of agents.

Taking all these factors into account, a methodology for the analysis and design of agent-based hybrid intelligent systems based on the Gaia methodology, coordination model, and organization abstraction is created.

We propose that such a methodology should consist of the construction of six main models: agent models, role models, skill models, knowledge models, an organizational model, and an interaction model. Each of the steps in the methodology below results in the construction of one (or more) of the corresponding models. The methodology for their elaboration and refinement can be expressed in five steps.

1. The first step consists of the identification of the *roles* in the application domain in terms of the corresponding goals or tasks. Consequently, a role is identified by the main tasks or responsibilities required by the system and forms the basis for a specification of *agent types*.
2. Secondly, the main *skills* associated with agent roles should be identified. Skills consist of the basic services required to be able to perform a role and ways to manipulate knowledge (reasoning techniques). The issue of agent-wrapping should be addressed in this step, which involves the integration of non-agent software components, and the design of an appropriate interface.
3. The third step consists of the modeling of the *knowledge* about the application domain associated with identified roles or skills and should result in the design of an adequate ontology. Techniques from knowledge engineering can be used here.
4. Fourthly, an *organizational* structure of the multi-agent system should be designed. The coordination among agents to perform a task and the required communication schemes need to be analyzed in this step.
5. Finally, the dynamics of the multi-agent system should be analyzed in terms of the flow of information, resulting in, for example, synchronization requirements derived from the roles associated with individual agents.

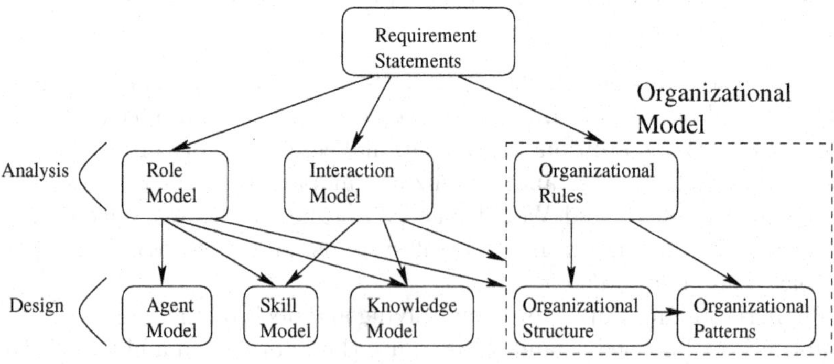

Fig. 4.1. Relationships between Models

With this methodology, analysis and design can be thought of as a process of developing increasingly detailed *models* of the system to be constructed. The main models used in this methodology are summarized in Fig. 4.1. More details are given in the following subsections. The descriptions of role models, interaction models, and agent models are based on [81]. The description of organizational model (organizational rules, organizational structure, and organizational patterns) is based on [87].

4.5.2 Role Model

The role model identifies the key roles in the system. Here a role can be viewed as an abstract description of an entity's expected function. A role is defined by four attributes: *responsibilities, permissions, activities* and *protocols.*

Responsibilities determine functionality and, as such, are perhaps the key attribute associated with a role. Responsibilities are divided into two types: *liveness properties* and *safety properties.* Liveness properties intuitively state that "something good happens". They describe those states of affairs that an agent must bring about, given certain environmental conditions. In contrast, safety properties are *invariants.* Intuitively, a safety property states that "nothing bad happens" (i.e., that an acceptable state of affairs is maintained across all states of execution).

In order to realize responsibilities, a role has a set of *permissions.* Permissions are the "rights" associated with a role. The permissions of a role thus identify the resources that are available to that role in order to realize its responsibilities. Permissions tend to be *information resources.* For example, a role might have associated with it the ability to read a particular item of information, or to modify another piece of information. A role can also have the ability to generate information. The *activities* of a role are computations associated with the role that may be carried out by the agent without interacting with other agents.

Finally, a role is also identified with a number of *protocols*, which define the way that it can interact with other roles. A role model is comprised of a set of *role schemata*, one for each role in the system. A role schema draws together the various attributes discussed above into a single place (see Fig. 4.2).

The formal notation for expressing protocols, activities, permissions, and responsibilities adopted by Gaia will be used. To introduce these concepts, the example of a PRICEWATCHER role will be used. The purpose of this role is to monitor whether the trading price of a specific security has exceeded the expected value of the share holder. The protocols and activities involved in the PRICEWATCHER role include: InformShareholder, GetInitializeInformation, GetPrice and <u>Compare</u>. The activity names (like <u>Compare</u>) are underlined to distinguish them from protocols.

The following is an illustration of the permissions associated with the role PRICEWATCHER:

reads supplied *SecurityCode* // Security code used in Share Exchanger
supplied *ExpectedValue* // The value the shareholder expected
supplied *TradingPrice* // The current trading price of the security

Role Schema:	*name of role*
Description	*short English description of the role*
Protocols and Activities	*protocols and activities in which the role plays a part*
Permissions	*"rights" associated with the role*
Responsibilities	
Liveness	*liveness responsibilities*
Safety	*safety responsibilities*

Fig. 4.2. Template for Role Schemata

This specification defines three permissions for PRICEWATCHER. It says that the agent carrying out the role has permissions to access the value of $SecurityCode$, $ExpectedValue$ and $TradingPrice$. The **supplied** keyword here is used to indicate that some roles are parameterized by certain values. Another two types of permission are `changes` (read and modify) and `generates` (produce a resource). Note that these permissions relate to the *knowledge* that the agent has.

The liveness responsibilities for the PRICEWATCHER role might be:

- whenever the share exchange is not closed, get the trading price of the specific security (indicated by the $SecurityCode$);
- whenever the trading price has exceeded the expected value, inform the share holder.

Following the Gaia notation, liveness properties are specified via a *liveness expression*, which defines the "life-cycle" of the role and is a regular expression. The general form of a liveness expression is:

$$\text{ROLENAME} = \mathit{expression}$$

where ROLENAME is the name of the role whose liveness properties are being defined, and $expression$ is the liveness expression defining the liveness properties of ROLENAME. The atomic components of a liveness expression are either *activities* or *protocols*. The operators for liveness expressions are shown in Table 4.1.

Thus the liveness responsibilities of the PRICEWATCHER role can be expressed as:

$$\text{PRICEWATCHER} = (\mathsf{GetInitializeInformation})+.(\mathsf{GetPrice}, \underline{\mathsf{Compare}})+.(\mathsf{InformShareholder})*.$$

This expression says that PRICEWATCHER consists of executing the protocol GetInitializeInformation, followed by the protocol GetPrice, followed by the activity <u>Compare</u> and the protocol InformShareholder.

Table 4.1. Operators for Liveness Expressions

Operator	Interpretation
$x.y$	x followed by y
$x \vert y$	x or y occurs
$x*$	x occurs 0 or more times
$x+$	x occurs 1 or more times
x^ω	x occurs infinitely often
$[x]$	x is optional
$x \Vert y$	x and y interleaved

Safety requirements are specified by means of a list of predicates. These predicates are typically expressed over the variables listed in a role's permission attribute. By convention, safety expressions are listed as a bulleted list, each item in the list expressing an individual safety responsibility.

When all these are put together, the schema for the PRICEWATCHER role results (Fig. 4.3).

Role Schema: PRICEWATCHER
Description: This role involves monitoring whether the trading price of a specific security has exceeded the expected value of the share holder.
Protocols and Activities: InformShareholder, GetInitializeInformation, GetPrice, <u>Compare</u>
Permissions: **reads supplied** *SecurityCode* // Security code used in Share Exchanger **supplied** *ExpectedValue* // The value the shareholder expected **supplied** *TradingPrice* // The current trading price of the security
Responsibilities Liveness: PRICEWATCHER = (GetInitializeInformation)+.(GetPrice, <u>Compare</u>)+.(InformShareholder)* Safety: • True

Fig. 4.3. Schema for Role PRICEWATCHER

4.5.3 Interaction Model

There are inevitably dependencies and relationships between the various roles in a multi-agent organization. Indeed, such interplay is central to the way in which the system functions. Given this fact, interactions obviously need to be captured and represented in the analysis phase. Such links between roles are represented in the *interaction model*. This model consists of a set of *protocol definitions*, one for each type of inter-role interaction. Here a protocol can be viewed as an institutionalized pattern of interactions.

A protocol definition consists of the following attributes:

- *purpose*: brief textual description of the nature of the interaction (e.g., 'information request', 'schedule activity', and 'assign task');
- *initiator*: the role(s) responsible for starting the interaction;
- *responder*: the role(s) with which the initiator interacts;
- *inputs*: information used by the role initiator while enacting the protocol;
- *outputs*: information supplied by/to the protocol responder during the course of the interaction;
- *processing*: brief textual description of any processing the protocol initiator performs during the course of the interaction.

As an illustration, the GetPrice protocol is considered, which forms part of the PRICEWATCHER role (Fig. 4.4). This states that the protocol GetPrice is initiated by the role PRICEWATCHER and involves the role SHAREEXCHANGER. This protocol involves PRICEWATCHER providing SHAREEXCHANGER with the *SecurityCode*, and results in SHAREEXCHANGER returning the value of the *Trading Price* for security designated by the *SecurityCode*.

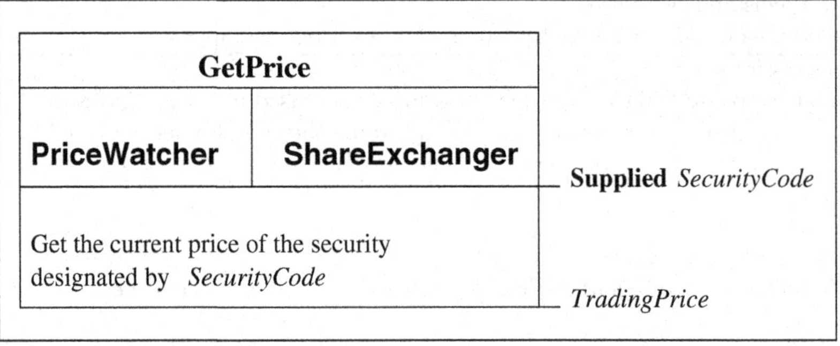

Fig. 4.4. The GetPrice Protocol Definition

4.5.4 Organizational Rules

Role models precisely describe all the roles that constitute the computational organization, in terms of their functionalities, activities, and responsibilities, as well as in terms of their interaction protocols and patterns, which establish the position of each role in the organization. However, such role models cannot be considered as the sole organizational abstraction upon which to base the entire development process. Rather, before the design process actually defines the role model and, consequently, the whole organization, the analysis phase should define how the organization is expected to work, i.e., the organizational rules. These describe the constraints that the actual organization, once defined, will have to respect.

The explicit identification of organizational rules is of particular importance in the context of open agent systems. With the arrival of new, and previously unknown, agents, the overall organization must somehow enforce its internal coherency despite the dynamic and untrustworthy environment. The identification of global organizational rules allows the hybrid system designer to explicitly define whether and when to allow newly arrived agents to enter the organization, and once accepted, what their position in the organization should be.

In summary, the analysis phase is tasked with collecting all the specifications from which the design of the computational organization can start. (Refer to Fig. 4.1.) The output of the analysis phase should be a triple, $\langle PR, PP, OL \rangle$, where PR are the preliminary roles of the system, PP are the preliminary protocols (which have already been discovered to be necessary for the preliminary roles), and OL are the organizational rules.

4.5.5 Agent Model

The purpose of the agent model is to document the various *agent types* that will be used in the system under development, and the *agent instances* that will realize these agent types at run-time.

An agent type is best thought of as a set of agent roles. There may, in fact, be a one-to-one correspondence between roles (as identified in the role model) and agent types. However, this need not be the case. A designer can choose to package a number of closely related roles in the same agent type for the purpose of convenience. Efficiency will also be a major concern at this stage – a designer will almost certainly want to optimize the design, and one way of doing this is to aggregate a number of agent roles into a single type.

The agent model is defined using a simple *agent type tree*, in which leaf nodes correspond to roles, and other nodes correspond to agent types. If an agent type t_1 has children t_2 and t_3, then this means that t_1 is composed of the roles that make up t_2 and t_3.

4.5.6 Skill Model

The aim of the skill model is to identify the main skills with each agent role. Skills mainly consist of the basic *services* required to be able to perform a role.

A service is defined as a *function* of the agent. For each service that may be performed by an agent, it is necessary to document its properties. Specifically, one must identify the *inputs, outputs, pre-conditions*, and *post-conditions* of each service. Inputs and outputs to services will be derived in an obvious way from the interaction model. Pre- and post-conditions represent constraints on services. These are derived from the safety properties of a role. Note that by definition, each role will be associated with at least one service.

The services that an agent will perform are derived from the list of protocols, activities, responsibilities and the liveness properties of a role. The inference mechanisms used by roles also need to be identified in this model.

4.5.7 Knowledge Model

The knowledge model identifies the different knowledge levels needed by each identified agent in the agent model. The first level of knowledge is for agent interaction and communication. This involves domain-specific and domain-independent terminologies and their relationships, an so on. The identified domain-specific terms and their relationships will result in the construction of a domain-dependent ontology for a specific application. The identified domain-independent terms and their relationships will result in customizing a domain-independent ontology from some available general-purpose ontologies.

The second level of knowledge is some domain knowledge related to specific problem solving techniques. This part of knowledge can be represented by typical $if-then$ rules. These rules are also domain-specific.

The third level of knowledge is meta knowledge that directs the activities of an agent. This part of knowledge can also be represented by $if-then$ rules. These rules are more abstract than those in the second level.

4.5.8 Organizational Structures and Patterns

In the design of a multi-agent system, as well as in the design of any organization, the role model should derive from the organizational structure that is explicitly chosen. Thus organizational structures should be viewed as first-class abstractions in the design of multi-agent systems.

The definition of the system's overall organizational structure can derive from the specifications collected during the analysis phase, as well as from other factors, related to efficiency, simplicity of application design, and organizational theory. In any case, a methodology cannot start the analysis phase by attempting to define a complete role model that implicitly sets the organizational structure. Rather, the definition of the organizational structure is a design choice that should not be anticipated during the analysis phase.

The obvious means by which to specify an organization is through the inter-agent relationships that exist within it. There is no universally accepted terminology set of organizational relationships: different types of organizations make use of entirely different organizational concepts.

The aim of organizational patterns is to encourage re-use of pre-defined components and architectures in order to ease and speed-up the work of both designers and developers. With the availability of catalogs of *organizational patterns*, designers can recognize in their multi-agent systems the presence of known patterns, and re-use definitions from the catalog. In addition, designers can also be guided by the catalog in the choice of the most appropriate organizational patterns for their multi-agent system. Of course, for patterns to be properly exploited, the organizational structure must have been explicitly identified in the design phase.

The design phase builds on the output of the analysis phase and produces a complete specification of the multi-agent system. The design stage can now be summarized.

- Create an agent model: (1) aggregate roles into agent types, and refine to form an agent type hierarchy; (2) document the instances of each agent type using instance annotations.
- Develop a skill model, by examining activities, protocols, and safety and liveness properties of roles.
- Develop an knowledge model from the interaction model and agent model.
- Identify organizational structures and organizational patterns that respect the organizational rules.

4.6 Summary

Agent-oriented methodologies are required to build agent-based systems, as there is a fundamental mismatch between the concepts used by other mainstream software engineering paradigms and the agent-oriented perspective.

Taking into account the characteristics of hybrid intelligent systems, a methodology for the analysis and design of agent-based hybrid intelligent systems was outlined, which is based on the Gaia methodology and organizational abstractions. These guidelines allow us to start the analysis and design an agent-based hybrid intelligent system. However, further work is needed to detail the proposed methodology, by:

- fully formalizing the concepts of organizational rules and organizational structures;
- fully formalizing the concepts of a knowledge model;
- providing suitable notations for expressing the expected outputs of the analysis and design phases.

5

Agent-Based Framework for Hybrid Intelligent Systems

Agents are good at dynamic interactions, a trait that is crucial for the success of hybrid intelligent systems. Meanwhile, to greatly facilitate the construction of hybrid intelligent systems from agent perspectives, a unifying agent-based framework is required. Under the support of such a framework, it is expected that any new capabilities (in the form of additional agents) can easily be added to a hybrid intelligent system, and any techniques no longer used can be dynamically deleted from a system. Such an agent-based framework is proposed in this chapter.

5.1 A Unifying Agent Framework for Hybrid Intelligent Systems

As discussed in Chap. 2, using current approaches to constructing hybrid intelligent systems results in non-adaptive organization. This shortcoming can be overcome with agent technology. With this technology, a special kind of agent (called a middle agent [41]) can be introduced into the system. Any other agents can add to the system by simply registering with the middle agent, or leave the system by unregistering with the middle agent.

One of the basic problems facing designers of open, multi-agent systems for the Internet is the connection problem, that is finding other agents who might have suitable information or other capabilities that one agent needs. To answer this question, different types of middle agents are usually employed [41]. Like middlemen in physical commerce, middle agents support the flow of information in electronic commerce, assisting in locating and connecting the ultimate information, or service provider, with the ultimate information, or service requester.

The performance of middle agents relies heavily on the matchmaking algorithms used. Matchmaking is the process of finding an appropriate provider for a requester through a middle agent. There has been substantial work carried out on "matchmaking" involving in different kinds of middle agents [114]. As

Z. Zhang, C. Zhang: Agent-Based Hybrid Intelligent Systems, LNAI 2938, pp. 57–64, 2004.

this is also crucial for the success of the proposed framework, we will discuss this topic in detail in Chap. 6.

To help agent-based hybrid intelligent systems to make decisions about the nature and scope of interactions at run-time, each agent should be autonomous. This is one of four main characteristics of agents [1]. Of course, it is important too that it is well designed. A planning agent with the capability to generate work plans based on the tasks received is also required. The hybrid intelligent systems can be reconfigured dynamically according to the work plans generated.

In order to add new problem solving techniques/capabilities to a system, they should be converted into agents. Generally, there are three main approaches to be taken: implementing a *transducer*, implementing a *wrapper*, and *rewriting* the original program as described in Sect. 3.5. Once they are converted into agents, they can be easily integrated into the system. In that way new capabilities are added to a system in the form of agents.

As any problem solving agent may only have limited capabilities, it needs the help of other agents when solving a complex problem. The problem solving agents can ask for help by sending requests to the middle agents in a system.

Of course, an interface is needed to communicate with users. All agents in a system should explain the meaning of received messages in the same way. This is accomplished by sharing a common ontology. Putting all these together results in the agent-based framework for hybrid intelligent systems which is shown in Fig. 5.1.

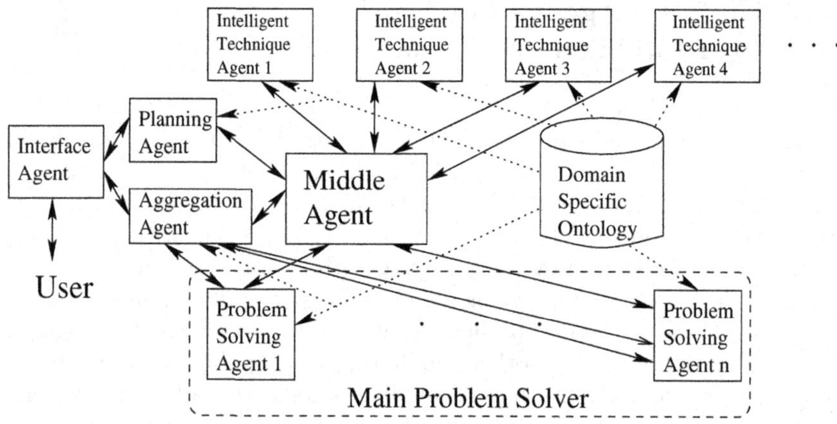

Fig. 5.1. General Framework of Agent-Based Hybrid Intelligent Systems

This framework is general, and can be applied to build agent-based hybrid intelligent systems for different applications. Some successful case studies based on the framework will be presented in Chaps. 7 and 8 to verify the applicability of this framework, and further justify that agent perspectives are well suited to building hybrid intelligent systems. These examples will be also used to demonstrate how to construct agent-based hybrid intelligent systems.

Compared with those agent-based hybrid systems described in Sect. 3.7, the framework has some crucial characteristics that differentiate this work from other hybrid intelligent systems.

- It has the ability to exchange comprehensible communications (interactions at knowledge level).
- Each service requester agent (decision making agent) can easily access all the intelligent techniques provided by service provider agents (e.g., soft computing agents) in the system.
- The presence of the middle agent in the framework allows adaptive system organization. For example, if we are sure that one hybrid soft computing agent can do a better job than a single technology soft computing agent, we can delete the single soft computing technology agent and add the hybrid agent to the society simply by adding or deleting a record in the database of the serving agent.
- Overall system robustness is facilitated through the use of the middle agent. For example, if a particular service provider (e.g., a soft computing agent) disappears, a requester agent (decision making agent) can find another one with the same or similar capabilities by interrogating the middle agent.
- Agent-based hybrid intelligent systems based on the framework can make decisions about the nature and scope of interactions at run time.

With the support of the agent-based intelligent technique society, the agent-based hybrid intelligent system developers need only to build the domain-specific parts and construct the ontologies used in the specific application field – rather than re-inventing the wheel as often happens at the moment. For demonstration purpose, an example ontology for finance that we have built is presented in the next section. It will be used in the system described in Chap. 7.

5.2 Issues on Ontologies

The American Heritage Dictionary defines "ontology" as "the branch of metaphysics that deals with the nature of being". The term has recently been adopted by the artificial intelligence community to refer to a set of concepts or terms that can be used to describe some area of knowledge, or build a representation of it [55]. An ontology can be very high-level, consisting of concepts that organize the upper parts of a knowledge base such as the WordNet [56, 59], or it can be domain-specific, such as an ontology for finance.

5.2.1 Why Ontologies?

To answer this question, consider the following scenario.

In a hybrid intelligent system for financial investment planning, one soft computing agent advertises its capability to a middle agent as "pattern watcher in the *stock* market", whereas another decision making agent requests a soft computing agent that is a "pattern watcher in the *share* market". In such a situation, problems arise when the middle agent tries to match them. How could the middle agent know the "*stock* market" and the "*share* market" are the same thing? Moreover, in complex problem solving and decision making, the agents in a multi-agent system need to coordinate, cooperate or communicate with each other. Communications among agents should be based on some common knowledge, as with human beings. When one talks about something, the other person must have the same background so that they can understand each other.

To this end, ontologies are employed. Ontologies are a key component in how different agents in a multi-agent system can communicate effectively, and how the knowledge of agents can develop [54]. Most methods to resolve semantic heterogeneities rely on using partial or global ontological knowledge which may be shared among agents [116].

When applying multi-agent systems to different application domains, different domain-specific ontologies are needed to support agent communications. This is one part of the knowledge model. This is also why we include a domain-specific ontology in the proposed agent-based framework for hybrid intelligent systems. (See Fig. 5.1.)

For different applications, specific ontologies in the corresponding application domains are needed. For financial investment planning problems, it is necessary to build an ontology used in the agent-based financial investment system [30].

Before discussing the construction of the financial ontology, the distinction between an ontology and a knowledge base should be clarified. An ontology provides the basic structure or armature around which a knowledge base can be built. An ontology provides a set of concepts and terms for describing some domain, while a knowledge base uses those terms to represent what is true about some real or hypothetical world. Thus, a financial ontology might contain working definitions of concepts like money, banks, and stocks, but it would not contain assertions that a particular investor bought certain securities, although a knowledge base might.

5.2.2 Ontologies in Finance

Interest in ontologies has grown as researchers and system developers have become more interested in reusing or sharing knowledge across systems. There are some general-purpose upper ontologies such as CYC [58] and Wordnet [59], and some domain-specific ontologies that focus on the domains of discourse such as chemicals ontology and air campaign planning ontology. (Refer to [54] for an overview of the recent development of the field of ontologies in artificial intelligence.) Until now, very few financial ontologies have been reported. In the Larflast project, a financial domain ontology is under construction and will be used for learning finance terminology (*http://www.linglink.lu/hlt/projects/larflast-inco/ar-99/ar99. html.* (See also [57].) In the I3 (Intelligent Integration of Information, *http://dc.isx.com/ I3*) project, there is a *financial ontology and databases* group. They are creating ontologies of financial knowledge in Loom that describe the contents of existing financial databases. Loom is a kind of knowledge-representation language (*http://www.isi.edu/isd/ LOOM/documentation/LOOM-DOCS.html.*) We failed to find an existing financial ontology that can be (re)used in multiagent environments. This lack directly motivated us to build such an ontology.

5.2.3 Construction of Financial Ontology

To facilitate the construction of multi-agent application systems in finance, to support communication among agents in the prototype multi-agent system, and to ease the implementation of the *Nearest Neighbor* matchmaking algorithm in the middle agent, a finance ontology was constructed. This ontology provides working definitions of concepts like money, banks, and stocks. This knowledge is expressed in computer-usable formalisms.

Ontolingua was used to construct the financial ontology. *Ontolingua* is an ontology development environment that provides a suite of ontology authoring and translation tools, and a library of modular reusable ontologies. (For details on *Ontolingua*, visit *http://ontolingua.stanford.edu.*) *Ontolingua* is based on a top ontology that defines terms such as *frames, slots, slot values* and *facets.* When building the ontology using *Ontolingua*, the terms such as *portfolio, security, share, stock, bond*, etc. must be defined by determining the slots and giving the slot values. Before this can be done, a difficult knowledge-acquisition problem is faced. Like knowledge-based-system development, ontology development faces a knowledge-acquisition bottleneck.

In addition to the knowledge acquisition problem, two more problems involved in the construction of financial ontology are coding and accessing the ontology.

Knowledge Acquisition

Because we are not experts in the financial domain, we first read literature on finance to acquire some basic concepts of financial investment. Then preliminary meetings were held with financial experts to look for general, not detailed, knowledge. After this, we studied the documentation very carefully and tried to learn as much as possible about the world of finance. Having obtained some basic and general knowledge, we gradually moved into more specific details in order to configure the full ontology. Sets of terms and their relationships were extracted, and then attributes and their values defined. At the later stage of knowledge acquisition, these were submitted to financial experts for inspection. During this knowledge acquisition, the following set of knowledge acquisition techniques were used in an integrated manner [11]:

- Non-structured interviews were held with experts to draw up a preliminary draft of the terms, definitions, classifications, and so on.
- We undertook informal text analysis to study the main concepts in books and handbooks;
- We then undertook formal text analysis. This was performed manually without using specialized environments. We analyzed the text to extract attributes, natural-language definitions, assignation of values to attributes, and so on.
- We held structured interviews with experts to get specific and detailed knowledge about concepts, their properties, and their relationships with other concepts.
- We studied detailed reviews by experts. At this later stage of knowledge-acquisition, we submitted the knowledge acquired to experts for detailed inspection. In this way, we could get some suggestions and corrections from financial experts before coding the knowledge.

We then constructed the financial ontology conceptual structures based on the acquired knowledge. The conceptual structure of *portfolio* is shown in Fig. 5.2. Unfortunately, this is a time consuming and potentially error containing process. Obviously, more efficient construction tools are needed.

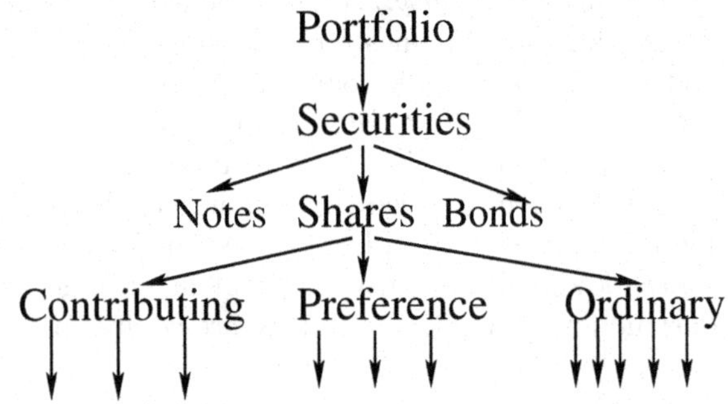

Fig. 5.2. Financial Ontology Conceptual Structure (Example)

Coding the Ontology

As mentioned previously, *Ontolingua* was used to construct the financial ontology. We manually coded the knowledge with *Ontolingua* based on conceptual structures. Currently, one can log on to *Ontolingua* and check the *financial investment ontology* in the unloaded category. Some terms of the financial ontology written in *Ontolingua* are as follows:

```
;;; Securities (Define-Class Securities (?X) "A term that covers
the paper certificates that are evidence of ownership of bonds,
debentures, notes and shares." :Def (And (Relation ?X)))

;;; Share (Define-Class Share (?X) "A unit of equity capital in a
company." :Def (And (Securities ?X)))
```

Accessing the Ontology

To use this ontology, we adopted the *Open Knowledge Base Connectivity* (OKBC) protocol [60] as a bridge between the agents in the multi-agent system for financial investment planning and the financial ontology. The ontology constructed using *Ontolingua* was in *Lisp* format. Before one could access the ontology through OKBC, one had to translate the ontology into OKBC format. This can be accomplished automatically by using the ontology server. One piece of the ontology in OKBC format is shown below:

```
(define-okbc-frame Securities
                   :frame-type
                   :class
                   :direct-superclasses
                   (Relation)
                   :direct-types
                   (Class Primitive)
                   :own-slots
                   ((Arity 1)))
               :template-slots
            ((Belongs_To)(Have-Some)(Has-One)
            :template-facets
    ((Belongs_To)(Value-Type Shareholders))
    (Have-Some (Some-Values Premium Share))
    (Has-One (Some-Values)(Minimum-Cardinality 1)
    (Value-Type Note))))
```

5.3 Summary

A flexible and unifying agent-based framework has been proposed in this chapter to facilitate the construction of hybrid intelligent systems. This framework has a few crucial characteristics that differentiate it from others.

When agents communicate with each other in a multi-agent system, and the middle agent performs matchmaking tasks, they all need to access the corresponding domain specific ontologies (part of the knowledge model). As an example, constructing an ontology for financial investment was discussed.

A question frequently asked in multi-agent systems is how to search efficiently for suitable agents to solve a specific problem. To answer this question, different types of middle agents that can assist in locating and connecting the ultimate service provider with the ultimate service requester are usually employed. For this purpose, we employed a middle agent in our agent based framework for hybrid intelligent systems. To our knowledge, almost all currently used matchmaking algorithms are only based on the advertised capabilities of providers. They do not consider the providers' practical outcomes in accomplishing delegated tasks at all. In fact, the practical performance of service provider agents has a significant impact on the matchmaking outcomes of middle agents. To this end, in Chap. 6 some algorithms are developed to consider the practical performance of service provider agents.

6 Matchmaking in Middle Agents

Middle agents play a very important role in the framework we propose. The main function of middle agents in an agent-based system is keeping track of the capabilities of other agents and retrieving them when required.

Generally, as far as the matchmaker, or broker is concerned, there are two relatively independent sub-problems to capability matchmaking:

- **Capability Storage** (corresponding to the CAPABILITYRECORDER role in both systems. Refer to Chaps. 7 and 8.): the matchmaker has to store the capability descriptions received. The most important question here is how capabilities can be described or represented in a way that is useful to the matchmaker.
- **Capability Retrieval** (corresponding to the CAPABILITYMATCHER role in both systems): the matchmaker has to find service provider agents that have the capabilities required to solve the given problem. The most important question here is how capability descriptions can be reasoned about, that is, capability matchmaking.

There has been some work related to capability descriptions as well as capability retrieval (matchmaking). The performance of middle agents relies heavily on the matchmaking algorithms used. To our knowledge, almost all the currently used algorithms have missed one point when carrying out matchmaking – the matchmaking is only based on the advertised capabilities of provider agents. The actual performance of provider agents in accomplishing delegated tasks is not considered at all. This results in inaccuracy of the matchmaking outcomes, as well as with the random selection of provider agents with the same advertised capabilities.

To this end, it is argued that the practical performance of service provider agents has a significant impact on the matchmaking outcomes of middle agents. Our idea is to consider the past track records of agents in accomplishing delegated tasks. This includes the acquisition of track records and the use of track records. As the track records of agents are accumulated gradually with the running of the agent system, there is no record available when

Z. Zhang, C. Zhang: Agent-Based Hybrid Intelligent Systems, LNAI 2938, pp. 65–90, 2004.

the system is just launched. For this reason, algorithms to provide "initial values" for track records are proposed. The improvements to matchmaking algorithms have been tested under the two agent-based hybrid intelligent systems which will be discussed in Chaps. 7 and 8, but there is no limitation to applying the improved algorithms in other applications.

This chapter starts by describing the matchmaking problem. Then some related work concerning matchmaking in middle agents is recounted, followed by the capability retrieval (matchmaking) algorithm on which the improvement is based. Based on these descriptions, the algorithms for the acquisition of track records and the use of track records are discussed.

6.1 Description of the Problem

One of the basic problems facing designers of the multi-agent systems used in open environments, such as the Internet, is the connection problem – finding suitable agents (service providers) that might have the information or other capabilities required by service requesters [41]. Because an agent may not have the necessary knowledge, or the necessary resources, the situation can arise (for both the problem division and the solution of sub-problems) that an agent would like to delegate a task to another agent. Generally, there are three possible ways of doing this:

- The meta-knowledge based approach. Provided the requester knows a suitable partner, no external assistance is required. The appropriate provider can be contacted and then the transfer of the task can be negotiated. However, it is difficult, or even impossible, for requesters to have comprehensive knowledge of providers in many application domains, especially in open, dynamic environments.
- The contract net based approach ([107] (pp. 96-100) and [108]). Within the contract net framework, the requester (manager) can make a public offer (broadcast) for bids in the form of a so-called contract for every pending sub-problem that is to be solved. The offer for bids is open to all agents (providers). Any agent in a contract net system can be a service requester as well as a service provider.
- The middle agent based approach [41]. Like middle-men in the physical world, middle agents can be employed to assist in locating and connecting the ultimate service provider with the ultimate service requester. This approach is very flexible. Agents (providers and/or requesters) can dynamically enter and exit open multi-agent systems.

In open multi-agent systems, the middle agent based approach is the most commonly used to efficiently search for suitable agents to solve a specific problem [41, 109]. Thus the discussion here concentrates on middle agents.

Different systems define their middle agents differently. For example, facilitators in Genesereth's federated systems [42] and SRI's Open Agent Architecture [19, 20], and matchmakers and brokers in Retsina [14] all differ in their interactions with providers and requesters. In [41], the authors identified different types of middle agents on the Internet, such as matchmakers (yellow page services), brokers, blackboard, etc., and experimentally evaluated different protocols for inter-operation between providers, requesters, and various types of middle agents. The results show that different types of middle agents exhibit different characteristics in terms of, for example, privacy, robustness, and adaptiveness. Regardless of which kinds of middle agents are used, their performance relies heavily on the matchmaking algorithms adopted. Matchmaking is the process of finding an appropriate provider for a requester through a middle agent, and has the following general form [110].

- Provider agents advertise their capabilities to middle agents.
- Middle agents store these advertisements.
- A requester asks some middle agent whether it knows of providers with desired capabilities.
- The middle agent matches the request against the stored advertisements and returns the result, a subset of the stored advertisements.

Matchmaking in middle agents is a crucial issue in multi-agent systems, especially those used in open environments such as the Internet. To improve the matchmaking performance of middle agents so that they can pick up the "right" service provider agents is of paramount importance.

6.2 Related Work of Matchmaking in Middle Agents

Agent matchmaking has been actively studied since the inception of software agent research. The earliest matchmaker we are aware of is the ABSI (Agent-Based Software Interoperability) facilitator [112], which is based on the KQML specification and uses the KIF (Knowledge Interchange Format) as the content language. The KIF expression is basically treated like Horn clauses. The matching between the advertisement and request expressed in KIF is simple unification with the equality predicate.

Kuokka and Harada presented the *SHADE* and *COINS* systems for matchmaking [111]. The content language of *COINS* allows for free text, and its matching algorithm utilizes the TF-IDF (Term Frequency-Inverse Document Frequency). The context language of the *SHADE* matchmaker consists of two parts: one is a subset of KIF, the other is a structured logic representation called MAX. MAX uses logic frames to store knowledge declaratively. The matchmaking algorithm used in *SHADE* is a Prolog-like unification process.

A more recent service broker-based information system is *InfoSleuth* [22]. The content language supported by *InfoSleuth* is KIF. The constraints for both user request and resource data are specified in terms of some given central ontology. It is the use of this common vocabulary that enables the dynamic matching of requests to the available resources. The advertisements specify agents' capabilities in terms of one or more ontologies. Constraint matching is an intersection function between the user query and the data resource constraints. If the conjunction of all the user constraints with all the resource constraints is satisfiable, then the resource contains data that is relevant to the user request.

In [41] Decker, Sycara, and Williamson presented matchmakers that store the capability advertisements of different agents. They concentrated their efforts on architectures that support load balancing and protection of privacy of different agents. In [113] a matchmaking system called *A-Match* is described. *A-Match* is a Web based interface to the Matchmaker that allows human users to find agents that can provide required services. Agents in the Matchmaker are represented on the bases of the inputs that they take and the outputs that they return. The Matchmaker matches the requirements of the user against the advertisements stored, and it reports the list of agents whose advertisements match the request of the user. The match performed by the Matchmaker is based on a taxonomy of terms. *A-Match* can store different types of advertisements coming from different applications. In [110, 114], Sycara et al. have proposed an agent capability description language, called LARKS (Language for Advertisement and Request for Knowledge Sharing), that allows for advertising, requesting and matching agent capabilities. There are three types of matching in LARKS: exact match (the most accurate type of match), plug-in match (a less accurate but most useful type of match), and relaxed match (the least accurate type of match). The matching engine of the matchmaker agent in LARKS contains five different filters: context matching, profile comparison, similarity matching, signature matching, and constraint matching. The computational costs of these filters are in increasing order. Users may select any combination of these filters on demand. The matchmaking process using LARKS has a good trade-off between performance and quality of matching.

Subrahmanian, Bonatti, Dix, et al. introduced an HTML-like Service Description Language (SDL), which is used by the agents to describe their services [21]. By restricting their language, they are able to very clearly articulate what they mean by *similar* matches in terms of nearest neighbor and range queries, as well as provide very efficient algorithms to implement these operations. However, they do not address issues such as load balancing which is addressed by Decker, Sycara, and Williamson.

A capability description language called CDL has been developed at the University of Edinburgh [115]. The syntax of CDL is KQML-like. Capabilities of, and requests for, services are described in CDL, either in terms of achievable objectives or as performable actions. Logic-based reasoning over descriptions in CDL is based on the notion of capability subsumption or through instantiation. *Capability subsumption* in CDL refers to the question of whether a capability description can be used to solve a problem described by a given task description in CDL. Both the CDL and the proposed matching of CDL descriptions have been implemented in Java under the support of JAT (Java Agent Template, the old version of JATLite) (*http://www.aiai.edu.ac.uk/~oplan/cdl*).

For a more comprehensive survey of matchmaking and brokering, see [116].

The above work has dealt with many important issues in agent capability description and capability matchmaking. However, almost all the work missed one point – matchmaking is only based on the advertised capabilities of provider agents. The actual performance of provider agents in accomplishing delegated tasks is not considered at all. This problem also exists in current contract net systems.

Usually, more than one service provider agent claims that they have the same, or very similar capabilities, to accomplish a task in an application. For example, in financial investment applications one usually needs to predict the interest rates. There are different techniques for interest rate prediction, such as neural network (NN) and fuzzy logic with genetic algorithm (FLGA) [49]. But their prediction performances are different. If there are two interest rate prediction agents, one based on NN, the other based on FLGA, which one should be chosen to predict the interest rate? In such cases, current matchmaking algorithms can only choose one provider agent randomly. As the quality of service of different service provider agents varies from one agent to another, even though they claim they have the same capabilities, it is obvious that the requirements of requester agents cannot be met by randomly choosing one.

We propose algorithms that can pick up the appropriate provider agents, based on past information about similar tasks that have been accomplished rather than choosing randomly. The focus of this discussion is on how to consider agents' actual performance based on the available capability description languages and capability matchmaking algorithms. The improvements to matchmaking algorithms are based on the **find_nn** and **range** algorithms in IMPACT [21, 53]. For convenience in future discussion, a brief introduction to these two algorithms is given below.

When an agent wants to find another agent providing a service, the serving agent must *match* the requested service with other service descriptions stored in its database, in order to find appropriate services. A service specification in IMPACT consists of: (1) a service name in terms of a verb-noun(noun) expression such as calculate:rate(interest), (2) typed input and output variables, and (3) attributes of services (e.g., the cost for using the service). Agents may request services in one of the following forms:

- *k-Nearest Neighbor Request:* find the k-nearest service names (pairs of verb and noun term) such that there exists an agent that provides that service, and identify this agent;
- *d-Range Search:* find all service names within a specified distance d.

Searching for appropriate services essentially relies on the exploitation of given weighted verb hierarchy and noun hierarchy, which are special cases of the general concept of a term hierarchy. Similarity between verbs and nouns in the verb and noun hierarchy, is computed via a given distance function on paths of weighted edges in the hierarchies. A composite distance function then combines both distance functions to calculate the combined similarity value for two word pairs (verb, noun) of service names. If a word cannot be found in the respective hierarchy a synonym will be searched in the ontology instead.

Suppose Σ_v is a set of verbs, and Σ_{nt} is a set of noun terms. A *noun term* is either a noun or an expression of the form $n_1(n_2)$, where n_1 and n_2 are both nouns. If $v \in \Sigma_v$ and $nt \in \Sigma_{nt}$, then $v : nt$ is called a *service name.*

Given a pair $\langle v, nt \rangle$ specifying a desired service, the **find_nn** algorithm will return a set of k agents that provide the most closely matching services. Closeness between $\langle v, nt \rangle$ and another pair $\langle v', nt' \rangle$ is determined by using the distance functions associated with the verb and noun-term hierarchies, together with a composite distance function *cd* specified by the agent invoking the **find_nn** algorithm. The algorithm uses the following internal data structures and/or subroutines.

- **Todo:** This is a list of verb/noun-term pairs, which are extended by their distances from the verb/noun-term pair, that is requested in the initial or recursive call, to the **find_nn** function. The list is maintained in increasing order of distance, and is not necessarily complete.
- **ANSTABLE:** This is a table consisting of, at most, k entries (k being the number of agents requested). At any given point in time during execution of the **find_nn** algorithm, *ANSTABLE* will contain the best answers found thus far, together with their distances from the requested service (v, nt). *ANSTABLE* will be maintained in increasing order with respect to this distance.
- **search_service_table:** This function, given a verb/noun-term pair (V, NT) and an integer k, returns the set of all agents which provide the service ($V : NT$); if their number exceeds k, it returns k of them, which are deliberately chosen.
- **num_ans:** This function merely keeps track of the number of answers in *ANSTABLE.*
- **next_nbr:** This function takes as input the list *Todo* mentioned above and a pair (V, NT). It returns as output the first member of the *Todo* list. If the *Todo* list is empty, it returns a special pair.
- **relax_ontology:** This function is called when either V or NT of the specified service name do not appear in the corresponding hierarchy. It returns a pair that is "similar" to (V, NT) whose components do appear in the hierarchies. This function accesses the financial ontology (see Sect. 5.2) and the verb/noun-term hierarchies.

The algorithm is shown below:

Algorithm find_nn(V:verb;NT:noun-term;k:integer)

```
/* Find the k agents offering the services closest to ⟨V, NT⟩, and output them with their */
/* distances; relax ⟨V, NT⟩ first, if it is not in the hierarchy. Output is either */
/* ANSTABLE (which contains a set of tuples of the form */
/* (agent name, service name, composite distance from ⟨V, NT⟩)) or ERROR */
create(Todo, V, NT);
ClosedList := NIL;
ANSTABLE := ∅;
if ⟨V, NT⟩ ∈ Σ_v × Σ_nt then
{ done := false;
Sol := search_service_table(V, NT, k);
while ¬done do
{ insert(⟨V, NT⟩, ClosedList);
insert(Sol, ANSTABLE);
n := num_ans(ANSTABLE);
if n ≥ k then done := true
else
{ ⟨V', NT'⟩ := next_nbr(Todo);
if error(V', NT') = true then done := true
else
{ ⟨V, NT⟩ := ⟨V', NT'⟩;
Sol := search_service_table(V, NT, k − n); }
}
}
}
else /* search ontology */
{ ⟨V', NT'⟩ := relax_ontology(V, NT);
if error(V', NT') = true then return ERROR
else return find_nn(V', NT', k); }
return ANSTABLE;
end.
```

Suppose $V \in \Sigma_v$ and $NT \in \Sigma_{nt}$. Also, let $\Sigma_v^V \subseteq \Sigma_v$ ($\Sigma_{nt}^{NT} \subseteq \Sigma_{nt}$) denote the set of all verbs (noun-terms) in our hierarchies whose distance from V (NT) is finite. Then, in the worst case, **find_nn**(V, NT, k) will need $O(|\Sigma_v^V| \cdot |\Sigma_{nt}^{NT}| + k)$ time. Note, however, that if there are k services whose composite distance from $\langle V, NT \rangle$ is finite, then one can obtain a tighter bound. Specifically, let d_V (d_{NT}) be the maximum distance from a verb (noun-term) of one of these k services to V (NT). Furthermore, let $\Sigma_v^{d_V} \subseteq \Sigma_v^V$ ($\Sigma_{nt}^{d_{NT}} \subseteq \Sigma_{nt}^{NT}$) denote the set of all verbs (noun-terms) in the hierarchies whose distance from V (NT) is less than, or equal to, d_V (d_{NT}). Then, in this case, **find_nn**(V, NT, k) will only need $O(|\Sigma_v^{d_V}| \cdot |\Sigma_{nt}^{d_{NT}}| + k)$ time.

The range search algorithm below allows the middle agent to answer queries of the form "Find all agents that provide a service $vnt = \langle V', NT' \rangle$ which is within a distance D of a requested service $vnt = \langle V, NT \rangle$".

In the **range** algorithm below, *Todo* is a list of nodes to be processed, each of which is a service vnt' extended by its distance from the service vnt. The algorithm has two steps:

- The first step is the **while** loop. It finds all pairs $vnt^* = \langle v^*, nt^* \rangle$ that are within the specified distance d from vnt. This step uses a procedure **expand** that behaves as follows: **expand**(vnt, vnt', d) first computes the set

  $$\{vnt^{\#} \mid d' = cd(vnt^{\#}, vnt) \leq d, vnt^{\#} \in \mathbf{cr}(vnt'), \langle vnt^{\#}, d' \rangle \notin RelaxList\}.$$

  Here, *RelaxList* contains the services which have already been considered. Then, **expand** inserts the elements of this set into *Todo*. $\mathbf{cr}(vn, t)$ is the candidate-relaxation of (vn, t). (Refer to [21] (p. 61) for the definition of **cr**.)
- The second step executes a "select" operation on the Service Table, finding all agents that offer any of the service names identified in the first step. As in the **find_nn** algorithm, if V or NT are not in the relevant verb or noun-term hierarchies, the algorithm **range** calls the **relax_ontology** procedure specified in the **find_nn** algorithm to find a similar pair which belongs to them.

Algorithm range(V:verb; NT:noun-term; D:real)

```
/* Find all agents offering a service within distance D to ⟨V, NT⟩. */
/* Output is either an ANSTABLE or an ERROR */
if D < 0 then return ERROR;
if ⟨V, NT⟩ ∈ Σ_v × Σ_nt then
{ RelaxList := NIL;
Todo := ⟨⟨V, NT⟩, 0⟩;
while Todo ≠ NIL do
{⟨⟨V', NT'⟩, D'⟩ := first element of Todo;
insert ⟨⟨V', NT'⟩, D'⟩ into RelaxList;
remove ⟨⟨V', NT'⟩, D'⟩ from Todo;
expand(⟨V, NT⟩, ⟨V', NT'⟩, D);
}
return π_{Agents,Dist}(RelaxList[Verb = V', NounTerm = NT']ServiceTable)
}
else
{ /* search ontology */
⟨V', NT'⟩ := relax_ontology(V, NT);
if error(V', NT') then return ERROR
else return range(V', NT', D − cd(⟨V, NT⟩, ⟨V', NT'⟩));
}
end.
```

Suppose $V \in \Sigma_v$ and $NT \in \Sigma_{nt}$. Also, let $vnt = \{\langle v, nt\rangle | v \in \Sigma_v \wedge nt \in \Sigma_{nt} \wedge cd(\langle v, nt\rangle, \langle V, NT\rangle) \leq D\}$ and let S be the set of all (agent name, $\langle v, nt\rangle$) pairs where $\langle v, nt\rangle \in vnt$. Then **range**$(V, NT, D)$ will need $O(|vnt| + |S|)$ time.

6.3 Improvements to Matchmaking Algorithms in Middle Agents

The algorithms discussed above can only find the agents that they claimed to offer the services closest to the services requested. The "best" agent in the **find_nn** or **range** algorithm only means that the service name advertised by this agent is closest to the service name requested, but has nothing to do with the actual performance of the agent in accomplishing a task. Here, we believe that the service providers make a binding commitment to perform the corresponding tasks (or provide the corresponding services) when they report the availabilities of their services to the matchmaker. That is, if an agent says it has a capability, then it can perform the tasks corresponding to the capability, and will do so when asked. If one really delegates the same task to different agents with the same or similar capabilities, the quality of service ($Q \circ S$) may vary from agent to agent. Some agents provide very good service, demonstrating an expert standard; some only reach a novice level. How can one choose the agents (service providers) that not only claim to offer the services but also do well in practice? We propose one solution to this problem – taking into account agents' track records in matchmaking. When the agents' "credit histories" are considered during the selection process, the selected agent is more appropriate for the task than the agent chosen by directly using **find_nn** or **range** algorithms. Before presenting the matchmaking algorithm that considers agents' track records, representation of track records is discussed.

6.3.1 Representation of Track Records

In the previous section it was mentioned that the specification of a single service consists of four components: service name, inputs, outputs and attributes. Here, one more component (track records) is added to the specification.

What should be put in the track records? The requester's evaluation for the service provided by the selected agent will be put in the track record field of the agent service specification. The requester's evaluation is actually the degree of satisfaction for the service received, just as when a person goes to a restaurant, and tips the waiter based on the service received. Here we assume that the requester agent can give an overall evaluation for the service it has received based on a set of criteria. The following linguistic values are allocated for the requester to describe overall evaluation (degree of satisfaction): *strong satisfaction, satisfaction, weak satisfaction, neutral, weak unsatisfaction, unsatisfaction,* and *strong unsatisfaction*. The track records consist of $2 - tuples$ with a form $[n^{th}$ *time service, evaluation*$]$. The first parameter in the $2 - tuple$ is the ordinal of the service provided, the second is the degree of satisfaction returned by the agent that received the service. For example, if an agent is delegated a task, and this is the third time the agent delegated the task deems the service is excellent, then a $2 - tuple$, $[3, strong\ satisfaction]$, will be added to the track record of the agent providing the service, the track record is kept in the database of the middle agent.

Such a representation has an extra advantage – it can keep track of agent aging. For example, if an agent's track record indicates that this agent received very good evaluations from the requesters with a small service ordinal number, and received bad evaluations with larger service ordinal numbers, this means the agent is aged. Its knowledge is out of date. When trying to choose a suitable agent to accomplish a task, the matchmaker should be very cautious with aged agents.

6.3.2 Accumulation of Track Records

To accumulate track records, we provide a special module for requester agents to allow them to give evaluation results for the services they received in the prototype. This module can also assemble the evaluation results in the KQML messages, which will be sent to middle agents by requester agents. When middle agents receive the messages, they interpret them and extract the evaluation result from the KQML message. The value (evaluation result) is assigned to the track record field of the corresponding agent, and then stored into the database of the middle agents.

6.3.3 Generation of Initial Values

Basic Idea for Initial Value Generation

Suppose we want to delegate a task to a person, but we have ten people all claiming they have the capability to accomplish the task. In such a case whom should we choose to delegate the task? If we have track records for the ten people in accomplishing similar tasks in the past, we can make the decision based on their performance/accomplishment history. If there is no any information about the ten people accomplishing similar tasks, one simple and efficient method in real life is to design a set of problems and ask all the candidates to solve these problems, just as we would in an examination. We assess the solutions provided by the candidates and delegate the task to the candidate with the best solutions. Here, we call such a set of problems "benchmark problems." The "specimen" solutions are called "benchmark results" or "benchmark values".

According to the above scenario, we can summarize the basic idea of initial value generation approach as follows. Before putting a multi-agent system into practical operation, the system is "trained" with a set of benchmark problems. That is, the middle agent is run with a matchmaking algorithm first. (For example, the **find_nn** algorithm in [53].) The middle agent then asks the agents with the same or similar capabilities (based on the results returned from a matchmaking algorithm, such as **find_nn**) to solve the benchmark problems. By comparing the results provided by these agents against the benchmarks, one obtains an evaluation of the performance for these agents. This evaluation is then used as the initial value of each of their track records.

Description of Benchmark Problems and Benchmark Values

In order to extract an appropriate description of benchmark problems and benchmark values, we take the software risk analysis as an example.

Assume we want to analyze the risk of a software project. From a software engineering risk management point of view, there are certain principal software risk factors that influence the risk of a software project [63]. These software risk factors include organization, estimation, monitoring, development methodology, tools, risk culture, usability, correctness, reliability and personnel. The software risk factor,

- *organization*, addresses risks associated with the maturity of the organization structure, communications, functions, and leadership.
- *estimation*, focuses on risks associated with inaccurate estimations of the resources, schedules and costs needed to develop software.
- *monitoring*, refers to risks associated with identifying problems.
- *development methodology*, identifies the methods by which software is developed.
- *tools*, focus on risks associated with the software tools used when software is developed, and so on.

We analyze the risk of a software project by determining the values (e.g., low, medium, high, etc.) of the risk factors, which can be viewed as attributes describing the software risk problem. More generally, we can say that to solve a problem is to find the attribute values related to that problem.

Formally, let $A = \{A_1, A_2, \ldots, A_k\}$ be the agent set with the same, or similar capabilities. We use $S = \{S_1, S_2, \ldots, S_m\}$ to denote the problem set. Each problem $S_i \in S$ $(i = 1, 2, \ldots, m)$ has a related attribute set $a = \{a_1, a_2, \ldots, a_n\}$. We say agent A_i has solved problem S_j if it returned the values of the n attributes related to the problem. The values can be numeric or non-numeric (linguistic). The benchmark values of these attributes are denoted by $B_i = \{b_{i1}, b_{i2}, \ldots, b_{in}\}(i = 1, 2, \ldots, m)$, and the values returned by agent A_j are denoted by $B_i^{A_j} = \{b_{i1}^{A_j}, b_{i2}^{A_j}, \ldots, b_{in}^{A_j}\}(i = 1, 2, \ldots, m, j = 1, 2, \ldots, k)$. The description of the benchmark problems is then summarized in Table 6.1.

The next step in the initial value generation process is to calculate the "distances" between the values returned by agent A_j and the benchmark values. There are many definitions of "distance". Here distance is defined in terms of standard Euclidean distance. The distance between B_i and $B_i^{A_j}$ is

Table 6.1. Description of Benchmark (BM) Problems

Agent	S_1				...	S_m			
	a_1	a_2	...	a_n	...	a_1	a_2	...	a_n
A_1	$b_{11}^{A_1}$	$b_{12}^{A_1}$	...	$b_{1n}^{A_1}$	...	$b_{m1}^{A_1}$	$b_{m2}^{A_1}$	...	$b_{mn}^{A_1}$
A_2	$b_{11}^{A_2}$	$b_{12}^{A_2}$	...	$b_{1n}^{A_2}$	...	$b_{m1}^{A_2}$	$b_{m2}^{A_2}$	...	$b_{mn}^{A_2}$
$\vdots$			$\vdots$		...			$\vdots$	
A_k	$b_{11}^{A_k}$	$b_{12}^{A_k}$	...	$b_{1n}^{A_k}$	...	$b_{m1}^{A_k}$	$b_{m2}^{A_k}$	...	$b_{mn}^{A_k}$
BM	b_{11}	b_{12}	...	b_{1n}	...	b_{m1}	b_{m2}	...	b_{mn}

defined to be d_j, where $d_j = \sqrt{\sum_{r=1}^{n}(b_{ir} - b_{ir}^{A_j})^2}$. Then these distances are added to the database of the middle agent as the initial values of the track records.

Considering that the initial values and the track records need to be combined when accumulated, the distances were mapped to the degrees of satisfaction. Suppose there are 7 levels of degrees of satisfaction – *strong satisfaction, satisfaction, weak satisfaction, neutral, weak unsatisfaction, unsatisfaction* and *strong unsatisfaction*, and each level accounts for 1/7 of the distance range. Therefore, if the distance is between 0 and 0.143, *strong satisfaction* will be the initial value of the agent's track record. If the distance is between 0.143 and 0.286, *satisfaction* will be the initial value, and so on. The mapping results are shown in Table 6.2.

Table 6.2. Mapping Results between Distance and Satisfactory Degree

Distance Range	Satisfactory Degree
0 to 0.143	*strong satisfaction*
0.143 to 0.286	*satisfaction*
0.286 to 0.429	*weak satisfaction*
0.429 to 0.572	*neutral*
0.572 to 0.715	*weak unsatisfaction*
0.715 to 0.858	*unsatisfaction*
0.858 to 1.0	*strong unsatisfaction*

In the process of initial value generation, there are two situations that need to be considered. One is that the benchmark values in Table 6.1 are known in advance, the other is that the benchmark values are unknown. We will discuss the two cases in the subsequent sections, together with examples.

Initial Value Generation with Known Benchmark Results

For different applications, benchmark problems are different. That is, the benchmark problems are application-dependent. In this section, we take a financial application as an example as we discuss the initial value generation problem with known benchmark values.

In financial applications, different models (e.g., the fuzzy logic and genetic algorithm model [49]) can be used for interest rate prediction. Here, two soft computing (SC) agents for interest rate prediction (one based on neural networks, SC_Agent_NN, the other based on fuzzy logic and genetic algorithm, SC_Agent_FLGA) are taken as examples to show how to determine the initial values for the two agents. The initial values are based on the predictive capabilities of these two SC agents.

Construction of Benchmark Problems

When predicting the interest rate (as represented by 91-day Treasury bill rates), both of the agents take the changes of previous Treasury-bill (T-bill) rates, real gross national product (GNP), consumer price index (CPI), M2 money supply, and personal wealth (W) as inputs. Personal wealth is the accumulation of the difference between personal income and personal consumption. The M2 money supply consists of all cash in circulation, and deposits in savings and check accounts, and represents readily available liquid assets. The consumer price index is a measure of the inflation trend. The outputs are the changes of the next T-bill rates (predicted interest rates). Quarterly data are used.

We use past financial data from the five factors (from 1966 to 1987) provided in Appendix B of [49] to construct the required benchmark problems, which listed here from Table 6.3 to Table 6.7.

Table 6.3. Change in Consumer Price Index

Year	Qtr1	Qtr2	Qtr3	Qtr 4	Year	Qtr1	Qtr2	Qtr3	Qtr 4
1966	0.30	0.30	0.30	0.30	1977	1.00	1.30	0.90	0.70
1967	0.00	0.30	0.30	0.30	1978	1.00	1.60	1.60	1.30
1968	0.40	0.30	0.50	0.40	1979	1.70	2.40	2.30	2.10
1969	0.40	0.60	0.60	0.50	1980	3.00	2.90	1.50	2.20
1970	0.50	0.60	0.50	0.50	1981	2.30	2.00	2.60	1.30
1971	0.30	0.40	0.50	0.20	1982	0.80	1.40	1.80	0.20
1972	0.30	0.30	0.40	0.40	1983	0.00	1.20	1.20	0.90
1973	0.50	1.00	1.00	1.00	1984	1.10	1.10	1.10	0.80
1974	1.30	1.30	1.50	1.50	1985	0.70	1.30	0.70	1.00
1975	0.90	0.80	1.20	0.80	1986	0.20	-0.20	0.80	0.60
1976	0.60	0.70	0.90	0.60	1987	1.20	1.50	1.30	1.00

There is some evidence to suggest that fundamental financial market characteristics change over a period of four to five years [117]. That is, the market "forgets" the influence of data that is more than five years old. For this reason, five-year data windows are used. Fifteen data windows are examined,

Table 6.4. Change in Gross National Product in 1982 US Dollars (Billions)

Year	Qtr1	Qtr2	Qtr3	Qtr 4	Year	Qtr1	Qtr2	Qtr3	Qtr 4
1966	42.50	5.70	22.50	10.90	1977	39.20	46.70	59.10	-7.70
1967	12.60	13.40	32.50	12.90	1978	26.40	95.40	26.70	39.00
1968	26.70	39.60	18.40	-2.30	1979	0.10	-3.00	28.70	-6.10
1969	33.50	3.30	13.40	-9.70	1980	32.10	-76.40	2.10	40.10
1970	-14.00	2.10	20.30	22.00	1981	61.90	-10.90	14.40	-45.60
1971	64.80	-0.20	12.70	-0.10	1982	-48.60	9.50	-25.40	4.80
1972	54.60	49.50	27.00	49.20	1983	27.30	71.70	48.10	58.70
1973	62.70	7.00	-2.70	24.50	1984	86.60	46.30	22.60	14.60
1974	-15.40	7.80	-35.90	-23.90	1985	42.30	21.70	36.60	26.60
1975	-52.70	26.90	45.30	37.80	1986	58.70	-16.50	7.80	21.20
1976	51.70	12.50	11.70	28.20	1987	49.40	40.50	49.30	62.80

Table 6.5. Change in M2 Money Supply in 1982 US Dollars (Billions)

Year	Qtr1	Qtr2	Qtr3	Qtr 4	Year	Qtr1	Qtr2	Qtr3	Qtr 4
1966	13.40	1.00	-2.70	2.10	1977	30.00	16.80	20.00	16.10
1967	19.40	24.20	28.50	16.20	1978	0.50	-7.50	-6.90	-3.40
1968	6.70	9.60	8.90	17.10	1979	-16.30	-22.10	-9.10	-30.00
1969	6.20	-9.00	-11.10	-9.50	1980	-43.10	-45.30	35.30	-8.70
1970	-14.30	-9.20	14.30	19.30	1981	-20.70	5.50	-5.90	16.90
1971	32.50	47.80	28.10	37.00	1982	23.90	4.30	14.20	37.90
1972	35.40	33.50	42.40	40.40	1983	95.00	30.30	19.00	20.70
1973	16.90	-7.40	-6.80	-23.00	1984	10.00	17.30	14.80	29.30
1974	-17.00	-24.10	-30.00	-31.20	1985	45.10	9.90	41.20	14.10
1975	-1.70	41.60	24.90	13.10	1986	20.30	66.80	50.50	39.80
1976	35.80	39.20	19.70	42.60	1987	5.50	-15.50	-1.30	7.20

Table 6.6. Personal Wealth in 1982 US Dollars (Billions)

Year	Qtr1	Qtr2	Qtr3	Qtr 4	Year	Qtr1	Qtr2	Qtr3	Qtr 4
1966	318.20	332.60	339.10	356.00	1977	507.00	518.80	537.30	537.10
1967	369.70	366.40	378.50	383.20	1978	553.80	560.10	578.80	593.10
1968	381.20	394.20	394.20	407.20	1979	601.60	598.10	597.80	593.60
1969	406.80	420.40	439.20	442.20	1980	597.60	600.70	603.60	625.90
1970	434.20	456.40	449.90	448.30	1981	626.30	627.30	655.10	650.20
1971	441.80	456.70	454.30	451.40	1982	629.20	638.20	614.10	601.40
1972	469.40	462.10	476.20	511.90	1983	591.80	578.90	558.60	592.20
1973	506.30	522.30	536.70	569.50	1984	630.60	611.00	632.80	635.90
1974	548.30	523.90	528.20	543.50	1985	642.80	637.00	597.90	618.50
1975	507.90	506.30	507.30	514.40	1986	632.50	651.60	608.80	620.70
1976	509.90	516.40	517.80	512.80	1987	633.60	614.80	604.80	678.30

Table 6.7. Two-Quarter Moving Average Change in T-Bill Discount Rate

Year	Qtr1	Qtr2	Qtr3	Qtr 4	Year	Qtr1	Qtr2	Qtr3	Qtr 4
1966	0.39	0.22	0.21	0.33	1977	-0.28	0.07	0.42	0.65
1967	-0.26	-0.79	-0.09	0.56	1978	0.47	0.17	0.46	1.10
1968	0.36	0.36	0.09	0.03	1979	1.02	0.34	0.14	1.22
1969	0.45	0.33	0.46	0.54	1980	1.91	-0.88	-2.11	1.83
1970	0.11	-0.29	-0.44	-0.69	1981	2.57	0.56	0.36	-1.40
1971	-1.26	-0.58	0.60	0.01	1982	-1.10	0.17	-1.59	-2.21
1972	-0.81	-0.24	0.40	0.55	1983	-0.82	0.25	0.55	0.18
1973	0.70	0.88	1.38	0.42	1984	-0.03	0.53	0.61	-0.43
1974	-0.40	0.41	0.34	-0.47	1985	-1.08	-0.73	-0.54	-0.18
1975	-1.20	-0.96	0.23	0.14	1986	-0.11	-0.51	-0.68	-0.39
1976	-0.69	-0.25	0.11	-0.24	1987	0.00	0.19	0.25	0.13

each starting in the first quarter of the years 1967 through to 1981. The ending quarter for each data window will be the fourth quarter of the years 1971 through to 1985. This means there are 15 benchmark problems. The inputs of benchmark problem S_1, for example, are the data from 1967 to 1971. The benchmark value for these inputs is the T-bill rate of the first quarter of 1972, -0.81.

Experimental Results

The 15 data windows are used to train these two agents (neural network and genetic algorithm). We then let the agents predict the interest rate of the first quarter following the training data windows. For example, for training data of 1967-1971, the outputs of the agents are the (predicted) T-bill rate of the first quarter of 1972. The prediction results of the two agents on the 15 benchmark problems are summarized in Table 6.8.

Table 6.8. Predicting Results on Benchmark Problems

Agent	S_1	S_2	S_3	S_4	S_5	S_6	S_7
SC_Agent_NN	-0.53	0.45	0.03	-0.93	-0.67	-0.14	0.43
SC_Agent_FLGA	-0.78	0.73	-0.16	-1.36	-0.60	-0.28	0.53
Benchmark	-0.81	0.70	-0.40	-1.20	-0.69	-0.28	0.47

S_8	S_9	S_{10}	S_{11}	S_{12}	S_{13}	S_{14}	S_{15}
0.79	1.41	2.15	-0.95	-1.16	-0.33	-0.45	-0.41
1.03	1.84	2.66	-1.17	-1.00	-0.22	-0.87	-0.53
1.02	1.91	2.57	-1.10	-0.82	-0.03	-1.08	-0.11

Figure 6.1 shows the predicted values of SC_Agent_NN and SC_Agent_FLGA, and the benchmark values from 1972 to 1986. The plot of the distances

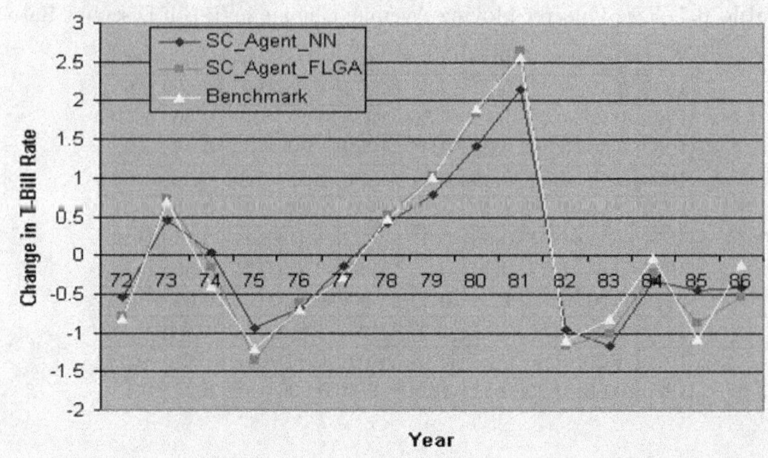

Fig. 6.1. Curves of Benchmark Values, SC_Agent_NN, and SC_Agent_FLGA

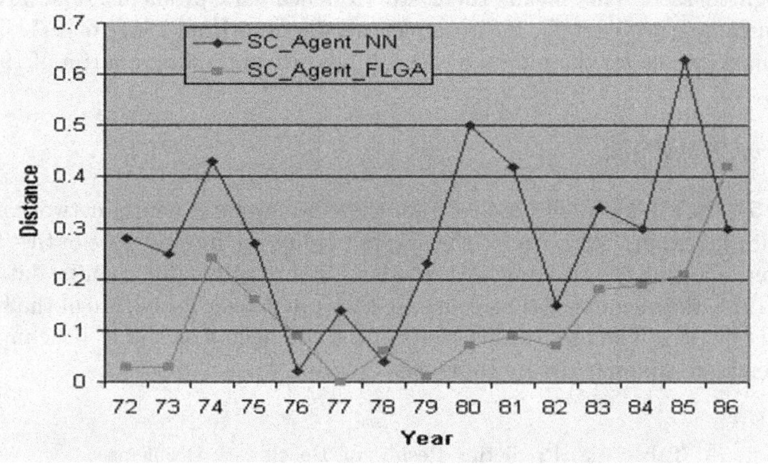

Fig. 6.2. Distances with Benchmark Values

from the prediction values to the benchmark values for each data windows is depicted in Fig. 6.2.

The average distance for the prediction values of SC_Agent _NN is 0.287. The value for SC_Agent_FLGA is 0.123. Based on Figs. 6.1 and 6.2 and the average distances, one can see that the prediction performance of SC_Agent_FLGA is better than that of SC_Agent_NN for the benchmark problems. Mapping the distances to the degrees of satisfaction (refer to Table 6.2), *weak satisfaction* is added to the track record of SC_Agent_NN as its initial value, and *strong satisfaction* to the track record of SC_Agent_FLGA as its initial value. Hence at this stage, if the middle agent needs to pick one agent for interest rate prediction, SC_Agent_FLGA would be chosen. Of course, the situation may change with the growth of the track records of these agents.

Initial Value Generation with Unknown Benchmark Results

In the case discussed in the previous section, one must know a *priori* of the attribute values of the benchmark problems. But this is not always the case. In some situations, it is impossible to obtain the attribute values in advance. The agents must then be asked to solve these problems first. One can then try to cluster the attribute values returned by agents using cluster analysis methods. In this way, "heuristic" attribute values can be obtained. One can then use these values as benchmark values and we return to the situation discussed in the previous section.

There are seven steps involved when using cluster analysis algorithms to determine benchmark results. Before presenting these steps in details, a brief introduction to the fuzzy cluster analysis algorithms [118] [119], which are used in our experiments, is given.

Introduction to Fuzzy Cluster Analysis

The aim of a cluster analysis is to partition a given set of data or objects into clusters (prototypes). This partition should have the following properties:

- homogeneity within the cluster, i.e., data that belong to the same cluster should be as similar as possible; and
- heterogeneity between clusters, i.e., data that belong to different clusters should be as different as possible.

The concept of "similarity" has to be specified according to the data. Since the data are in most cases real-valued vectors, the Euclidean distance between data can be used as a measure of the dissimilarity.

The fuzzy clustering algorithms that we will use classify the elements of the data set $X = \{x_1, x_2, \ldots, x_j, \ldots, x_n\} \subset \chi$ into classes $P = \{p_1, p_2, \ldots, p_i, \ldots, p_c\} \subset \wp$ by means of a membership matrix $U \subset [0,1]^{|P| \times |X|}$. A membership grade $u_{i,j}$ denotes the degree of belongingness of datum x_j to class p_i. The algorithms minimize the following objective function by means of *alternating optimization* (AO):

$$J(X, W; U, P) = \Sigma_{i=1}^{c} \Sigma_{j=1}^{n} u_{i,j}^{m} w_j d^2(k_i, x_j)$$

where $d : \chi \times \wp \to R$ measures the distance between data vectors and prototypes, and w_j is the weight for the data vector x_j. The term *alternating optimization* comes from the fact that J is minimized by updating prototypes and membership alternatively. If $X = \{x_1, x_2, \ldots, x_j, \ldots, x_n\}$ and $P = \{p_1, p_2, \ldots, p_i, \ldots, p_c\}$ are finite, an analysis result $f : X \to F(P)$ can be represented as a $c \times n$ matrix U, where $u_{i,j} := f(x_j)(p_i)$. The algorithm used is shown below.

Fuzzy Clustering Algorithm

Let a data set $X = \{x_1, x_2, \ldots, x_j, \ldots, x_n\}$ be given. Let each cluster be uniquely characterizable by an element of a set P.

Choose the number c of clusters, $2 \leq c < n$
Choose an $m \in R$ $(m > 1)$
Choose a precision for termination ε
Initialize $U^{(0)}$, $i := 0$
REPEAT
  Increase i by 1
  Determine $P^{(i)}$ such that J is minimized by $P^{(i)}$ for fixed $U^{(i-1)}$
  Determine $U^{(i)}$ according to certain conditions
UNTIL $||U^{(i-1)} - U^{(i)}|| \leq \varepsilon$

There are many ways to determine $U^{(i)}$. Different ways result in different fuzzy clustering algorithms. (Refer to [118] for more details.)

In the next subsection, we will discuss the steps for determining benchmark values by using this fuzzy clustering algorithm.

Determining Benchmark Values by Fuzzy Clustering

As discussed previously, finding a solution to any problem can be viewed as determining the attribute values related to the problem. With this observation in mind, a set of benchmark problems can be designed, but the solutions to all these problems are unknown. (For example, we do not know what the risk exactly is for a software project.) Some agents that claim to have the capabilities, are asked to solve these problems and return the solutions, on the attribute values. These attribute values are then used as inputs to the fuzzy clustering algorithm. The algorithm partitions the solutions into different clusters (called prototypes). We then choose the center of the cluster with the highest weight as the benchmark values for the problems. This implies that we should accept most agents' opinions if their solutions are similar. It is reasonable to do so. Specifically, this process involves the following steps.

- Preparation: Given k similar problems (benchmark problems), choose m agents having the capability to solve the k problems. The solution of each problem consists of n attributes.
- Use the fuzzy clustering algorithm to determine the clusters (prototypes) of the solutions for each of the k problems returned by the m agents. That is, the input of the algorithm is an $m \times n$ data matrix. There are k such matrices. The outputs of the algorithm have the following format:

  (cluster
  (prototype (weight *value*) (center (*values for all the attributes*) ...
  (prototype (weight *value*) (center (*values for all the attributes*))

- Choose the prototype with the highest weight as the benchmark values for this problem. Repeat this step for k problems.
- Calculate the distances (using Euclidean distance) of the solutions given by the agents and the found benchmark values.
- Find the average distances of all the solutions provided by the m agents with the found benchmark values of the k problems.
- Normalize the distances to $[0, 1]$. Sort the m agents according to the average distances. Map the average distances to the seven satisfaction degrees (refer to Table 6.2), and use the degrees of satisfaction as the initial values of these agents.

Average distances are used as the measurement of agents' performance in accomplishing benchmark problems. Such a measurement meets the "majority principle". That is, if one agent can solve most of the benchmark problems very well, and another agent can only accomplish a few of the benchmark problems with high quality, the average distance of the first agent is shorter than that of the second. Therefore, the results obtained according to the above process are convincing. The key in this process is step 2. In this step a fuzzy clustering algorithm is used to cluster the solutions provided by different agents. Based on the clustering results, the "heuristic" attribute values, which are reasonable benchmark values, are determined.

Experimental Results

We recall the software project risk example in this subsection. Suppose some experts in this field are invited to assess the risks of certain software projects. The experts are asked to give their assessment results by providing a number ($\in [0, 10]$) for each of the ten software risk factors. The bigger the number, the higher the risk concerning that risk factor. According to the process described in the previous subsection, some experiments were conducted with $k = 30$, $m = 20$, and $n = 10$. That is, 20 agents with similar capabilities were delegated to assess 30 software projects (benchmark problems). The answer for each problem consists of 10 attributes. The data for the risk factors used in the experiments is randomly generated. For demonstration purposes, Table 6.9 shows the solutions of the 20 agents for one of the 30 benchmark problems.

Taking this as input, the clustering algorithm produces the following output for this problem:

(cluster
(prototype(weight 2.67437) (center (7.052511.84176 3.82815 5.14071 3.05296 1.94812 8.18994 6.23528 4.76634 4.21243)))
(prototype(weight 2.01146) (center (6.92752 2.09169 4.33178 5.17589 2.66185 2.1582 8.16927 5.69102 5.11877 3.92546)))
(prototype(weight 5.45996) (center (6.99357 1.95553 3.98165 5.02628 3.01206 2.00627 7.99989 6.01413 5.01984 3.9859))))

Table 6.9. Agents' Solutions to One Benchmark Problem

Agent	S_{22}									
	a_1	a_2	a_3	a_4	a_5	a_6	a_7	a_8	a_9	a_{10}
A_1	6.94	1.85	3.89	5.38	3.24	1.99	8.21	5.84	5.02	3.85
A_2	6.93	2.04	4.07	4.96	2.97	1.95	8.06	6.0	4.97	3.97
A_3	6.99	1.99	4.0	5.0	3.0	2.0	8.0	5.99	5.0	4.01
A_4	7.12	1.9	4.08	4.87	3.14	2.01	8.07	5.99	5.15	3.87
A_5	7.06	1.93	4.22	5.21	3.31	2.14	8.14	5.76	4.88	3.8
A_6	7.15	1.65	3.65	4.82	3.42	2.01	7.66	6.03	5.16	3.57
A_7	6.7	2.41	4.44	5.14	2.65	2.27	8.42	5.54	4.9	3.8
A_8	6.93	2.03	3.69	5.28	2.99	1.75	8.45	6.46	4.45	4.34
A_9	6.86	1.9	3.73	4.78	3.21	2.15	7.87	6.02	5.17	4.29
A_{10}	6.93	1.62	3.68	4.98	2.88	1.74	8.13	6.39	4.97	4.38
A_{11}	6.75	1.98	4.0	5.23	2.75	2.08	7.86	6.26	5.04	4.05
A_{12}	7.27	1.87	3.78	5.09	3.14	1.94	8.26	6.12	4.64	4.24
A_{13}	6.9	2.04	4.34	4.89	2.28	1.98	8.14	5.53	5.16	4.32
A_{14}	7.05	1.95	3.97	4.94	3.0	1.99	7.92	6.0	5.02	4.01
A_{15}	7.15	2.09	4.25	5.03	2.79	2.06	8.07	5.76	5.13	3.79
A_{16}	6.87	1.93	4.13	5.16	2.77	1.89	8.17	6.17	5.02	4.02
A_{17}	7.15	1.63	3.96	5.27	3.24	2.16	8.3	6.45	4.55	4.36
A_{18}	6.91	1.95	3.69	5.14	2.64	1.89	7.91	6.2	5.05	3.97
A_{19}	7.14	2.21	3.93	5.24	3.08	2.09	7.84	6.07	4.88	4.11
A_{20}	6.96	1.96	4.64	5.63	2.49	2.41	8.13	5.59	5.46	3.82

There are three different clusters (prototypes). Choosing the prototype with the highest weight (5.45996), we obtain the benchmark values for this problem. The attribute values are $a_1 = 6.99357$, $a_2 = 1.95553$, $a_3 = 3.98165$, $a_4 = 5.02628$, $a_5 = 3.01206$, $a_6 = 2.00627$, $a_7 = 7.99989$, $a_8 = 6.01413$, $a_9 = 5.01984$, and $a_{10} = 3.9859$, respectively. Table 6.10 lists the benchmark values for the first 10 benchmark problems determined by the fuzzy clustering approach.

Table 6.10. Partial Benchmark Values for Benchmark Problems

Problems	a_1	a_2	a_3	a_4	a_5	a_6	a_7	a_8	a_9	a_{10}
P_1	3.016	6.027	4.972	4.013	2.958	1.987	3.913	1.926	6.035	2.947
P_2	7.076	5.016	3.972	9.051	4.005	4.009	2.977	2.987	4.042	3.975
P_3	4.012	6.949	2.937	3.021	5.011	4.934	2.072	6.978	3.06 2	2.011
P_4	2.888	2.998	8.035	7.036	8.002	2.001	4.992	3.013	8.069	9.009
P_5	7.983	3.922	7.071	7.013	1.968	7.041	1.995	3.988	7.017	5.000
P_6	2.956	6.039	9.043	4.078	2.022	7.960	8.959	5.059	8.959	5.960
P_7	2.097	8.019	1.961	4.969	1.915	2.968	6.027	6.016	8.073	6.954
P_8	2.052	8.964	1.929	7.016	2.991	1.986	3.033	7.976	4.993	4.946
P_9	2.997	1.979	4.943	8.012	2.976	9.036	8.068	1.984	1.976	5.049
P_{10}	7.018	4.012	6.026	2.935	6.950	3.977	9.023	9.005	2.965	7.973

We then calculate the Euclidean distances between the solutions provided by the agents and the found benchmark values. The results are shown in Table 6.11. As space is limited, only the distances between 10 agents' solutions and the benchmark results of 10 benchmark problems are listed.

Table 6.11. Distances between Agents' Solutions and Benchmark Values

Agents	P_1	P_2	P_3	P_4	P_5	P_6	P_7	P_8	P_9	P_{10}
A_1	0.2148	0.2611	0.2258	0.2229	0.2522	0.1715	0.1772	0.189	0.2533	0.1963
A_2	0.0554	0.0389	0.0622	0.0749	0.0403	0.0654	0.0579	0.0612	0.0509	0.0385
A_3	0.0467	0.0364	0.0486	0.0428	0.0394	0.0435	0.0559	0.0342	0.0341	0.0303
A_4	0.0795	0.1035	0.0904	0.088	0.0813	0.0899	0.072	0.0831	0.1101	0.0627
A_5	0.1604	0.2026	0.1785	0.1585	0.17	0.1788	0.1578	0.1864	0.1554	0.2265
A_6	0.3327	0.3513	0.3586	0.3297	0.327	0.3387	0.4119	0.4304	0.3209	0.4033
A_7	0.2995	0.2927	0.3013	0.2075	0.2304	0.2463	0.2738	0.2756	0.2432	0.2722
A_8	0.3357	0.308	0.1936	0.253	0.3237	0.2986	0.3267	0.4162	0.34	0.2774
A_9	0.2173	0.1651	0.1915	0.1678	0.207	0.2318	0.1707	0.0989	0.1498	0.2095
A_{10}	0.3203	0.2963	0.2318	0.2911	0.326	0.236	0.2214	0.2483	0.2767	0.2333

To measure the performance in solving benchmark problems, the average distances between agents' solutions and the benchmark values of all benchmark problems are used. The shorter the average distance, the better the performance. The average distance between agent A_i and the benchmark values is denoted by d_{A_i}. Based on the experimental data, these distances are $d_{A_1} = 0.2141$, $d_{A_2} = 0.0631$, $d_{A_3} = 0.0482$, $d_{A_4} = 0.0941$, $d_{A_5} = 0.1795$, $d_{A_6} = 0.3442$, $d_{A_7} = 0.2591$, $d_{A_8} = 0.3157$, $d_{A_9} = 0.1824$, $d_{A_{10}} = 0.2666$, $d_{A_{11}} = 0.2181$, $d_{A_{12}} = 0.215$, $d_{A_{13}} = 0.3946$, $d_{A_{14}} = 0.077$, $d_{A_{15}} = 0.1818$, $d_{A_{16}} = 0.1353$, $d_{A_{17}} = 0.2724$, $d_{A_{18}} = 0.2097$, $d_{A_{19}} = 0.1442$, $d_{A_{20}} = 0.4322$. From the average distances, it is obvious that agent 3 (A_3) demonstrates the best performance, agent 2 (A_2) the second best performance, and so on. Mapping these average distances to the degrees of satisfaction according to Table 6.2, the initial values of agents 2, 3, 4, 14, and 16 are *strong satisfaction* as their average distances are within $[0, 0.143]$; the initial values of agents 1, 5, 7, 9, 10, 11, 12, 15, 18, and 19 are *satisfaction* as their average distances are between 0.143 and 0.286; the initial values of agents 6, 8, 13, and 17 are *weak satisfaction*; and the initial value of agent 20 is *neutral*.

6.3.4 Use of Track Records

Based on the representation of track records and the accumulated track records (including the initial values of track records), the matchmaking algorithm that can consider agents' track records are now ready to be presented.

This algorithm is based on the returned results, *ANSTABLE*, of **find_nn** or **range** algorithm, and processes as follows.

- For each agent $A_j \in ANSTABLE$, let A_j solve the benchmark problems in S.
- Calculate the distances between the returned values $B_i^{A_j}$ and the benchmark values B_i, and add the corresponding 2-tuple $[0, satisfactory\ degree]$ to A_j's track records.
- Sum up the numbers of different satisfactory degree (*strong satisfaction*, *satisfaction*, etc.) for each agent in $ANSTABLE$. The result for each agent is a vector, EV_j ($j = 1, \ldots, k = |ANSTABLE|$), $EV_j = ([strong\ satisfaction, n_{1j}],$ $[satisfaction, n_{2j}], [weak\ satisfaction, n_{3j}], [neutral, n_{4j}],$ $[weak\ unsatisfaction, n_{5j}], [unsatisfaction, n_{6j}],$ $[strong\ unsatisfaction, n_{7j}])^t,$ $n_{ij} \geq 0$ $(i = 1, \ldots, 7; j = 1, \ldots, k)$.
- Construct evaluation matrix of agents $M_{7\times k}$. The matrix looks like:

$$M = \begin{array}{c|cccc|} & A_1 & A_2 & \ldots & A_k \\ strong\ satisfaction & n_{11} & n_{12} & \ldots & n_{1k} \\ satisfaction & n_{21} & n_{22} & \ldots & n_{2k} \\ \vdots & \vdots & \vdots & \vdots & \vdots \\ strong\ unsatisfaction & n_{71} & n_{72} & \ldots & n_{7k} \end{array}$$

  where A_i ($i = 1, \ldots, k$) are agent names in the returned results of **find_nn** or **range** algorithm, i.e., they have the same or closely similar capabilities.
- Select the *most promising* agent to provide the requested service based on the evaluation matrix M.

In the last item above, different criteria may be used to describe *most promising.* Two reasonable approaches we tested are given below.

The first one is based on a collection of heuristic rules. These rules are derived from examples in typical international conference paper choosing procedures in practice. Some example rules are listed below.

- **Rule 1: If** n_{1l} (the number of *strong satisfaction* for agent A_l) is the largest among n_{1j} ($j = 1, \ldots, k$) and $n_{5j} = n_{6j} = n_{7j} = 0$ **then** choose A_l.
- **Rule 2: If** all n_{1j} ($j = 1, \ldots, k$) are equal and n_{2l} (the number of *satisfaction* for agent A_l) is the largest among n_{2j} ($j = 1, \ldots, k$) and $n_{5j} = n_{6j} = n_{7j} = 0$ **then** choose A_l.
- **Rule 3: If** all $n_{ij} = 0$ except n_{4j}, **then** randomly choose one agent, A_l.
- and so on.

The alternative is to map each satisfaction degree (*strong satisfaction, satisfaction,* etc.) to a weighting value. Then the total score of each agent is calculated, and the agent with the highest score is chosen. If there is more than one agent with the same highest score, then one is randomly chosen to accomplish the delegated task. For example, one can map an element in the evaluation vector to a value in $[-1, 1]$. The weight for *strong satisfaction* is 1, for *satisfaction* is 2/3, for *weak satisfaction* is 1/3, for *neutral* is 0, for *weak unsatisfaction* is $-1/3$, for *unsatisfaction* is $-2/3$, and for *strong unsatisfaction* is -1. The second approach is easier to implement than the first.

The algorithm uses the following variables and subroutines:

- **initial_value_generation**: This subroutine takes $ANSTABLE$ and benchmark problem set S as inputs, and generates the initial values of track records for all agents in $ANSTABLE$ as outputs. The initial values are stored in the database of middle agents;
- TR_j: The track record of agent $A_j \in ANSTABLE$. This consists of $2-tuples$ like $[5, satisfaction]$;
- **aging_check**: This subroutine checks the aging status of agent A_j based on its track record, TR_j. It will mark an agent "aged" if it satisfies the pre-set aged conditions;
- **take_one_tuple**: This function takes one tuple from TR_j, and assigns it to the variable *tr*;
- **evaluation_part**: This function returns the satisfactory degree part of $2 - tuple$, *tr*, and assigns the corresponding value (*strong satisfaction, satisfaction,* etc.) to the variable *sd*;
- **sum_up**: This function counts the numbers of different satisfactory degrees, n_{ij} $(i =, 1 \ldots, 7; j = 1, \ldots, k)$, and adds $[strong\ satisfaction, n_{1j}]$, $[satisfaction, n_{2j}]$, and so on to EV_j $(j = 1, \ldots, k)$. It is actually a **case** statement;
- **construct_evaluation_matrix**: This function constructs the evaluation matrix based on the evaluation vectors, EV_j $(j = 1, \ldots, k)$;
- **most_promise**: This function chooses the best agent, $FINAL\_ANS$, using one of the approaches mentioned above. Here, $FINAL\_ANS$ is the best agent based on its advertised capabilities and its actual ability to accomplish delegated tasks.

As a summary, the algorithm that considers agents' track records is given as follows:

Algorithm find_most_promise(V,NT,k,D)

/* Find the most promising agent based on the agents' track records and */

/* the returned results of **find_nn** or **range** algorithm. */

1. $ANSTABLE := find\_nn(V, NT, k)$;
2. **if** $ANSTABLE = \emptyset$ **then**
3. $ANSTABLE := range(V, NT, D)$;
4. **if** $ANSTABLE = \emptyset$ **then**
5. **return** NO_ANSWER
6. **else**
7. For all agents in $ANSTABLE$, call *initial_value_generation*

8. { **for** $j := 1$ to $k = |ANSTABLE|$ **do**
9. { $TR_j := A_j$'s track records;
10. $aging\_check(TR_j)$;
11. **while** $TR_j \neq NIL$ **do**
12. { $tr := take\_one\_tuple(TR_j)$;
13. $sd := evaluation\_part(tr)$;
14. $EV_j = sum\_up(sd)$;
15. remove tr from TR_j; } }
16. $M = construct\_evaluation\_matrix(EV_j)$;
17. $FINAL\_ANS := most\_promise(M)$;
18. **return** $FINAL\_ANS$; }

end.

Suppose the maximum number of elements $(2 - tuples)$ in TR_j is m, then the time complexity from line 7 to line 15 is $O(mk)$. Both lines 16 and 17 will need $O(7k)$ time. In the worst case, **find_nn**(V, NT, k) will need $O(|\Sigma_v^V| \cdot |\Sigma_{nt}^{NT}| + k)$ time [21]. Thus, in the worst case, **find_most_promise** will need $O(|\Sigma_v^V| \cdot |\Sigma_{nt}^{NT}| + (15+m)k)$ time (when calling **find_nn**). As $15+m$ is a small constant, the time complexity of **find_most_promise** only increases a little compared with that of **find_nn**.

With the **find_most_promise** algorithm, if one service provider agent keeps performing well, the algorithm always returns that agent as its matchmaking result. This is natural. Just as in human society, if someone always does their work well, there is no reason to terminate their employment.

6.3.5 Impact of Track Records on Matchmaking

To evaluate the impact of different track records on the final matchmaking results, we conducted some simulations. All the data here were generated by a special designed C program calling the $rand()$ function.

Suppose the returned results of **find_nn** have 10 agents,

$$ANSTABLE = [A_1, A_2, A_3, A_4, A_5, A_6, A_7, A_8, A_9, A_{10}].$$

That is, these 10 agents have the same or closely similar capabilities. Assume there are n (similar) tasks. For each task, we randomly delegate to an agent, A_i, from $ANSTABLE$, and randomly attach an evaluation result (satisfactory degree) to A_i. The track records of these 10 agents with $n = 40$ are shown in Table 6.12.

The corresponding evaluation matrix is as follows:

$$M = \begin{pmatrix} 0&0&0&0&0&1&0&0&1&0 \\ 0&0&0&1&1&1&1&0&1&1 \\ 0&2&1&0&1&0&0&1&0&1 \\ 0&0&0&1&1&0&0&1&0&0 \\ 0&0&1&0&0&0&1&1&1&0 \\ 0&0&3&0&2&1&1&0&1&0 \\ 2&4&0&0&1&1&0&1&0&2 \end{pmatrix}$$

Table 6.12. Track Records with n = 40

(s-s: strong satisfaction, s: satisfaction, w-s: weak satisfaction, n: neutral w-u: weak unsatisfaction, u:unsatisfaction, s-u: strong unsatisfaction)

Agent	*Track Records*
A_1	[1,s-u], [2,s-u]
A_2	[1,s-u], [2, s-u], [3,s-u], [4,s-u],[5,w-s], [6,w-s]
A_3	[1,u], [2,w-u], [3,u], [4,u], [5,w-s]
A_4	[1,s], [2, n]
A_5	[1,s-u], [2,s], [3, n], [4,u], [5,w-s], [6,u]
A_6	[1,s], [2,s], [3,s-u], [4,u]
A_7	[1,s], [2, w-u], [3, u]
A_8	[1,w-s], [2, n], [3,w-u], [4,s-u]
A_9	[1,w-u], [2,u], [3,s], [4,s-s]
A_{10}	[1,s-u], [2,s], [3,w-s], [4,s-u]

Using the second approach (mapping each satisfactory degree to a weighting value in $[-1, 1]$), we can calculate the total score of each agent in *ANSTABLE*. For example, agent A_9 has 4 items in its track records when $n = 40$. The evaluation (satisfactory degree) for its first delegated task is *weak unsatisfaction* (the mapped weight is $-1/3$), the second delegated task is *unsatisfaction* (corresponding weight is $-2/3$), the third is *satisfaction* (corresponding weight is $2/3$), and the fourth is *strong satisfaction* (corresponding weight is 1). Thus the total score for A_9 with $n = 40$ is

$$1 \times 1 + 1 \times (2/3) + 1 \times (-1/3) + 1 \times (-2/3) \approx 0.7$$

The higher the total score, the better the actual performance. Table 6.13 summarizes the results when task number n is 20, 40, 60, 80, 100, 200, and 300.

Table 6.13. Agents' Scores with Different Track Records

n	A_1	A_2	A_3	A_4	A_5	A_6	A_7	A_8	A_9	A_{10}
20	-1.0	-4.0	-1.0	0.7	-1.0	**1.7**	0.7	0.3	-0.3	-0.3
40	-2.0	-3.3	-2.0	**0.7**	-1.3	0.0	-0.3	-1.0	0.7	-1.0
60	-2.0	-4.3	-1.7	0.7	-2.0	-0.3	-1.3	-1.0	**1.0**	0.0
80	-2.3	-4.3	-2.0	0.3	-2.3	0.0	0.7	-1.0	**1.0**	0.7
100	-2.3	-5.3	-3.3	**2.0**	-1.7	-0.3	0.0	-1.0	0.7	-0.3
200	**1.7**	-2.3	1.0	0.0	-5.3	-3.0	0.7	-0.3	-0.3	-3.0
300	0.7	-0.3	-1.7	-3.3	-7.3	-2.0	**2.3**	-3.3	2.0	-7.7

Following "choosing the agent with highest score" principle, the selected agents are A_6 ($n = 20$), A_4 ($n = 40$), A_9 ($n = 60$), A_9 ($n = 80$), A_4 ($n = 100$), A_1 ($n = 200$), and A_7 ($n = 300$). If we do not consider agents' track records, the selected agent is always A_1. The simulation results indicate that the selected agent is different, based on different track records. This shows that agents' track records have a strong impact on the outcome of matchmaking. Therefore, it is best to consider agent's track records whenever possible.

6.4 Discussion

There is an underlying assumption for the proposed matchmaking algorithm. That is, all requesters (agents receiving services) should be able to present evaluations and be willing to do so after they receive services. This represents a small commitment, but it is not too onerous a task. What a requester agent needs to do is send a short message reporting a degree of satisfaction to the middle agent. The middle agent then stores the information in a database. No action is required of provider agents. Thus the cost for collecting the evaluation data is very low and need not be seriously taken into account.

In this algorithm, both the representation of track records and the satisfactory degree values can be changed to suit the needs of different applications. The criteria for "most promising" can also be defined according to specific applications. What is emphasized here is that agents' track records in matchmaking should be considered, as well as ways to provide initial values for track records. The issue of trustworthiness of agents in the matchmaking process is subject to further research.

7

Agent-Based Hybrid Intelligent System for Financial Investment Planning

Based on the framework proposed in Chap. 5, two agent-based hybrid intelligent systems have been successfully developed. One is for financial investment planning, and will be described in this chapter. The other is for data mining, and will be discussed in the next chapter.

In financial investment planning, a large number of components that interact in varying and complex ways are involved. This leads to complex behavior that is difficult to understand, predict and manage. Take one sub-task of financial planning – financial portfolio management – as an example. The task environment has many interesting features [5], including:

- the enormous amount of continually changing, and generally unorganized, information available;
- the variety of kinds of information that can, and should, be brought to bear on the task (market data, financial report data, technical models, analysts' reports, breaking news, etc.); and
- the many sources of uncertainty and dynamic change in the environment. It is obvious that financial planning is typically a complex problem for which hybrid solutions are crucial.

In the agent-based financial investment planning system we have implemented, the following models (techniques) have been integrated:

- a client financial risk tolerance model and a client asset allocation model – both are based on fuzzy logic [47];
- two interest rate prediction models – one based on neural networks, the other based on fuzzy logic and genetic algorithms [49];
- three portfolio selection models: Markowitz's model [104], the fuzzy probability model, and the possibility distribution model [105];
- ordered weighted averaging(OWA) operators for result aggregation [99]; and
- expert systems with explanation mechanisms.

Z. Zhang, C. Zhang: Agent-Based Hybrid Intelligent Systems, LNAI 2938, pp. 93–125, 2004.

In addition to these models, an operations research software package called *LINDO*, used for solving quadratic programming (*http://www.lindo.com/*) and a matrix software package called *MatrixLib* for solving eigenvalues of matrices (*http://www. mathtools.com/*), were also integrated.

Before discussing how to analyze, design, and implement this system, the main integrated techniques are briefly described first.

7.1 Introduction to Some Models Integrated in the System

Diverse models were integrated in the agent-based hybrid intelligent system for financial investment planning.

7.1.1 Financial Risk Tolerance Model

When giving investment advice to a client, the first thing a financial investment planning system needs to do is to determine the client's investment policy. Based on this (aggressive or conservative etc.), the system can then decide in which categories (stock market, real estate, etc.) the client should invest.

To make a decision about a client's investment policy (IP), decision making agents need the information about the client's financial *risk tolerance* (RT) ability, the falling or rising of *interest rates* (P_1), the state of the stock market (P_2), and the unemployment rate (P_3), and so on. Decision making agents use rules in their domain knowledge bases such as

$$If\ RT\ is\ H\ and\ P_1\ is\ B_1\ and\ \ldots\ then\ IP\ is\ C$$

to make decisions. Here, C is a fuzzy subset indicating the aggressive or conservative nature of the investment policy. H and B_1 are fuzzy subsets.

The agents use the client's annual income and total net-worth to evaluate the client's financial risk tolerance ability. In our example, assume the agents agree to describe the input variables *annual income* and *total net-worth* and the output variable *risk tolerance* by the sets:

annual income $= \{L, M, H\}$, *total networth* $= \{L, M, H\}$, *risk tolerance* $= \{L, MO, H\}$.

The terms have the following meaning: L = low, M = medium, H = high, and MO = moderate. They are fuzzy numbers whose supporting intervals belong to the universal sets $U_1 = \{x \times 10^3 | 0 \leq x \leq 100\}$, $U_2 = \{y \times 10^4 | 0 \leq y \leq 100\}$, $U_3 = \{z | 0 \leq z \leq 100\}$. The real numbers, x and y, represent dollars in thousands and hundreds of thousands, correspondingly, while z takes values on a psychometric scale from 0 to 100, measuring risk tolerance. The numbers on that scale have specified meaning for the financial experts (agents).

For a simplified client financial risk tolerance model, the following nine approximate reasoning rules are used to determine a client's risk tolerance [47]:

Rule 1: If the client's annual income (AI) is low (L), and the client's total networth (TN) is low (L), then the client's risk tolerance (RT) is low (L);
Rule 2: If AI is L and TN is M, then RT is L;
Rule 3: If AI is L and TN is H, then RT is MO;
Rule 4: If AI is M and TN is L, then RT is L;
Rule 5: If AI is M and TN is M, then RT is MO;
Rule 6: If AI is M and TN is H, then RT is H;
Rule 7: If AI is H and TN is L, then RT is MO;
Rule 8: If AI is H and TN is M, then RT is H;
Rule 9: If AI is H and TN is H, then RT is H.

In this application, approximate reasoning (part of the skill model) is used for determining the client's investment policy and risk tolerance ability.

7.1.2 Asset Allocation Model

The inputs (linguistic variables) in the fuzzy logic client asset allocation model are *age* and *risk tolerance* (*risk*). It is assumed that the risk is already estimated. There are three outputs (linguistic variables), *savings*, *income* and *growth*. The control objective for any given pair ($age, risk$) which reflects the state of a client is to find how to allocate the asset to *savings*, *income*, and *growth*. For a detailed description of this model, see [47].

Assume that the financial experts (agents) describe the two input and three output variables in terms of triangular and trapezoidal shape as follows:

$$Age = \{Y(young), MI(middle\ age), OL(old)\},$$
$$Risk = \{L(low), MO(moderate), H(high)\},$$
$$Saving = \{L(low), M(medium), H(high)\},$$
$$Income = \{L(low), M(medium), H(high)\},$$
$$Growth = \{L(low), M(medium), H(high)\}.$$

Similar to the risk tolerance model, there are nine $if - then$ rules. Each inference rule produces not one but three conclusions, one for *savings*, one for *income*, and one for *growth*. Consequently, the financial experts (agents) have to design three decision tables. Figures 7.1, 7.2 and 7.3 are decision tables for *savings*, *income* and *growth*.

Based on these tables, the first two $if - then$ rules read:

If a client's age is young and risk tolerance is low, then asset allocation is: medium in savings, medium in income, medium in growth.

If a client's age is young and risk tolerance is moderate, then asset allocation is: low in savings, medium in income, high in growth.

Age \ Risk tolerance	Low	Moderate	High
Young	M	L	L
Middle	M	L	L
Old	H	M	M

Fig. 7.1. Decision Table for Output *savings*

Age \ Risk tolerance	Low	Moderate	High
Young	M	M	L
Middle	H	H	M
Old	H	H	M

Fig. 7.2. Decision Table for Output *income*

Age \ Risk tolerance	Low	Moderate	High
Young	M	H	H
Middle	L	M	H
Old	L	L	M

Fig. 7.3. Decision Table for Output *growth*

7.1.3 Portfolio Selection Models

Portfolio selection involves determining the most suitable portfolio for either private or institutional investors. It is a key step in financial investment. There are many portfolio selection models available. It is too difficult to choose the "best" model to use in real-world financial investment applications. Each model has its own strengths and weaknesses. One model may put emphasis on some factors or attributes during portfolio selection but may ignore others. No single model can take all factors into consideration.

In this system, to select portfolios independently based on the data, three typical models are employed – Markowitz's model [104], the fuzzy probability model, and the possibility portfolio selection model [105, 106]. The ordered weighted averaging (OWA) operator is then used to aggregate these three different portfolios into a final one.

After Markowitz proposed the first portfolio selection model in the 1950s [104], many portfolio selection models appeared based on different techniques. Here, a brief introduction of three typical models is given – Markowitz's model, the fuzzy probability model, and the possibility portfolio selection model. Markowitz's model is based on a probability distribution. The fuzzy probability model can be regarded as a natural extension of Markowitz's model because it extends probability into fuzzy probability. The possibility portfolio selection model is based on a possibility distribution that is used to characterize experts' knowledge. A possibility distribution is identified using the returns of securities associated with possibility grades offered by portfolio experts.

Markowitz's Portfolio Selection Model

Assume that there are n securities, denoted by $S_j(j = 1, \ldots, n)$. The return of the security S_j is denoted as r_j and the proportion of total investment funds devoted to this security is denoted as x_j. Thus, the equation $\sum_{j=1}^{n} x_j = 1$ holds.

Since the returns from securities $r_j(j = 1, \ldots, n)$ vary from time to time, those are assumed to be random variables which can be represented by a pair of the average vector and the covariance matrix. For instance, it is assumed that the observation data on returns is denoted as $\mathbf{r_i} = [r_{i1}, ..., r_{in}]^t$. Thus, the total data over m periods are denoted as the following matrix:

$$\begin{pmatrix} r_{11} & r_{12} & \cdots & r_{1n} \\ r_{21} & r_{22} & \cdots & r_{2n} \\ \vdots & \vdots & \ddots & \vdots \\ r_{m1} & r_{m2} & \cdots & r_{mn} \end{pmatrix}$$

where r_{ij}, denoting the return of the jth security at the time i, is defined as (Closing price of the jth security at the time i) minus (Its closing price at time $i-1$) plus (Its dividends at the time i) all divided by (Its closing price at time $i-1$). The average vector of returns over m periods denoted as $\mathbf{r^0} = [r_1^0, ..., r_n^0]^t$ is defined as

$$\mathbf{r^0} = \begin{bmatrix} \sum_{i=1}^{m} r_{i1}/m \\ \vdots \\ \sum_{i=1}^{m} r_{in}/m \end{bmatrix}$$

Also, the corresponding covariance matrix $\mathbf{Q} = [q_{ij}^2]$ is defined as $q_{ij}^2 = \sum_{k=1}^{m}(r_{ki} - r_i^0)(r_{kj} - r_j^0)/m(i = 1, \ldots, n, j = 1, \ldots, n)$.

Therefore, random variables can be represented by the average vector $\mathbf{r^0}$, and the covariance matrix $\mathbf{Q}$, denoted as $(\mathbf{r^0}, \mathbf{Q})$. Now, the return associated with a portfolio $\mathbf{x} = [x_1, ..., x_n]^t$ is given by $z = \mathbf{x^t r}$. The average and variance of z are given as:

$$E(z) = E(\mathbf{x^t r}) = \mathbf{x^t} E\mathbf{r} = \mathbf{x^t r^0}$$
$$V(z) = V(\mathbf{x^t r}) = \mathbf{x^t Q x}$$

Since the variance of a portfolio return is regarded as a risk of investment, the best investment is one with the minimum variance subject to a given average return r_s. This is the famous Markowitz's model as described in [1]. It can be formalized as the following quadratic programming (QP) problem:

$Min_x\ \mathbf{x^t Q x}$
s.t. $\mathbf{x^t r^0} = r_s, \sum_{i=1}^{n} x_i = 1, x_i \geq 0.$

The Fuzzy Probability Portfolio Selection Model

In this model, the data are given as $(\mathbf{r_i}, h_i)(i = 1, \ldots, m)$, where h_i is a possibility grade to reflect a similarity degree between the future state of stock markets and the state of the ith sample offered by experts. These grades, $h_i(i = 1, \ldots, m)$, are graded as weights to determine the fuzzy average vector and covariance matrix in fuzzy probabilities.

Given the data $(\mathbf{r_i}, h_i)(i = 1, \ldots, m)$, the fuzzy weighted average vector $\alpha = [\alpha_1, ..., \alpha_n]^t$ can be defined as follows:

$$\alpha = \sum_{i=1}^{m}(h_i \mathbf{r_i}) / \sum_{i=1}^{m} h_i$$

Similarly, the fuzzy weight covariance matrix $\Sigma = [\sigma_{ij}]$ can be defined by $\sigma_{ij} = \{\sum_{k=1}^{m}(r_{ki} - \alpha_i)(r_{kj} - \alpha_j)h_k\} / \sum_{k=1}^{m} h_k (i = 1, \ldots, n, j = 1, \ldots, n)$.

Thus, the given data $(\mathbf{r_i}, h_i)(i = 1, \ldots, m)$ can be summarized as the parametric representation (α, Σ), which is used to construct the fuzzy portfolio selection model.

Given the weighted average vector and covariance matrix, (α, Σ), the average and covariance of the return z are given as follows:

$$E(z) = \mathbf{x^t} \alpha$$
$$V(z) = \mathbf{x^t} \Sigma \mathbf{x}$$

Thus, the fuzzy probability portfolio selection problem can be obtained as:

$Min_x\ \mathbf{x^t} \Sigma \mathbf{x}$
s.t. $\mathbf{x^t} \alpha = r_s, \sum_{i=1}^{n} x_i = 1, x_i \geq 0.$

It should be noted that the average vector and covariance matrix in Markowitz's model are replaced by the weight-average vector and covariance, respectively, in which the expert judgment h_i is contained. It is still a QP problem.

The Possibility Portfolio Selection Model

Assume that the returns $\mathbf{r_i}(i = 1, \ldots, m)$ are governed by a possibility distribution. The possibility distribution, denoted as $\mathbf{\Pi_A}(\mathbf{r}) = (\alpha, \mathbf{D_A})_\mathbf{e}$, where α is a center vector, and $\mathbf{D_A}$ is a symmetric positive-definite matrix. The possibility return of a portfolio $\mathbf{x} = [x_1, \ldots, x_n]^t$ can be written as $z = \mathbf{x^t r}$.

The possibility distribution of Z, denoted as $\Pi_Z(z)$, can be defined by the extension principle as follows:

$$\Pi_Z(z) = Max_{\{r|z=x^t r\}} \Pi_A(\mathbf{r})$$

Solving this simple optimization problem produces the following:

$$\Pi_Z(z) = exp\{-(z - \mathbf{x^t}\alpha)^2 \cdot (\mathbf{x^t D_A x})^{-1}\}$$

where $\mathbf{x^t}\alpha$ is the center value and $\mathbf{x^t D_A x}$ is the spread of the possibility return Z. Following Markowitz's model, the following possibility portfolio selection model is given:

$Min_x \; \mathbf{x^t D_A x}$

s.t. $\mathbf{x^t}\alpha = r_s, \sum_{i=1}^{n} x_i = 1, x_i \geq 0$, which is also a QP problem minimizing the spread of possibility return, subject to a given center return r_s.

7.1.4 Interest Prediction Models

Two interest prediction models are integrated into the system, one is based on the feedforward network and the other based on the combination of fuzzy logic and genetic algorithms [49]. Here we will not discuss the basic concepts of neural networks, fuzzy logic, and genetic algorithms, but the major factors that affect interest rates.

Interest rates are usually represented by the rates for 91-day Treasury bills, or so-called T-bills. In [141], Larrain employs statistical analysis to establish that five factors account for roughly 90 percent of the variation in interest rates (as represented by 91-day Treasury bill rates). These five factors are:

- previous T-bill rates;
- real gross national product (GNP);
- consumer price index (CPI);
- M2 nominal money supply; and
- personal wealth

Personal wealth is the accumulation of the difference between personal income and personal consumption. The M2 money supply consists of all cash in circulation and deposits in savings and checking accounts, and represents readily available liquid assets. The consumer price index is a measure of the inflation trend.

The interest rate prediction models based on neural networks or fuzzy logic and genetic algorithms take the changes of these five factors as inputs, and output the changes of T-bill rates as the predicted interest rates. This is shown in Fig. 7.4.

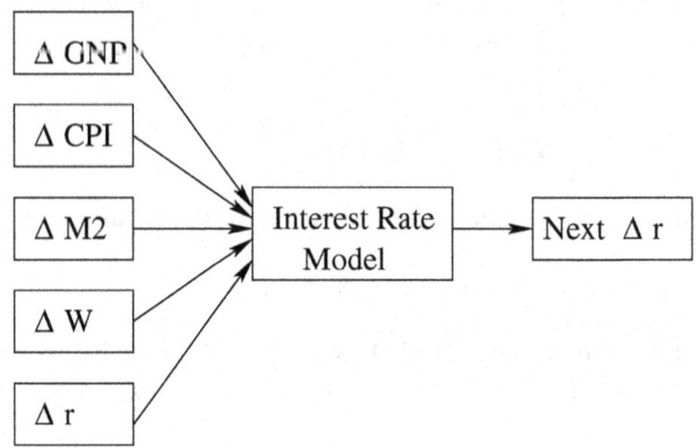

Fig. 7.4. Block Diagram for the Interest Rate Model

7.1.5 Ordered Weighted Averaging Operation

In multi-agent systems, each of the agents may have its own expertise. When they are asked to make a decision on the same task, the results may be different. In such situations, different decisions need to be aggregated to obtain a final result. To better understand the problem, here is an example based on financial investment planning.

Suppose a user (investor) wants to know whether his investment policy (IP) should be aggressive or conservative. First, the user gives his *annual income* (AI) and *total net-worth* (TN) to the decision making agents through the interface agent. The decision making agents use their own knowledge (with the help of intelligent technique agents) to evaluate the user's *risk tolerance* (RT) ability using rules such as: *If user's AI is low (L) and TN is L, then user's RT is L.* Note that different decision making agents may have different rules similar to this.

The decision making agents then delegate the information gathering agents to collect data concerning the rise or fall of interest rates, the state of the stock market, the trade balance, the unemployment rate, the level of inventory stock, etc. These data are called parameters, and are represented as $P = \{P_1, P_2, \ldots\}$. The parameters collected by different information gathering agents may differ.

Assume there are k parameters to be collected: $P = \{P_1, P_2, \ldots, P_k\}$, and m information gathering agents are asked to collect the k parameters independently. The gathered results are $\{P_{i1}, P_{i2}, \ldots, P_{ik}\}$ $(i = 1, 2, \ldots, m)$. The first aggregation problem involves combining $\{P_{i1}, P_{i2}, \ldots, P_{ik}\}$ $(i = 1, 2, \ldots, m)$ in some reasonable way to obtain $P = \{P_1, P_2, \ldots, P_k\}$.

Now, suppose there are n decision making agents. Each agent has rules in its knowledge base such as

$$If\ RT\ is\ H\ and\ P_1\ is\ B_1\ and\ \ldots\ then\ IP\ is\ C_i \tag{7.1}$$

where $C_i (i = 1, 2, \ldots, n)$ is a fuzzy subset indicating the aggressive or conservative degree of the investment policy.

Because the knowledge of the decision making agents and their decision attitudes may be different, the answers to the same question may also be different, and differ in various degrees. They have to be combined or reconciled in order to produce a final decision.

There are many aggregation algorithms. Different aggregation algorithms are needed for different applications. In this financial application, there exists much fuzzy or uncertain information, so approaches are needed that can deal with such information to do the aggregation. There are three main classes of aggregation operation that can deal with fuzzy or uncertain information – the t–norm and t–conorm, *generalized means*, and *ordered weighted averaging* (OWA). After comparing the three class aggregation operations, OWA is used in this system.

Yager has introduced the OWA operator to provide a family of aggregators having the properties of mean operators [99, 100, 101].

A mapping $F : R^n \longrightarrow R$ is called an OWA operator of dimension n if it has an associated weighting vector W of dimension n such that its components satisfy

(1) $w_j \in [0, 1]$;
(2) $\sum_{j=1}^{n} w_j = 1$; and
(3) $F_w(a_1, a_2, \ldots, a_n) = \sum_{j=1}^{n} w_j b_j$, where b_j is the jth largest of the a_i.

A fundamental feature of this operator is the reordering process which associates the arguments with the weights. This aggregation can be expressed in a vector notation as $F_w(a_1, a_2, \ldots, a_n) = W^T B$. In this expression, W is the OWA weighting vector associated with the aggregation, and B is the ordered argument vector; where the jth component in B, b_j is the jth largest of the a_i.

Expressing the OWA operator $F_w(a_1, a_2, \ldots, a_n)$ in its vector notation form, $W^T B$ makes very clear the distinct components involved in the performance of this operation. First, there is a weighting vector W; this is required to have components w_j which lie in the unit interval and sum to one. The second part of the OWA aggregation is the vector B, known as the ordered argument vector. This vector is composed of the arguments of the aggregation. To solve a specific problem using the OWA operator, we need to find out the appropriate weighting vector W and the ordered argument vector B.

There are two characterizing measures associated with the weighting vector W. (See [99] and [100].)

The first of these, the α value of an OWA operator, is defined as

$$\alpha(W) = \frac{1}{n-1}\sum_{j=1}^{n} w_j(n-j) \tag{7.2}$$

This measure, which takes its values in the unit interval, is determined by the weighting used in the aggregation. The actual semantics associated with α are dependent upon the application in which it is being used. In our case, the α can be the degree that the aggregation prefers decisions with high confidence, or the attitude of the decision making agent.

The second measure is called the dispersion (or entropy) of W and is defined as

$$H(W) = -\sum_{j=1}^{n} w_j \ln(w_j) \tag{7.3}$$

Equation (7.3) helps measure the degree to which W takes into account all of the information in the aggregation.

One method of determining these weights, $w_1, \ldots, w_n$, requires the solution of the following mathematical programming problem:

Maximize $-\sum_{j=1}^{n} w_j \ln(w_j)$ subject to
(1) $\alpha(W) = \frac{1}{n-1}\sum_{j=1}^{n} w_j(n-j)$;
(2) $w_j \in [0,1]$;
(3) $\sum_{j=1}^{n} w_j = 1$.

Assume that the agents' decisions are still represented by trapezoidal numbers. If $C_i = (a_{i1}, b_{i1}, b_{i2}, a_{i2}), i = 1, 2, \ldots, n$, are trapezoidal numbers, then

$$\begin{aligned} C_{OWA} = (&F_w(a_{11}, \ldots, a_{n1}), F_w(b_{11}, \ldots, b_{n1}), \\ &F_w(b_{12}, \ldots, b_{n2}), F_w(a_{12}, \ldots, a_{n2})) \end{aligned} \tag{7.4}$$

where F_w is an OWA operator. We now discuss how to decide the weighting vector W and the ordered argument vector B in different situations when aggregating use (7.4).

Suppose that the three agents present their decisions on the investment policy by the fuzzy numbers

$$C_1 = (-100, -100, -50, -30), C_2 = (-10, 10, 10, 30), C_3 = (60, 90, 100, 100)$$

and the weighting vector can be obtained: $W = [w_1, w_2, w_3] = [1/3, 1/3, 1/3]$. The arguments are ordered by their values.

Corresponding to the weighted case, if the arguments are ordered using the values of r_i, i.e., let b_j be the a_i value which has the jth largest of r_i, and let $W = [w_1, w_2, w_3] = [u_3, u_2, u_1] = [0.5, 0.3, 0.2]$. Formula (7.4) is then used to aggregate. In both cases, the same results are obtained as those using fuzzy averaging.

The problem here is that the degrees of importance in aggregation were not used directly. Actually in this case, the arguments which need to be aggregated are pairs such as

$$(u_1, a_{11}), (u_2, a_{21}), \ldots, (u_n, a_{n1})$$

Here, the formula $G(u, a) = \bar{\alpha}\bar{u} + ua$ is used to transform the tuple into a single value [101] (pp. 41-49), where α is defined by (7.2). The following are the steps of the procedure:

1. Calculate the α value of the OWA operator:

$$\alpha = \sum_{j=1}^{3} \frac{3-j}{3-1} w_j = w_1 + w_2/2 = 0.5 + 0.3/2 = 0.65$$

2. Transform each of the argument tuples using $G(u_j, a_j) = \bar{\alpha}\bar{u_j} + u_j a_j$, hence

$$G(u_1, a_{11}) = -49.72, G(u_2, a_{21}) = -2.755, G(u_3, a_{31}) = 30.175$$

$$G(u_1, b_{11}) = -49.72, G(u_2, b_{21}) = 3.245, G(u_3, b_{31}) = 45.175$$
$$G(u_1, b_{12}) = -9.72, G(u_2, b_{22}) = 3.245, G(u_3, b_{32}) = 50.175$$
$$G(u_1, a_{12}) = -5.72, G(u_2, a_{22}) = 9.245, G(u_3, a_{32}) = 50.175$$

3. Calculate C_{OWA}

$$\begin{aligned} C_{OWA} &= (F_w(-49.72, -2.755, 30.175), F_w(-49.72, 3.245, 45.175), \\ &\quad F_w(-9.72, 3.245, 50.175), F_w(-5.72, 9.245, 50.175)) \\ &= (4.32, 13.62, 24.12, 26.72) \end{aligned}$$

The defuzzification value is 18.87. This still indicates a very cautious investment policy – much more cautious than one not using the degrees of importance.

The concept of agents' decision making attitudes is also important. Because the agents usually have different knowledge, this results in different attitudes when making decisions. Some are aggressive, some conservative. Here, α_i ($\alpha_i \in [0, 1]$) is used to indicate the agents' attitudes. The bigger the value of α_i, the more aggressive the attitude of the decision making agent DA_i.

Suppose there are still three agents, and their attitudes are $\alpha_1 = 0.3, \alpha_2 = 0.5$ and $\alpha_3 = 0.8$. The decisions they make, and their degrees of importance, remain unchanged, as described above.

To aggregate, the first step is to decide the attitude α of all the agents (in this case three). The OWA operator is still used. Degrees of importance are mapped to unit interval as the weighting vector for combining α_i, called $W(\alpha)$, and

$$W(\alpha) = [w(\alpha)_1, w(\alpha)_2, w(\alpha)_3] = [0.5, 0.3, 0.2]$$

Then

$$\alpha = F_{W(\alpha)}(\alpha_1, \alpha_2, \alpha_3) = \alpha_3 \times w(\alpha)_1 + \alpha_2 \times w(\alpha)_2 + \alpha_1 \times w(\alpha)_3 = 0.61$$

By solving the mathematical programming problem with $\alpha = 0.61$, the weighting vector W is obtained for the final aggregation as follows:

$$W = [w_1, w_2, w_3] = [0.45, 0.32, 0.23]$$

The arguments are ordered according to the values of r_i. The final aggregation using (7.4) gives $C_{OWA} = (0.8, 20.7, 36.7, 47.3)$. The defuzzification value according to the *mean of maximum method* in fuzzy averaging is 28.7 [47]. This suggests a policy on the aggressive side of the scale, but a cautious one – more cautious than that using fuzzy averaging. This is because the decision attitude of DA_1 is slightly conservative, but its decision is very conservative. Taking all the information into account, the investment policy should be cautiously aggressive.

If the degrees of importance are used directly in the aggregation in this case, $C_{OWA} = (1.26, 9.93, 21.38, 24.22)$ is obtained. The defuzzification value is 15.66.

7.2 Analysis of the System

In order to identify which components should be contained in a typical financial investment planning system, without loss of generality, consider a financial establishment house providing investment advice for clients. In such a place, there are: an up-front administrator, one or more personnel officer(s), and many financial investment experts (decision makers). The advice giving (decision making) process is initiated by a user contacting the up-front administrator with a set of requirements. The administrator asks the personnel officer to provide the experts' profiles, and then delegates the task to one or more experts based on the experts' profiles. The experts then work on the task and try to give their recommendations with or without external help. After the experts finish preparing a recommendation (if the task was assigned to more than one expert, the recommendations from different experts must be combined to form a final one), they pass it to the front desk clerk. Finally, the administrator sends the advice to the user. Such a typical process can help us analyze and design an agent-based hybrid system for financial investment planning.

Based on the above description and the methodology proposed in Sec. 4.5, it is comparatively straightforward to identify the roles in the hybrid intelligent system for financial investment planning.

The up-front administrator's behavior falls into two distinct roles: one acting as an interface to the user (USERHANDLER, Fig. 7.5) and one overseeing

Role Schema: USERHANDLER
Description: Receives request/inquiry from the user and oversees process to ensure appropriate decision is returned
Protocols and Activities: AwaitCall, InformUser, ProduceAssignments, ReceiveDecision
Permissions: **reads supplied** *UserDetails* // personal information of the user **supplied** *UserRequirements* // what user wants *Decision* // final decision or nil
Responsibilities Liveness: USERHANDLER = AwaitCall. ProduceAssignments. ReceiveDecision. InformUser Safety: • True

Fig. 7.5. Schema for Role USERHANDLER

Role Schema: WORKPLANNER
Description: This role elaborates a work plan for decision making and is in charge of ensuring that such a work plan is fulfilled.
Protocols and Activities: GetUserRequirements, <u>ProducePlan</u>, GetCapabilities, DelegateTasks
Permissions: **reads supplied** *UserDetails* // personal information of the user **supplied** *UserRequirements* // detailed service requirements *Capabilities* // capabilities of other roles **generates** plan // work plan
Responsibilities Liveness: WORKPLANNER = GetUserRequirements.GetCapabilities.<u>ProducePlan</u>.DelegateTasks Safety: • *UserDetails* and *UserRequirements* are available

Fig. 7.6. Schema for Role WORKPLANNER

the process inside the organization (WORKPLANNER, Fig. 7.6). The personnel officer's behavior falls into another two roles: one keeping track of the profiles (CAPABILITYRECORDER, Fig. 7.7) and one checking the profiles (CAPABILITYMATCHER, Fig. 7.8). The experts' behaviors are covered by DECISIONMAKER (Fig. 7.9), HELPPROVIDER (Fig. 7.10), and DECISIONAGGREGATOR (Fig. 7.11) roles. The final role is that of the USER (Fig. 7.12) who requires the decision.

Role Schema: CAPABILITYRECORDER
Description: Add capabilities advertised by roles to CapabilityDatabase, or delete capabilities unadvertised by roles from the database
Protocols and Activities: ReceiveAdvertisement, AddCapability, DeleteCapability
Permissions: **reads supplied** *CapabilityInfo* // Advertised or unadvertised capability information **changes** *CapabilityDatabase* // add or delete capability
Responsibilities Liveness: CAPABILITYRECORDER = ReceiveAdvertisement.(AddCapability|DeleteCapability) Safety: • CapabilityDatabase exists

Fig. 7.7. Schema for Role CAPABILITYRECORDER

Role Schema: CAPABILITYMATCHER
Description: Matches capabilities requested by a role with those capabilities in CapabilityDatabase. Informs requester role with the ROLENAME whose capability matched with the requested one.
Protocols and Activities: GetRequestedCapability, AccessCapabilityDatabase, InformRequester, CompareCapability
Permissions: **reads supplied** *RequestedCapability* // capability requested by a role **supplied** *CapabilityDatabase*
Responsibilities Liveness: CAPABILITYMATCHER = GetRequestedCapability. (AccessCapabilityDatabase.CompareCapability)+.InformRequester Safety: • True

Fig. 7.8. Schema for Role CAPABILITYMATCHER

With the respective role definitions in place, the next stage is to define the associated interaction models for these roles. Here we focus on the interactions associated with the DECISIONMAKER role.

This role interacts with the WORKPLANNER role to obtain the task this role will accomplish (ReceiveTask protocol, Fig. 7.13a). It interacts with the INFOGATHER role to gather some relevant information (known facts) for the task (GetInformation protocol, Fig. 7.13b). It also interacts with the CAPABIL-

Role Schema: DECISIONMAKER
Description: Reaches a conclusion for the delegated task based on the information gathered and knowledge the role has.
Protocols and Activities: ReceiveTask, GetInformation, AskforHelp, InformDecisionAggregator, <u>Reasoning</u>
Permissions: **reads supplied** *Task* // Task delegated by other roles **supplied** *Knownfacts* // Gathered information **generates** *Decision* // one alternative decision
Responsibilities Liveness: DECISIONMAKER = ReceiveTask.GetInformation.(<u>Reasoning</u>.AskforHelp)+.InformDecisionAggregator Safety: • True

Fig. 7.9. Schema for Role DECISIONMAKER

Role Schema: HELPPROVIDER
Description: Provides appropriate help for other roles (e.g., DECISIONMAKER) when asked.
Protocols and Activities: ReceiveHelpRequirements, ReturnProcessedResults, AskforHelp, <u>Processing</u>
Permissions: **reads supplied** *HelpRequirements* // one role asks another role for help **generates** *ProcessedResults* // do the requested processing and // generate results
Responsibilities Liveness: HELPPROVIDER = ReceiveHelpRequirements.(<u>Processing</u>.AskforHelp)*.ReturnProcessedResults Safety: • HELPPROVIDER has the requested capability

Fig. 7.10. Schema for Role HELPPROVIDER

ITYMATCHER role to provide some roles for data pre- and/or post-processing and so on when accomplishing the task (AskforHelp protocol, Fig. 7.13c). When the DECISIONMAKER role finishes making decision for the task, it informs the DECISIONAGGREGATOR role of its alternative decision for the task (InformDecisionAggregator protocol, Fig. 7.13d).

In this system, the most important organizational rule in the organizational model is that *if a role says it has a capability then it can perform the tasks corresponding to the capability and will do so when asked.*

Role Schema: DECISIONAGGREGATOR
Description: Produces the final decision based on currently received alternative decisions for a task.
Protocols and Activities: ReceiveDecisions, InformUserHandler, ChooseDecision, AggregateDecisions
Permissions: **reads supplied** *Decision* // alternative decision **generates** *FinalDecision* // The "best" one of all alternative decisions or aggregated decision
Responsibilities Liveness: DECISIONAGGREGATOR = ReceiveDecisions.(ChooseDecision| AggregateDecisions).InformUserHandler Safety: • alternative decisions are available

Fig. 7.11. Schema for Role DECISIONAGGREGATOR

Role Schema: USER
Description: Organization or individual requesting a decision.
Protocols and Activities: MakeCall, GiveRequirements
Permissions: **generates** *UserDetails* // Owner of user information *UserRequirements* // Owner of user requirements
Responsibilities Liveness: USER = (MakeCall.GiveRequirements)+ Safety: • True

Fig. 7.12. Schema for Role USER

7.3 Design of the System

Having completed the analysis of the system, the design phase follows. The first model to be generated is the agent model (Fig. 7.14). This shows, for most cases, a one-to-one correspondence between roles and agent types. The exception is for the CAPABILITYRECORDER and CAPABILITYMATCHER roles which, because of their high degree of interdependence, are grouped into a single agent type.

The second model is the skill model. Again, to avoid redundance, the focus is on the DECISIONMAKER role and the Decision Making Agent. Based on the DECISIONMAKER role, six distinct services can be identified (Table 7.1).

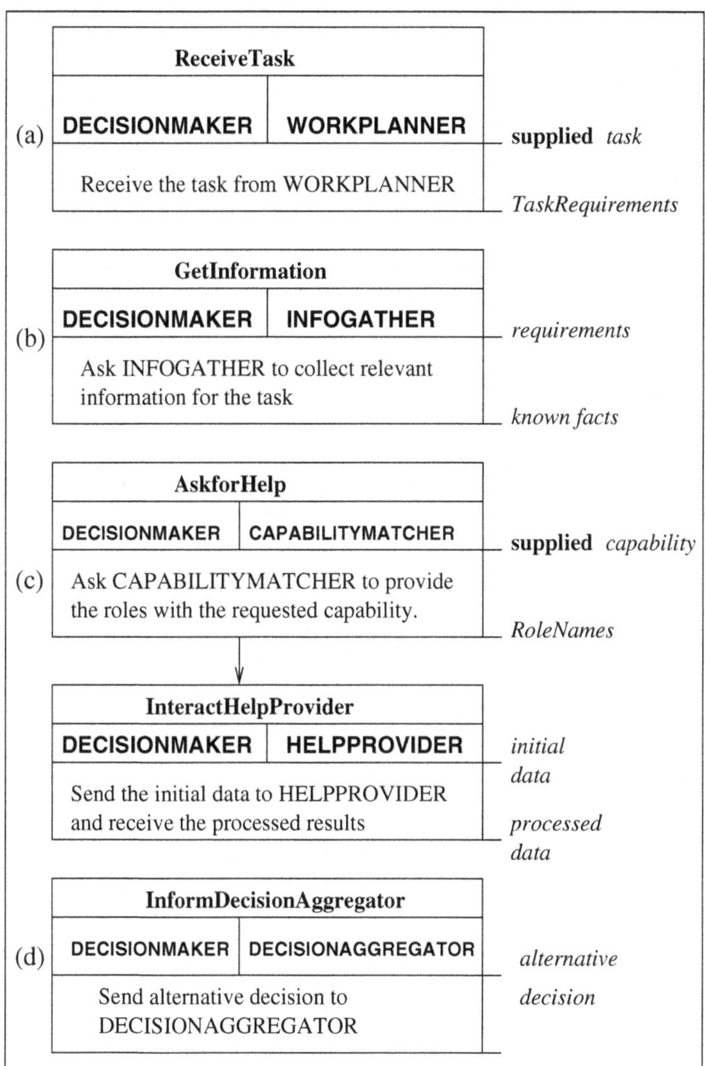

Fig. 7.13. Definition of Protocols Associated with the DecisionMaker Role: (**a**) ReceiveTask, (**b**) GetInformation, (**c**) AskforHelp, and (**d**) InformDecisionAggregator

From the ReceiveTask protocol, the service 'obtain task' is derived. This service returns the *TaskRequirements* as output. It has a pre-condition that the agent or role has the corresponding capability to perform the task, but has no post-condition.

The service associated with the GetInformation protocol is 'get information'. Its inputs, derived from the protocol definition (Fig. 7.13b), are the

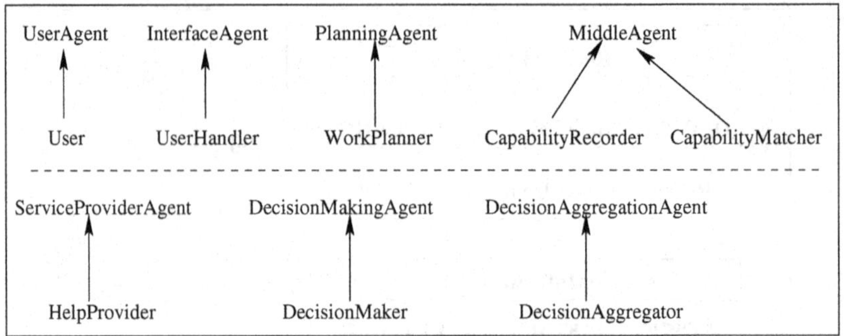

Fig. 7.14. Agent Model of the Financial Planning System

Table 7.1. Services in Skill Model

Service	Inputs	Outputs	Pre-condition	Post-condition
obtain task		task requirements	agent or role has corresponding capability	true
get information	requirements for gathering	gathered information	information sources are available	relevant information returned
accomplish reasoning	known facts	conclusions (decisions)	known facts are enough	conclusions reached
call for help	capability description	agent names or nil	true	agent name with matched capability returned
provide initial data	agent name and initial data	processed results	initial data are ready	data processed
inform aggregator	alternative decision		true	aggregator knew decision

requirements for information gathering, and its outputs are known facts (gathered information). The pre-condition for this service is that some information sources are available, and the post-condition is that relevant information is returned.

The third service, 'accomplish reasoning', is related to the Reasoning activity. The inputs for this service are known facts, and outputs are some conclusions. This service has a pre-condition that the known facts are sufficient to reach conclusions (post-condition).

The next two services, 'call for help' and 'provide initial data', are derived from the AskforHelp protocol. The 'call for help' service takes a specific capability description as input, and returns the agent name with matched capability, or nil (if not matched) as outputs. The 'provide initial data' service takes the agent name and initial data as inputs, and returns the processed data as outputs.

The final service involves informing the decision aggregator of the alternative decisions. Then the inference mechanisms in the skill model are checked. To make decisions, the agents must accomplish some reasoning based on their knowledge, and on other available information. The final model is the knowledge model, which indicates the different levels of knowledge that agents should have. In this system, the agents should have three levels of knowledge. The first level of knowledge is for agent interaction and communication. This involves, for example, domain-specific and domain-independent terminologies and their relationships. The identified domain-specific terms and their relationships will result in the construction of a domain-dependent ontology for a specific application. The second level of knowledge is some domain knowledge related to specific problem solving techniques. The third level of knowledge is meta knowledge that directs the activities of an agent.

7.4 Architecture of the System

From the above analysis and design phases it is clear that there are seven types of agents in the financial investment planning system – user agent, interface agent, planning agent, middle agent (called *serving agent* here), service provider agent, decision making agent, and decision aggregation agent.

Based on the proposed framework (refer to Fig. 5.1), the architecture of the financial planning system is determined. This is shown in Fig. 7.15. The behaviors of each kind of agent in the system (except the user agent) are now briefly described.

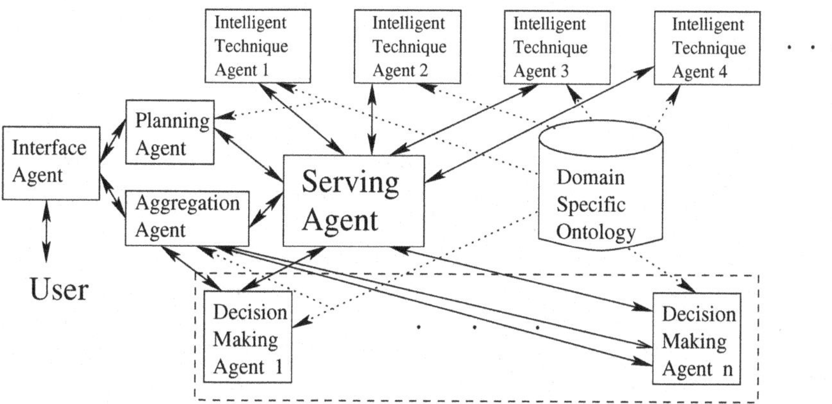

Fig. 7.15. Architecture of Agent-Based Financial Investment Planning System

- **Interface Agent** This agent interacts with the user (or user agent). It asks the user to provide their personal information and requirements, and provides the user with a final decision (or advice) that best meets the user's requirements.
- **Planning Agent** The planning agent is in charge of the activation and synchronization of the different agents. It elaborates a work plan and is in charge of ensuring that such a work plan is fulfilled. It receives assignments from the interface agent.
- **Decision Making Agent** It is application-specific, i.e., it has its own knowledge base; it must have some meta-knowledge about when it needs the help of intelligent technique agents (e.g., pre- or post-processing some data); and it can ask intelligent technique agents to accomplish some subtasks.
- **Serving Agent** The serving agent is a matchmaker – a kind of middle agent [41]. It keeps track of the names, ontologies, and capabilities of all registered intelligent technique agents in the system. It can reply to the query of a decision making agent with appropriate intelligent technique agent's name and ontology.
- **Service Provider Agent** Most of the service provider agents in the system are intelligent technique agents. Each intelligent technique agent can provide services for decision making agents with one or some kind of combined intelligent techniques. It can send back the processed results to decision making agents; it must advertise its capabilities to the serving agent.
- **Decision Aggregation Agent** When decision making agents finish the assigned tasks they return the results to the decision aggregation agent. The aggregation agent chooses one of the alternative decisions, or performs an aggregation of the different results to produce a final result.

The ontology is the foundation for agent communication. All agents in the system interpret the content of received messages based on the ontology (refer to Sec. 5.2).

7.5 Implementation of the System

The most important implementation criterion for such a system is platform independent. With this observation in mind, the JATLite (Java Agent Template, Lite, *http://java. stanford.edu/*) was chosen to support the implementation. JATLite provides a set of Java templates and a ubiquitous Java agent infrastructure that makes it easy to build systems in a common way. JATLite facilitates, in particular, construction of agents that send and receive messages using the emerging standard agent communication language KQML (Knowledge Query and Manipulation Language) [46]. JATLite does not impose any particular theory on agents. All agents implemented have the ability to exchange KQML messages. This greatly increases the interoperability of the system.

7.5.1 Internal Structures of Agents

Under the framework, all decision making agents or intelligent technique agents must register and connect to the serving agent.

Each decision making agent has its own domain-specific knowledge base as well as meta-knowledge about when to use intelligent technique agents. The serving agent records the capabilities, ontologies, and names, etc. of all the intelligent technique agents in a multi-agent system. The scenario goes as follows.

At a certain stage of the decision making process, the decision making agent sends a KQML message using the *recommend-one* performative to the serving agent, according to its meta-knowledge. The serving agent then retrieves its service provider agent database and replies with an appropriate service provider agent's name and ontology, which has the capability asked for using the *reply* performative. After that, the decision making agent communicates directly with the service provider agent to solve a specific problem. In most cases, service provider agents in the society are intelligent technique agents. The decision making agent provides the intelligent technique agent with some parameters according to the *ontology*, and the intelligent technique agent sends the results to the decision making agent.

Based on the above description, the internal structures of agents in the system can be identified. Figures 7.16 to 7.21 show the internal structures of these agents.

As one can see from Figures 7.16 to 7.21, all the agents have a common part – a KQML Message Interpreter (KMI). That is because KQML is used

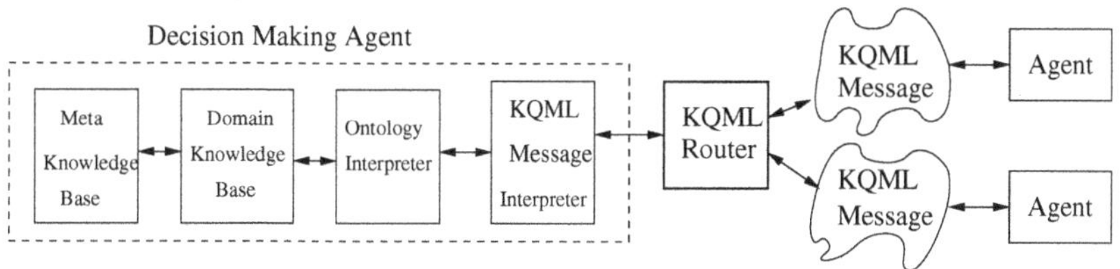

Fig. 7.16. Decision Making Agent Structure

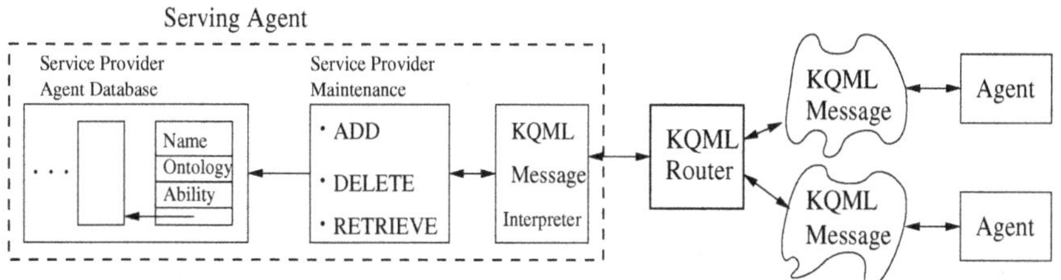

Fig. 7.17. Serving Agent Structure

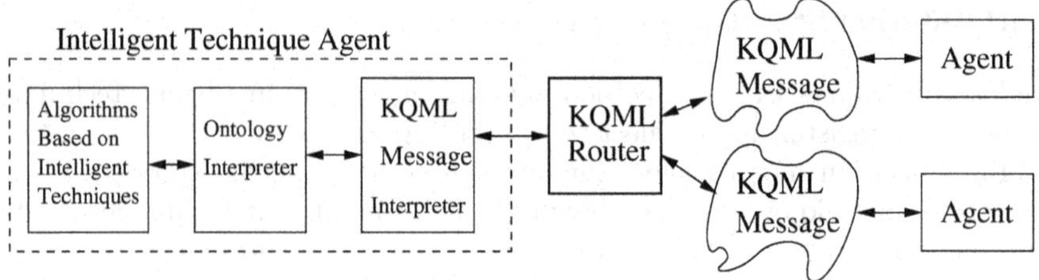

Fig. 7.18. Intelligent Technique Agent Structure

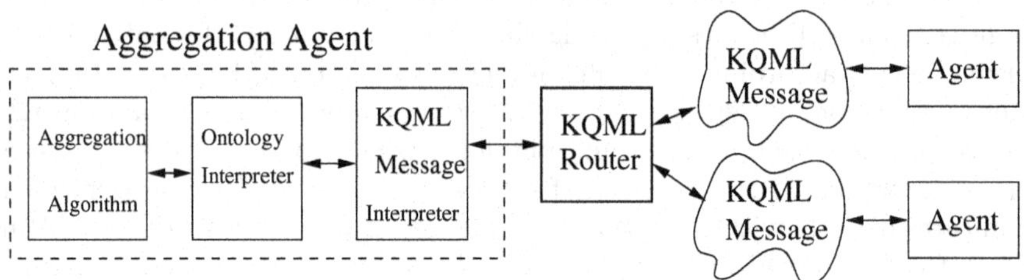

Fig. 7.19. Aggregation Agent Structure

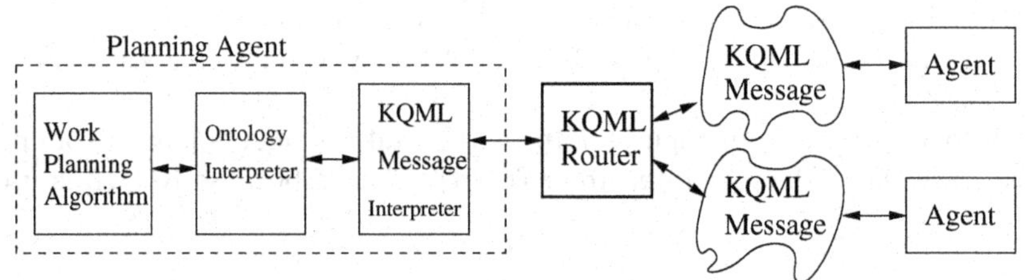

Fig. 7.20. Planning Agent Structure

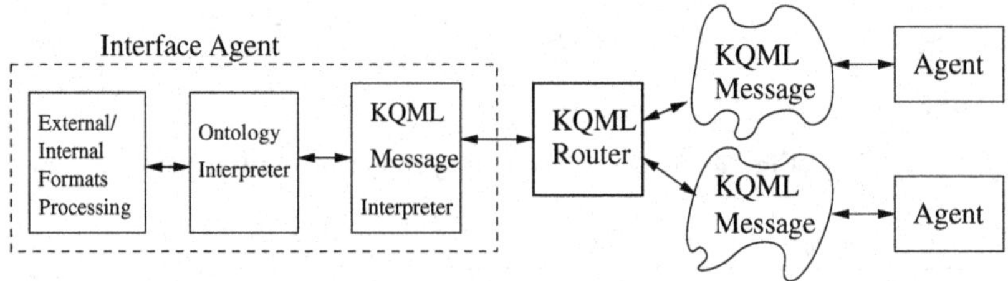

Fig. 7.21. Interface Agent Structure

for inter-agent communication. The KMI represents the interface between the KQML router and the agents. Once an incoming KQML message is detected, it will be passed to the KMI. The KMI transfers incoming KQML messages into a form that agents can understand. The implementation of KMI is based on JATLite KQMLLayer Templates.

All the agents, except the serving agent, have an ontology interpreter. They need to decrypt and process the *:content* part of the KQML message when they solve a problem. There is no ontology interpreter in the serving agent because it is not concerned with the *:content*.

The domain knowledge in decision making agents is not usually adequate to make a decision. Relevant information and skills to use the knowledge and information are also needed. The help of intelligent technique agents and other service provider agents for data pre- and/or post-processing is often required. The meta-knowledge of decision making agents advises them when help is required from intelligent technique agents.

The intelligent technique agent maintenance module in the serving agent has three functions: to add an entry that contains the intelligent technique agent's name, capability and ontology to the database; to delete an entry from the database; and to retrieve the database to find intelligent technique agents with a specific capability. The last function is usually called *matchmaking*.

Algorithms based on intelligent techniques in intelligent technique agents, if the agent is under control, will be built using KQML as a communication language. If not, the Java Native Interface is used to connect the legacy system to the agent system [50] .

The kernel part of the system is the serving agent, which is one kind of middle agent [41]. The introduction of a middle agent in the system facilitates flexibility and robustness. With the middle agents, other agents can appear or disappear dynamically by simply registering or unregistering themselves with the middle agents. Therefore they can improve the flexibility and robustness of an agent-based system.

7.5.2 Practical Architecture of the System

Under the support of JATLite, the practical architecture of the system is depicted in Fig. 7.22. Figure 7.23 shows the user interface of the system, which can start from any Internet Browser or appletviewer.

Following the analysis and design phases of the proposed methodology, we worked out that the prototype consists of the following agents:

- one interface agent;
- one middle (serving) agent;
- one planning agent;
- one aggregation agent;
- four decision making agents – investment policy agent, portfolio selection agent based on the Markowitz model, portfolio selection agent based on the fuzzy model, and portfolio selection agent based on the possibility model; and

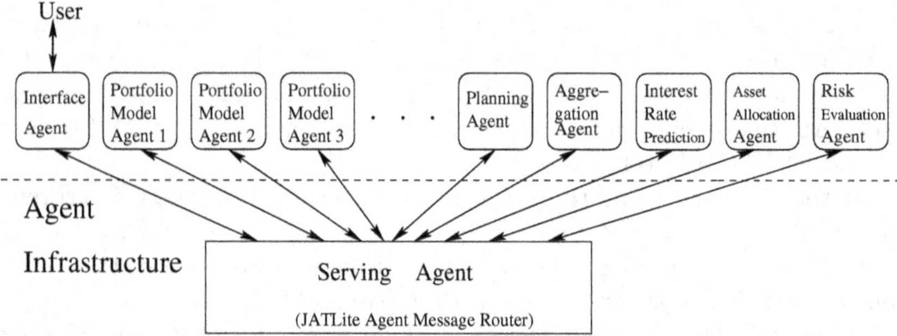

Fig. 7.22. Practical Architecture of Financial Investment Planning System

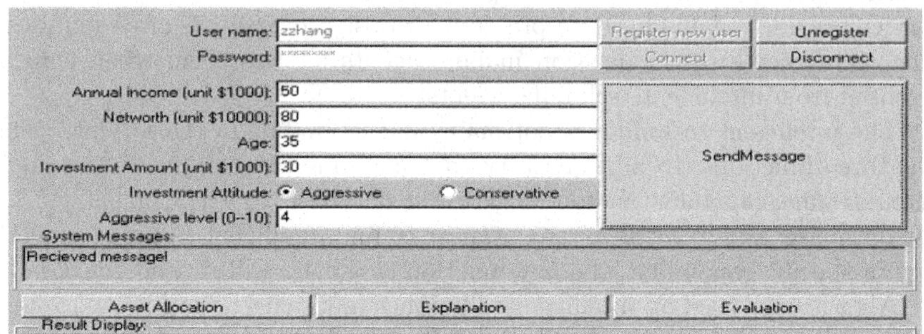

Fig. 7.23. User Interface of Financial Investment Planning System

- four service provider agents – financial risk tolerance ability evaluation agent, interest rate prediction agent based on neural network, interest rate prediction agent based on fuzzy logic and genetic algorithm, and an approximate reasoning agent.

To register for the first time, a user needs to type the user name and password in the corresponding fields and click 'register new user'. Thereafter they simply input the user name and password and click 'connect'. They can then input information about their annual income, networth etc. and click the 'sendmessage' button. The system provides asset allocation information, explanations of how to get the results, and evaluation of different portfolios in the 'result display' window. (See the next subsection.) If the user wants to leave the system, then click 'disconnect' and 'unregister'.

7.6 Case Study

To demonstrate how the system works, we first examine a typical scenario for investment. We then present an example to show how the agent-based financial investment planning system gives advice to the investor.

7.6.1 A Typical Scenario for Investment

When a person wants to invest some money, they usually go to a financial investment adviser for advice. The first thing the adviser needs to do is to understand the client's individual circumstances. The adviser may ask the client to provide the following information about himself: his financial position (for example, annual income and total net-worth), age, tax effectiveness, etc. Based on the information, the adviser will evaluate the financial risk tolerance ability as well as the client's investment goals.

If the client's primary goal is income, then investments that provide interest or dividend payments regularly and dependably are required. If the primary goal is growth, then investments that are likely to increase in value are appropriate so that they may be resold for more than their initial cost. If, however, the primary goal is to avoid risk, then investments that offer the greatest safety of principal, and protection from inflation, are required. Unfortunately, there is no single investment that simultaneously offers maximum income, maximum growth and minimum risk.

Suppose the adviser, after evaluating the client's financial risk tolerance ability, suggests they invest in the stock market. How can they select a portfolio for the client taking into account the individual constraints of that particular client? (For example, risk tolerance level and return rate.) The adviser must first gather some information about the stock market. The information would include such information as market data, financial report data, technical models, analysts' reports, breaking news. After gathering the information, the adviser then makes a portfolio selection decision based on certain models (for example, the Markowitz model or the fuzzy probability model.)

In short, the overall task of investment advice has several component tasks: eliciting (or learning) user profile information, collecting information on the user's initial portfolio position, and suggesting and monitoring a reallocation to meet the user's current profile and investment goals.

7.6.2 Example

Suppose the investor provides the interface agent with the following personal information:

Amount of money to invest: $ 150,000
Annual income: $ 70,000
Total net-worth: $ 200,000
Age: 40
Investment goal: *growth* (for example, *income, growth* and *avoid risk.* This reflects the investor's attitude towards risk.)

The interface agent passes the investor's information to the planning agent. (See Fig. 7.15.) The planning agent will delegate subtasks to different decision making agents. During the decision making process, decision making agents may ask different service provider agents for help. (Most would be soft computing agents.) Finally, the prototype gives its advice to the investor through the interface agent. The whole process (from receiving input to giving advice) consists of the following five steps.

Step 1: Determining the investor's investment policy (aggressive or conservative).

The investment policy agent will use the fuzzy rules in its knowledge base to determine the investor's investment policy. One example of a fuzzy rule is as follows:

If the investor's risk tolerance is *high*, and the interest rate is *falling*, and the investor's investment goal is *growth*, **then** the investor can take an *aggressive investment policy.*

The investment policy agent will then ask for help based on its meta-knowledge. Thus, the investment policy agent sends KQML messages using the *recommend-one* performative to the serving agent:

```
(recommend-one
 :sender investment_policy_agent
 :receiver serving_agent
 :language KQML
 :content (ask
            :ability risk_tolerance_evaluation
            :name ?
            :ontology ?
           )
 )

(recommend-one
 :sender investment_policy_agent
 :receiver serving_agent
 :language KQML
 :content (ask
            :ability interest_rate_prediction
            :name ?
            :ontology ?
           )
 )
```

The serving agent then retrieves its database and replies with an appropriate service provider agent's name and ontology which has the capability asked for, using the *reply* performative. In the prototype, there is a risk tolerance ability evaluation agent based on fuzzy logic, and two interest rate prediction agents based on feedforward neural network and fuzzy-genetic algorithm. The serving agent will choose the interest rate prediction agent based on the fuzzy genetic model according to the initial values of the agents' track records [94].

```
(reply
 :sender serving_agent
 :receiver investment_policy_agent
 :content (:name SC_agent_FL
           :ontology Financial_investment
          )
)

(reply
 :sender serving_agent
 :receiver investment_policy_agent
 :content (:name SC_agent_FLGA
           :ontology Financial_investment
          )
)
```

The investment policy agent then communicates with SC_agent_FL (for risk tolerance evaluation) and SC_agent_FLGA (for interest rate prediction) directly.

The risk tolerance evaluation agent (based on fuzzy logic) uses rules such as:

If the investor's annual income is *high* and total net-worth is *high* and the investor is *young* **then** the investor's risk tolerance ability is *high*;

If annual income $> \$50,000$ **then** annual income is *high*;

If age ≤ 35 **then** the investor is *young* etc.

Based on the investor's information and the financial risk tolerance model [47], the risk tolerance evaluation agent obtains the result that the investor's risk tolerance ability is *high*. During this process, the risk tolerance evaluation agent needs the help of an approximate reasoning agent.

The fuzzy-genetic based interest rate prediction agent will ask for the following parameters as input: change of real gross national product ΔGNP, change of consumer price index ΔCPI, change of M_2 nominal money supply ΔM_2, change of personal wealth ΔW, and change of previous T-bill rates Δr. All the data needs to be gathered by information gathering agents.

Suppose the gathered data is as follows: $\Delta GNP = 0.50$, $\Delta CPI = -0.10$, $\Delta M_2 = 47.80$, $\Delta W = 456.70$, and $\Delta r = 0.01$. The predicted result is -0.76. Thus the interest rate prediction agent reaches the conclusion that the interest rate will *fall*.

Combining the results of the two soft computing (SC) agents and the investor's investment goal, the investment policy agent reaches the conclusion that the investor's investment policy can be *aggressive*.

Step 2: Determining the investment category. Investment categories can be the stock market, real estate, fixed term deposit, etc. A decision making agent based on a fuzzy model is used to accomplish this task. Example rules used are:

If the investor's risk tolerance ability is *high* and the investment policy is *aggressive* **then** the suggested investment category is the *stock market*;

If the investor's risk tolerance ability is *high* and the investment policy is *conservative* **then** the suggested investment category is, say, *real estate*.

Based on the model, the agent gives the suggestion that the investor can invest in the *stock market*.

Step 3: Delegating information gathering agents to obtain stock market information. (This step has not been implemented in the system.) Here we assume information gathering agents gathered the returns of nine securities in the past 18 years. (See Table 7.2.)

Table 7.2. Returns on Nine Securities

Year	S_1	S_2	S_3	S_4	S_5	S_6	S_7	S_8	S_9
1982	-.305	-.173	-.318	-.477	-.457	-.065	-.319	-.400	-.435
1983	.513	.098	.285	.714	.107	.238	.076	.336	.238
1984	.055	.200	-.047	.165	-.424	-.078	.381	-.093	-.295
1985	-.126	.030	.104	-.043	-.189	-.077	-.051	-.090	-.036
1986	-.280	-.183	-.171	-.277	.637	-.187	.087	-.194	-.240
1987	-.003	.067	-.039	.476	.865	.156	.262	1.113	.126
1988	.428	.300	.149	.225	.313	.351	.341	.580	.639
1989	.192	.103	.260	.290	.637	.233	.227	.473	.282
1990	.446	.216	.419	.216	.373	.349	.352	.229	.578
1991	-.088	-.046	-.078	-.272	-.037	-.209	.153	-.126	.289
1992	-.127	-.071	.169	.144	.026	.355	-.099	.009	.184
1993	-.015	.056	-.035	.107	.153	-.231	.038	.000	.114
1994	.305	.038	.133	.321	.067	.246	.273	.223	-.222
1995	-.096	.089	.732	.305	.579	-.248	.091	.650	.327
1996	.016	.090	.021	.195	.040	-.064	.054	-.131	.333
1997	.128	.083	.131	.390	.434	.079	.109	.175	.062
1998	-.010	.035	.006	-.072	-.027	.067	.210	-.084	-.048
1999	.154	.176	.908	.715	.469	.077	.112	.756	.185

Step 4: Selecting portfolios from these nine securities that satisfies the investor's risk tolerance level and maximizes the return. The selected portfolios (with the expected average return of $r_s = 0.17$) based on the three portfolio selection models: the Markowitz model, the fuzzy probability model, and the possibility distribution model, are shown in Fig. 7.26 (denoted by P_{mar}, P_{fuz}, and P_{pos}, respectively).

Step 5: Aggregating the portfolios based on different models and giving a final portfolio to the investor.

How can we aggregate the portfolios from different models and finally produce one that is the best? This is a very tough question to answer. Currently, we have aggregated such portfolios using the ordered weighted averaging (OWA) aggregation algorithm based on fuzzy logic [99, 33]. Based on the OWA aggregation ($\alpha = 0.7$), the final portfolio is obtained (P_{owa} in Fig. 7.26).

7.6.3 Running the System

The system can provide reasonable financial investment planning information based on data provided by the user, and some relevant models. Figure 7.24 shows asset allocation results when the annual income is \$50,000, networth \$800,000, age 35, investments \$30,000, and investment attitude is aggressive (level 4).

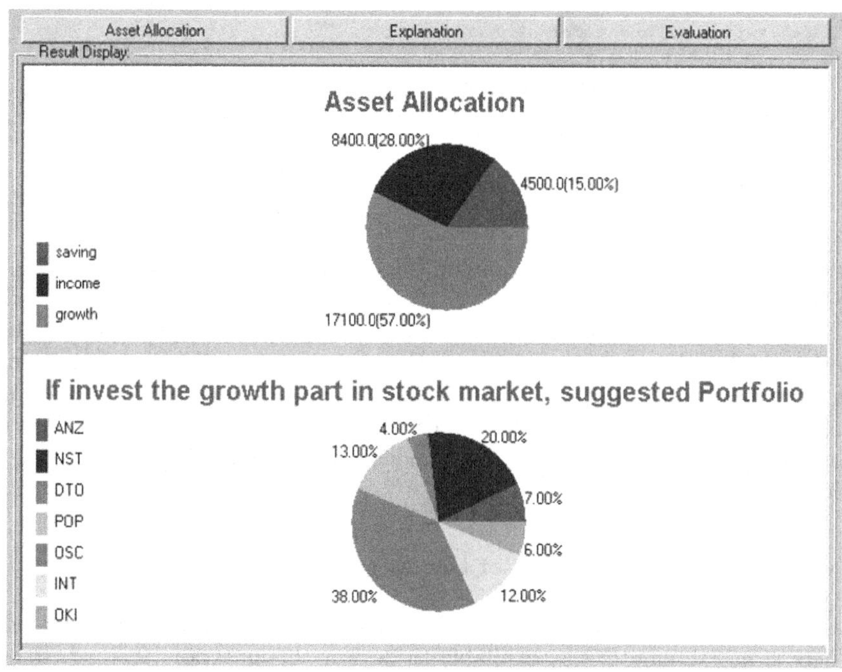

Fig. 7.24. Example Asset Allocation Results

By clicking the 'explanation' button, the corresponding explanation of how to get the results is displayed in the 'result display' window. (See Fig. 7.25.)

If the growth section is invested in the stock market, the system can provide a portfolio for the user (Fig. 7.24). The portfolio is the aggregated result of three portfolios based on the Markowitz portfolio selection model, the fuzzy probability portfolio selection model, and the possibility distribution portfolio selection model. The four portfolios are recorded as Powa, Pmar, Pfuz, and Ppos, respectively. The aggregation algorithm used is the ordered weighted averaging (OWA) aggregation algorithm [33]. By clicking the 'evalu-

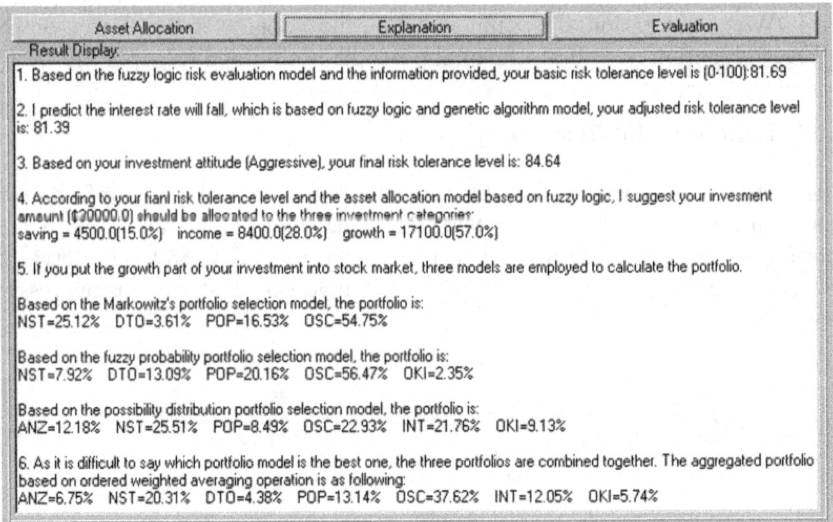

Fig. 7.25. Example Explanations of Financial Planning System

ation' button, the system will provide the comparisons of the four portfolios. (See Fig. 7.26.)

The lower part of Fig. 7.26 represents the realized average returns of the four portfolios. From this, one can see that in some years the average returns of Ppos is better than those of Pfuz or Pmar, or vice versa. Considering the overall results, the average returns of the aggregated portfolio, Powa, are better. To verify this, more experiments were conducted. The results are presented below.

7.6.4 Empirical Evaluation of the Aggregated Results

At this stage, one important problem is how to verify the aggregated portfolio. There is no systematic way available to answer this question. Instead, some experiments were conducted.

The first experiment was to use the first 12 years (1982 to 1993) return data as in Table 7.2, to produce three portfolios based on the three models. Based on the analysis in [105, 106], it is known that the fuzzy model is a direct extension of Markowitz's model, while the possibility model is more reasonable than the fuzzy model. Thus the three portfolios are ordered as P_{POS}, P_{FUZ}, and P_{MAR}, and $\alpha = 0.7$ (the degree that the aggregation prefers decisions with high confidence) is chosen when using an OWA operator to aggregate the three portfolios. The weight vector with $\alpha = 0.7$ is $W = [0.554, 0.292, 0.154]$. The selected portfolios and the corresponding risks of investment are shown in Table 7.3. The portfolios in Table 7.3 are also selected with an expected average return $r_s = 17\%$.

Asset Allocation | Explanation | Evaluation

Result Display:

Portfolios and Variances Based on 18 Years Return Data:

Portfolios	Ppos	Pfuz	Pmar	Powa
ANZ	12.18			6.75
AOL				
NST	25.51	7.92	25.12	20.31
DTO		13.09	3.61	4.38
POP	8.49	20.16	16.53	13.14
RIC				
OSC	22.93	56.47	54.75	37.62
INT	21.76			12.05
OKI	9.13	2.35		5.74
RISK:	18	2	3	11.02

Realized Average Returns of the Portfolios:

Year	Ppos	Pfuz	Pmar	Powa
1	16.76	21.5	20.55	18.73
2	27.2	23.4	25.9	25.88
3	17.76	17.69	18.34	17.83
4	17.11	18.46	18.12	17.66
5	13.85	16.52	16.43	15.03
6	18.81	18.81	19.55	18.92

Fig. 7.26. Comparison of the Portfolios

Table 7.3. Portfolios and Variances Based on 12 Years Return Data

P	S_1	S_2	S_3	S_4	S_5	S_6	S_7	S_8	S_9	Variance
P_{POS}	5.15			13.95	19.53			39.75	21.62	0.30
P_{FUZ}					23.05		46.55		30.40	0.04
P_{MAR}					23.14		46.60		30.26	0.05
P_{OWA}	2.85			7.73	21.12		20.77	22.02	25.51	0.18

The last 6 years (1994 to 1999) return data in Table 7.2 is used to verify the realized average returns of the four portfolios. The realized average returns of the four portfolios from one to six years are listed in Table 7.4.

From Table 7.4, one can see that the average returns of P_{OWA} are better than those of P_{FUZ} and P_{MAR}, and slightly less than those of P_{POS}. The variance (risk or uncertainty degree of the investment) of P_{OWA} is greatly reduced (from 0.30 to 0.18) compared with that of P_{POS}.

To further verify the aggregated portfolio, 12 securities listed in the Australian Stock Exchange Limited (ASX) were selected, and 12 years average returns (from 1986 to 1997) were collected. (See Table 7.5.) The ASX security codes of S_1 to S_{12} are AKC, AFI, AGL, BPC, CSR, EML, GUD, SMI, HAH, OPS, PDP, and WYL, respectively. The data has been taken from [124, 125].

Similar to the first experiment, the first 8 years (1986 to 1993) return data was used to generate the portfolios, while the last 4 years (1994 to 1997) data

Table 7.4. Realized Average Returns of the Portfolios (%)

Year(s)	P_{POS}	P_{FUZ}	P_{MAR}	P_{OWA}
1	11.421	7.501	7.554	9.681
2	27.694	15.665	15.700	22.334
3	18.748	14.457	14.467	16.836
4	19.684	14.990	15.006	17.593
5	14.005	13.318	13.334	13.701
6	19.703	14.590	14.607	17.425

Table 7.5. Returns on Twelve Securities from ASX

Yr	S_1	S_2	S_3	S_4	S_5	S_6	S_7	S_8	S_9	S_{10}	S_{11}	S_{12}
86	.675	.33	.053	.946	.081	1.026	.42	.198	.405	.249	.75	.08
87	.648	.93	.864	1.097	.826	.897	.535	.207	1.023	.333	.994	.684
88	.248	.432	-.157	.656	.515	1.044	.623	.05	.132	.174	.338	.403
89	-.007	.405	.838	.698	.136	.544	.358	1.296	.468	.271	.355	.467
90	-.087	-.08	-.168	-.029	-.228	-.115	.243	-.233	-.203	-.251	-.208	.096
91	.314	.291	.787	.341	.37	.598	.577	.57	.037	.391	.382	.263
92	.246	.004	.025	-.161	.01	-.148	-.116	-.03	.018	-.127	-.177	-.138
93	.105	.126	.107	-.091	-.105	-.126	.133	-.013	.011	.005	-.164	-.03
94	.133	.135	.264	-.17	.058	.112	0	.292	.232	.129	.014	-.006
95	.385	.433	.543	.042	.167	.293	.675	.646	.55	.62	.42	.361
96	.053	.105	.319	-.947	.121	-.179	-.487	-.214	.226	-.046	-.299	-.265
97	-.2	.109	-.046	1.192	-.305	-.168	-.06	.259	-.213	-.088	-.111	0

was used for verification. With the expected average return $r_s = 17\%$, the selected portfolios based on the three models, and the aggregated portfolio based on OWA with $\alpha = 0.7$, are listed in Table 7.6.

Table 7.6. Portfolios and Variances Based on ASX 8 Years Return Data

P	S_1	S_2	S_3	S_4-S_6	S_7	S_8	S_9	S_{10}	S_{11}	S_{12}	Variance
P_{POS}	22.2	26.45	12.06		9.95	0.07		28.65		0.62	0.26
P_{FUZ}	59.11				12.10	6.19				22.60	0.03
P_{MAR}	43.10				33.77	12.58				10.55	0.04
P_{OWA}	36.20	14.66	6.68		14.25	3.78		15.87		8.56	0.15

Based on the four portfolios, the realized average returns from one to four years are shown in Table 7.7.

The results in Table 7.7 are consistent with those in Table 7.4. Thus the same conclusion can be reached. The average returns of P_{OWA} are greater than those of P_{FUZ} and P_{MAR}, and slightly less than those of P_{POS}. The variance (risk) of P_{OWA} is greatly reduced (from 0.26 to 0.15) compared with that of P_{POS}.

Table 7.7. Realized Average Returns of the Portfolios Based on ASX Data (%)

Year(s)	P_{POS}	P_{FUZ}	P_{MAR}	P_{OWA}
1	13.432	9.556	9.351	11.672
2	30.833	25.035	28.315	28.752
3	19.584	11.304	8.524	15.463
4	12.644	4.887	3.919	9.035

Finally, different expected average return values (from 10% to 20%) were used to test the four portfolios, based on the two sets of return data. The same conclusion was reached.

8

Agent-Based Hybrid Intelligent System for Data Mining

Data mining, the central activity in the process of knowledge discovery in databases, is concerned with finding patterns in data. Many data mining techniques/algorithms that are used to look for such patterns have been developed, one at a time, in domains that range from space exploration to financial analysis. However, no single data mining technique has been proved appropriate for every domain and data set. Instead, several techniques may need to be integrated into hybrid systems, and used cooperatively during a particular data mining operation. That is, hybrid solutions are crucial for the success of data mining.

Recently, agent techniques have been applied to distributed data mining. In [130] and [131], Kargupta, Stafford, and Hamzaoglu describe a parallel/distributed data mining system PADMA (PArallel Data Mining Agents) that uses software agents for local data accessing and analysis, and a Web based interface for interactive data visualization. PADMA has been used in medical applications. In [132], an agent-based meta-learning system for large-scale data mining applications, which is called JAM (Java Agents for Meta-learning), is described. JAM was empirically evaluated against real credit card transaction data, where the target data mining application was to compute predictive models that detect fraudulent transactions. However, these works focus on only one of the many steps in data mining.

Kerber, Livezey, and Simoudis have reported a hybrid system (Recon) for data mining [136], where inductive, clustering, case-based reasoning, and statistical packages are integrated and used collaboratively. Recon adopted a typical client/server architecture, however, its the adaptability and robustness do not meet the requirements arising in real-world applications.

The emphasis of this chapter will be to try to combine the two cutting edge technologies, agent and data mining, applying the proposed agent-based hybrid framework to construct hybrid intelligent systems for data mining. The work presented in this chapter further verifies the proposed agent framework, and provides an easy way to construct hybrid systems for data mining. This will drive applications of data mining in real-world problems. The hybrid

Z. Zhang, C. Zhang: Agent-Based Hybrid Intelligent Systems, LNAI 2938, pp. 127–142, 2004.

systems for data mining based on this framework have two essential characteristics that differentiate our work from that done in the past:

- New data mining techniques can be plugged into the system and out-of-date techniques can be deleted from the system dynamically.
- Data mining technique agents can interact at run-time with ease under this framework, but in other non-agent based systems, these interactions must be determined at design-time.

Before discussing why hybrid solutions are required in data mining, some typical data mining techniques are introduced first.

8.1 Typical Data Mining Techniques

There are many variety of data mining techniques used for different applications, and at different stages of a data mining task. The typical techniques covered in this section, which are also core topics in data mining, are classification, clustering, and association rules. These three are viewed as the major data mining functions. Other data mining concepts such as prediction, regression, and pattern matching may be viewed as special cases of these three [145].

8.1.1 Classification

Classification is perhaps the most familiar and most popular data mining technique. Examples of classification applications include image and pattern recognition, medical diagnosis, loan approval, detecting faults in industry applications, and classifying financial market trends. Estimation and prediction may be viewed as types of classification. When someone estimates your age or guesses the number of marbles in a jar, these are actually classification problems. Prediction can be thought of as classifying an attribute value into one of a set of possible classes. it is often viewed as forecasting a continuous value, while classification forecasts a discrete value.

All approaches to performing classification assume some knowledge of the data. Often a training set is used to develop the specific parameters required by the techniques. *Training data* consist of sample input data as well as the classification assignment for the data. Domain experts may also be used to assist in the process.

The classification problem can be stated as follows:

Given a database $D = \{t_1, t_2, \ldots, t_n\}$ of tuples (items, records) and a set of classes $C = \{C_1, C2, \ldots, C_m\}$, the *classification problem* is to define a mapping $f : D \longrightarrow C$ where each t_i is assigned to one class. A *class*, C_j, contains precisely those tuples mapped to it; that is, $C_j = \{t_i | f(t_i) = C_j, 1 \leq i \leq n$, and $t_i \in D\}$.

The definition views classification as a mapping from the database to the set of classes. Actually, classification is a two-step process:

- Create s specific model by evaluating the training data. This step has as input the training data (including defined classification for each tuple) and as output a definition of the model developed. The model created classifies the training data as accurately as possible.
- Apply the model developed in step one by classifying tuples from the target database.

There are various categories of classification algorithms. Statistical algorithms are based directly on the use of statistical information, which include regression and Bayesian classification. Distance-based algorithms such as K nearest neighbors use similarity or distance measures to perform the classification. Decision tree-based algorithms including ID3, C4.5 and C5.0, CART, and scalable DT techniques use the corresponding structures to perform the classification. Neural network-based algorithms also use the structures to perform the classification. Rule-based classification algorithms generate $if - then$ rules to perform the classification.

Before applying any classification algorithms, the following preprocessing steps may be applied to the data in order to help improve the accuracy, efficiency, and scalability of the classification.

- **Data cleaning:** This refers to the preprocessing of data in order to remove or reduce *noise* (by applying smoothing techniques, for example) and the treatment of *missing values* (e.g., by replacing a missing value with the most commonly occurring value for that attribute, or with the most probable value based on statistics). Although most classification algorithms have some mechanisms for handling noisy or missing data, this step can help reduce confusion during learning.
- **Relevance analysis:** Many of the attributes in the data may be *irrelevant* to the classification task. For example, data recording the day of the week on which a bank loan application was filed is unlikely to be relevant to the success of the application. Furthermore, other attributes may be *redundant.* Hence, relevance analysis may be performed on the data with the aim of removing any irrelevant or redundant attributes from the learning process.
- **Data transformation:** The data can be *generalized* to higher-level concepts. Concept hierarchies may be used for this purpose. This is particularly useful for continuous-valued attributes. For example, numeric values for the attribute *income* may be generalized to discrete ranges such as *low*, *medium*, and *high*. Similarly, nominal-valued attributes, like *street*, can be generalized to higher-level concepts, like *city*. Since generalization compresses the original training data, fewer input/output operations may be involved during learning. The data may also be normalized, particularly when neural networks or algorithms involving distance measurements are used in the learning step. Normalization involves scaling all values for a given attribute so that they fall within a small specified rang.

Different classification algorithms can be compared and evaluated according to the following criteria:

- Classification accuracy: This refers to the ability of the model to correctly predict the class label of new or previously unseen data.
- Speed: This refers to the computation costs involved in generating and using the model.
- Robustness: This is the ability of the model to make correct classifications given noisy data or data with missing values.
- Scalability: This refers to the ability to construct the model efficiently given large amounts of data.
- Interpretability: This refers to the level of understanding and insight that is provided by the model.

No one classification technique is always superior to the others in terms of classification accuracy. However, there are advantages and disadvantages to the use of each. The regression approaches force the data to fit a predefined model. If a linear model is chosen, then the data are fit into that model even though it might not be linear. It requires that linear data be used. The K nearest neighbor technique requires only that the data be such that distances can be calculated. This can then be applied even to nonnumeric data. Outliers are handled by looking only at the K nearest neighbors. Bayesian classification assumes that the data attributes are independent with discrete values. Thus, although it is easy to use and understand, results may not be satisfactory. Decision tree techniques are easy to understand, but they may lead to overfitting. To avoid this, pruning techniques may be needed. ID3 is applicable only to categorical data. Improvements on it, C4.5 and C5, allow the use of continuous data and improved techniques for splitting. CART creates binary trees and thus may result in very deep trees.

8.1.2 Clustering

In Sect. 6.3.3, a fuzzy clustering algorithm has been employed for initial value generation of agents' track records. More details on clustering are given in this section.

Clustering is similar to classification in that data are grouped. However, unlike classification, the groups are not predefined. Instead, the grouping is accomplished by finding similarities between data according to characteristics found in the actual data. The groups are called *clusters*. The clustering problem can be stated as follows:

Given a database $D = \{t_1, t_2, \ldots, t_n\}$ of tuples and an integer value k (the number of clusters to be created), the *clustering problem* is to define a mapping $f : D \longrightarrow \{1, \ldots, k\}$ where each t_i is assigned to one cluster $K_j, 1 \leq i \leq k$. A *cluster*, K_j, contains precisely those tuples mapped to it; that is, $K_j = \{t_i | f(t_i) = K_j, 1 \leq i \leq n, \text{ and } t_i \in D\}$.

A classification of the different types of clustering algorithms is shown in Fig. 8.1 (adapted from [145]).

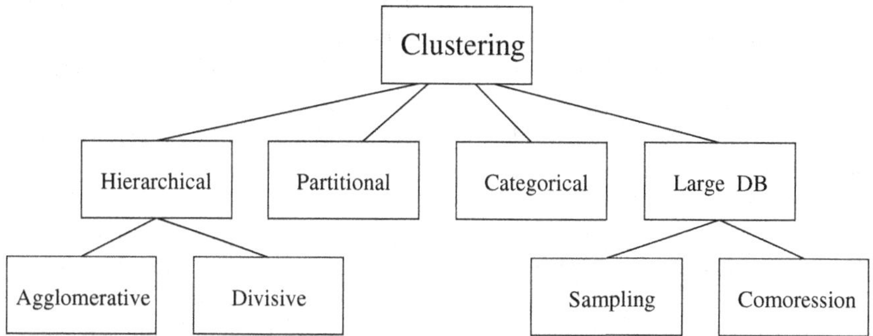

Fig. 8.1. Classification of Clustering Algorithms

Clustering algorithms themselves may be viewed as hierarchical or partitional. With *hierarchical* clustering, a nested set of clusters is created. Each level in the hierarchy has a separate set of clusters. At the lowest level, each item is in its own unique cluster. At the highest level, all items belong to the same cluster. With hierarchical clustering, the desired number of clusters is not input. With *partitional* clustering, the algorithm creates only one set of clusters. These approaches use the desired number of clusters to drive how the final set is created. traditional clustering algorithms tend to be targeted to small numeric databases that fit into memory. There are, however, more recent clustering algorithms that look at categorical data and are targeted to larger, perhaps dynamic, databases. Algorithms targeted to larger databases may adapt to memory constraints by either sampling the database or using data structures, which can be compressed or pruned to fit into memory regardless of the size of the database. Clustering algorithms may also differ based on whether they produce overlapping or nonoverlapping clusters. The types of clustering algorithms can be furthered classified based on the implementation technique used. Hierarchical algorithms can categorized as agglomerative or divisive. "*agglomerative*" implies that clusters are created in a bottom-up fashion, while *divisive* algorithms work in a top-down fashion.

In data mining, efforts have focused on finding methods for efficient and effective cluster analysis in *large databases.* Active themes of research focus on the *scalability* of clustering methods, the effectiveness of methods for clustering *complex shapes and types of data*, high-dimensional clustering techniques, and methods for clustering *mixed numerical and categorical data* in large database.

8.1.3 Association Rules

The purchasing of one product when another product is purchased represents an association rule. Association rules are frequently used by retail stores to assist in marketing, advertising, floor placement, and inventory control. Although they have direct applicability to retail businesses, they have been used for other purposes as well, including predicting faults in telecommunication networks. Association rules are used to show the relationships between data items. These uncovered relationships are not inherent in the data, as with functional dependencies, and they do not represent any sort of causality or correlation. Instead, association rules detect common usage of items.

Association rule mining finds interesting association or correlation relationships among a large set of data items. Rule *support* and *confidence* are two measures of rule interestingness. Typically, association rules are considered interesting if they satisfy both a *minimum support threshold* and a *minimum confidence threshold.* Such thresholds can be set by users or domain experts.

Given a set of *items* $I = \{I_1, I_2, \ldots, I_m\}$ and a database of transaction $D = \{t_1, t_2, \ldots, t_n\}$ where $t_i = \{I_{i1}, I_{i2}, \ldots, I_{ik}\}$ and $I_{ij} \in I$, an *association rule* is an implication of the form $X \Rightarrow Y$ where $X, Y \in I$ are sets of items and $X \cap Y = \emptyset$. The *support* (s) for an association rule $X \Rightarrow Y$ is the percentage of transactions in the database that contain $X \cup Y$. This is taken to be the probability, $P(X \cup Y)$. The *confidence or strength* (α) for an association rule $X \Rightarrow Y$ is the ratio of the number of transactions that contain $X \cup Y$ to the number of transactions that contain X. This is taken to be the conditional probability, $P(Y|X)$. That is,

$$support(X \Rightarrow Y) = P(X \cup Y) \tag{8.1}$$

$$confidence(X \Rightarrow Y) = P(Y|X) \tag{8.2}$$

Rules that satisfy both a minimum support threshold (min_sup) and a minimum confidence threshold (min_conf) are called *strong.*

A set of items is referred to as an *itemset.* An itemset that contains k items is a $k-itemset$. The set $\{computer, financial\_management\_software\}$ is a $2 - itemset$. The *occurrence frequency of an itemset* is the number of transactions that contain the itemset. An itemset satisfies *minimum support* if the occurrence frequency of the itemset is greater than or equal to the product of min_sup and the total number of transactions in D. The number of transactions required for the itemset to satisfy minimum support is therefore referred to as the *minimum support count.* If an itemset satisfies minimum support, then it is a *frequent* itemset.

Association rule mining is a two-step process:

1. **Find all frequent itemsets:** By definition, each of these itemsets will occur at least as frequently as a pre-determined minimum support count.
2. **Generate strong association rules from the frequent itemsets:** By definition, these rules must satisfy minimum support and minimum confidence.

Additional interestingness measures can be applied, if desired. The second step is the easiest of the two. The overall performance of mining association rules is determined by the first step.

8.2 Data Mining Requires Hybrid Solutions

Data mining is concerned with finding patterns in data. It is about exploring unknown patterns in large data sets. Data is a set of facts (e.g., cases in a database). The output of a data mining algorithm is typically a pattern, or a set of patterns, that are valid in the given data. A pattern is an expression, or statement, in a given language, which describes relationships among the facts in a subset of given data and is, in some sense, simpler than the enumeration of all facts in the subset. Typical representative patterns are equations, classification and regression trees, classification and regression rules, and positive and negative association rules.

The principal data mining tasks include: predictive modeling (classification and regression), clustering (grouping similar objects) and summarization (as exemplified by association rule discovery). According to the main tasks, data mining techniques can be divided into five classes as follows [135]:

- Predictive modeling. The goal is to predict some field(s) in a database based on other fields. If the field being predicted is a numeric (continuous) variable then the prediction problem is a regression problem. If the field is categorical, then it is a classification problem. *There is a wide variety of techniques for classification and regression.*
- Clustering. Unlike classification, we do not know the number of desired "clusters" in clustering. Thus clustering algorithms typically employ a two-stage search: an outer loop over possible cluster numbers and an inner loop to fit the best possible clustering for a given number of clusters. Given the number k of clusters, clustering methods can be divided into three classes: metric-distance based methods, model-based methods, and partition-based methods.
- Data summarization. One common method in data summarization is to take vertical (fields) slices of the input data. This class of methods is distinguished from the above in that, rather than predicting a specified field (e.g, classification) or grouping cases together (e.g., clustering), the goal is to find relations among fields (e.g., association rules).
- Dependency modeling. Insight into data is often gained by deriving some causal structure within the data. Models of causality can be probabilistic or they can be deterministic, as in deriving functional dependencies between fields in the data. Density estimation methods in general fall into this category, as do methods for explicit causal modeling.
- Change and deviation detection. These methods account for sequence information, be it time-series or some other ordering. The distinguishing feature of this class of methods is that ordering of observations is important and must be accounted for.

In a nutshell, there are variety of methods related to different principal tasks in data mining, and outputs of different data mining methods also have different forms. However, a single data mining technique has not been proven appropriate for every domain and data set. Instead, several techniques may need to be integrated into hybrid systems and used cooperatively during a particular data mining operation. Therefore, hybrid intelligent systems are required for data mining tasks. To further justify this statement, a simple example is now provided.

How do we identify a set of "promising" securities to be included in an investment portfolio based on the historical fundamental and technical data about securities? This is a very appropriate domain for data mining for two reasons. First, because the number of available securities being traded in the various exchanges is very large. Identifying appropriate securities for the goals of a particular portfolio is based on close examination of the performance of these securities. Without the use of data mining techniques, analysts can only closely examine small amounts of data. Second, analysts are able to state criteria for identifying securities that can potentially meet a set of investment goals. However, they cannot identify all the necessary criteria. Furthermore, even after a set of securities is identified, large volumes of data relating to these securities still have to be examined in order to fine-tune the stated performance criteria, as well as identify others not previously considered by the analyst. For this simple task, no single data mining technique is adequate. Methods are needed to formulate a pattern (hypothesis) and test its validity on the target databases. Methods to discover other relevant patterns from target databases are also required. Some other methods, including classification methods to classify each security, inductive learning methods, and visualization techniques are also helpful for this task. If we construct a computer system to perform this task, it is evident that this system is a hybrid system integrating different techniques.

Once again, data mining is an iterative sequence of many steps, while many techniques are involved in each step. These techniques need to be integrated into hybrid systems and used cooperatively for data mining tasks.

8.3 Requirements of the Agent-Based Hybrid Systems for Data Mining

As discussed previously, there are many well established data mining techniques. However, neither of the techniques is a panacea for solving problems involving hundreds of thousands of highly dimensional records. A data mining technique can work well in some domains but fail in others [128]. To be able to integrate different data mining techniques into hybrid systems and use them cooperatively is of paramount importance. For one data mining task, three techniques may be required to be put together, for another task, five techniques might need to be integrated, and so on. Thus, the requirements for such hybrid systems can be identified as follows.

- Different agents based on different data mining techniques can be dynamically tailored to different agent-based hybrid intelligent systems for different data mining tasks.
- Agents based on newly invented data mining techniques can be added to the systems and agents with out-of-date techniques can be deleted from the systems dynamically. That is, agents can be added to the systems or deleted without changing the design.
- Interactions at run-time are allowed.

8.4 Analysis and Design of the System

Based on the framework and methodology described in Chap. 5, the first step in the analysis process is to identify the roles in the hybrid system for data mining. Keeping the requirements in mind, the following roles can be identified. (To avoid redundancy, only the schema for some of the identified roles are given.)

- One role acting as an interface to the users (UserHandler, which is the same as Fig. 7.5).
- One role overseeing the whole process inside the system (WorkPlanner, which is also the same as Fig. 7.6).
- Two roles which meet the requirements of dynamic tailoring: one keeping track of the profiles of other roles performing data mining related tasks (CapabilityRecorder, see Fig. 7.7) and one checking the profiles (CapabilityMatcher, refer to Fig. 7.8).
- One role to visualize the mined results in certain situations (ResultVisualier).
- The behavior of all the data mining is covered by the AttributeSelector (Fig. 8.2), FrequentItemsetIdentifier, DataCleanser, AssociationRuleMiner (Fig. 8.3), DecisionTreeInducer, ClassificationRuleGenerator, CrossValidator, PredictionEvaluator, and ResultAccuracyAnalyzer (Fig. 8.4) roles, etc.
- The final role is that of the User (refer to Fig. 7.12) who requires the data mining results.

With the respective role definitions in place, the next stage is to define the associated interaction models for these roles. Here we focus on the interactions associated with the AssociationRuleMiner role.

This role interacts with the WorkPlanner role to obtain the task that this role will accomplish (ReceiveTask protocol, Fig. 8.5a). It interacts with the DataPreparer role (maybe AttributeSelector, FrequentItemsetIdentifier, etc.) from where it can access the data for mining (AccessItemsets protocol, Fig. 8.5b). When the AssociationRuleMiner role finishes mining association rules, it sends the ResultAccuracyAnalyzer role its mined results for the task (SendMinedResults protocol, Fig. 8.5c). For some

Role Schema: ATTRIBUTESELECTOR
Description: Access the databases for mining and determine the lists of attributes that are important for a specific task
Protocols and Activities: ReceiveTask, AccessDatabase, AskforHelp, InformRelevantRole
Permissions: **reads supplied** *Task* // Task delegated by other roles **supplied** *Databases* // Databases to be mined **generates** *Attributelists* // Important attributes for the mining task
Responsibilities Liveness: ATTRIBUTESELECTOR = ReceiveTask.AccessDatabase.AskforHelp)+.InformRelevantRole Safety: • True

Fig. 8.2. Schema for the Role ATTRIBUTESELECTOR

Role Schema: ASSOCIATIONRULEMINER
Description: Mines association rules from the itemsets prepared by other roles (e.g., ATTRIBUTESELECTOR)
Protocols and Activities: ReceiveTask, AccessItemsets, SendMinedResults, InformVisualizer, Processing
Permissions: **reads supplied** *Itemsets* // Data prepared by other roles **generates** *MinedResults* // processing the data and // generate results
Responsibilities Liveness: ASSOCIATIONRULEMINER = RECEIVETASK.AccessItemsets.(Processing)+. (SendMinedResults| INFORMVISUALIZER) Safety: • ASSOCIATIONRULEMINER has the requested capability

Fig. 8.3. Schema for Role ASSOCIATIONRULEMINER

roles, the outputs are also sent to the RESULTVISUALIER role to visualize and display, but not in the case of ASSOCIATIONRULEMINER.

In such a system, the most important organizational rule in the organizational model is that *if a role says it has a capability then it can perform the tasks corresponding to the capability and will do so when asked.*

Having completed the analysis of the system, the design phase follows. The most important model to be generated is the agent model (Fig. 8.6). In some

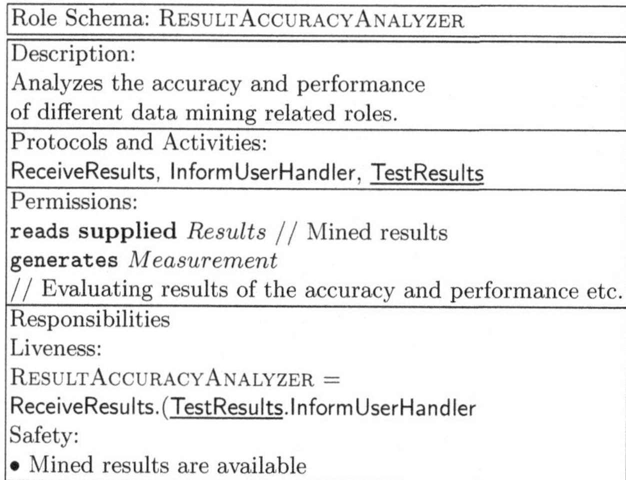

Role Schema: RESULTACCURACYANALYZER
Description: Analyzes the accuracy and performance of different data mining related roles.
Protocols and Activities: ReceiveResults, InformUserHandler, <u>TestResults</u>
Permissions: **reads supplied** *Results* // Mined results **generates** *Measurement* // Evaluating results of the accuracy and performance etc.
Responsibilities Liveness: RESULTACCURACYANALYZER = ReceiveResults.(<u>TestResults</u>.InformUserHandler Safety: • Mined results are available

Fig. 8.4. Schema for Role RESULTACCURACYANALYZER

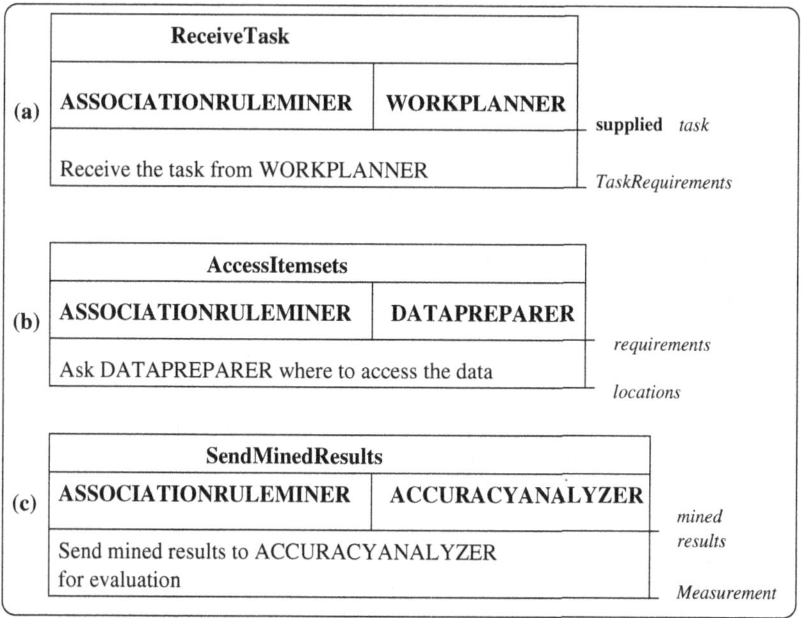

Fig. 8.5. Definition of Protocols Associated with the ASSOCIATIONRULEMINER Role: (a) ReceiveTask, (b) AccessItemsets, and (c) SendMinedResults.

cases, there is a one-to-one correspondence between roles and agent types (e.g., USERHANDLER role and **InterfaceAgent**, WORKPLANNER and **PlanningAgent**). In some cases, two or more roles are grouped into a single agent

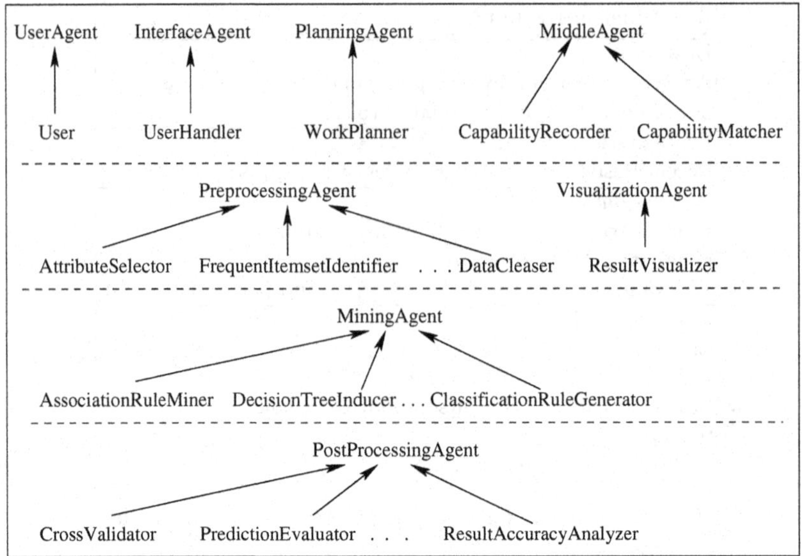

Fig. 8.6. Agent Model for the Data Mining System

type. For example, the CAPABILITYRECORDER and CAPABILITYMATCHER roles are grouped into a **MiddleAgent** because of their high degree of interdependence; the ATTRIBUTESELECTOR, FREQUENTITEMSETIDENTIFIER, and DATACLEANSER are grouped into the **PreprocessingAgent**; and so on.

8.5 Implementation of the System

From the above analysis and design phases, it is clear that there are eight types of agents in the system – user agent, interface agent, planning agent, visualization agent, middle agent, preprocessing agent, mining agent, and postprocessing agent. To meet the requirements of such systems, the architecture shown below (Fig. 8.7) is employed to put all these agents together. It is assumed that there are k preprocessing agents, m mining agents, and n postprocessing agents. These numbers (k, m, and n) can be increased or decreased dynamically. The behavior of each kind of agent in the system (except the user agent) is briefly described below:

- **Interface Agent** This agent interacts with the user (or user agent). It asks the user to provide his requirements, and provides the user with mined results. (These may be visualized.)
- **Planning Agent** The planning agent is in charge of the activation and synchronization of different agents. It elaborates a work plan, and is in charge of ensuring that such a work plan is fulfilled. It receives assignments from the interface agent.

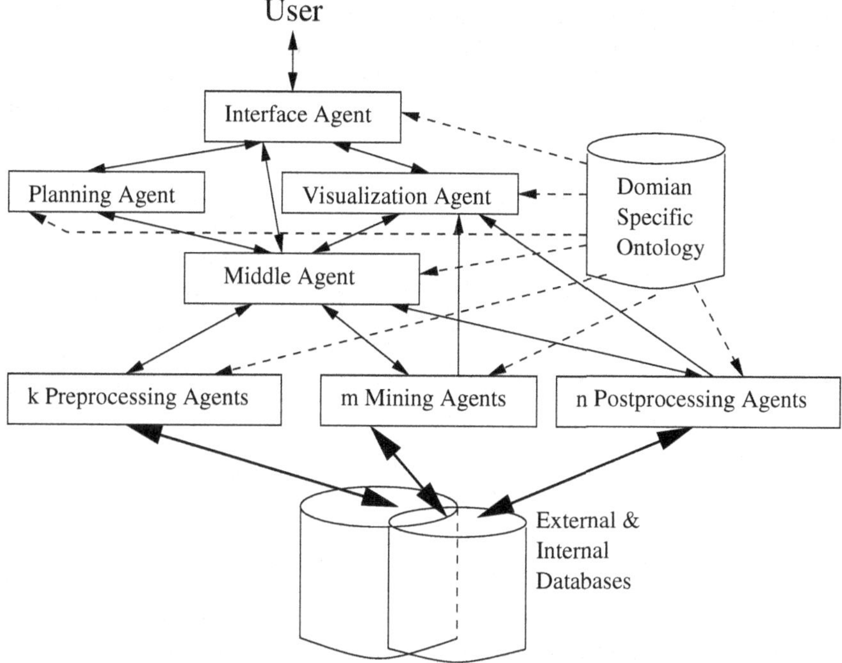

Fig. 8.7. Architecture of Agent-Based Data Mining System

- **Visualization Agent** Visualizes certain mined results and passes them to interface agent.
- **Middle Agent** Keeps track of the names, ontologies and capabilities of all registered agents in the system; it can reply to the query of an agent with the name and ontology of an appropriate agent having the capabilities requested. Once again, the introduction of a middle agent in the system facilitates flexibility and robustness.
- **Preprocessing Agent** Prepares data for mining.
- **Mining Agent** Mines the data prepared by preprocessing agents and generates relevant patterns.
- **Post-processing Agent** Evaluates the performance and accuracy, etc., of mining agents.

The ontology is the foundation of agent communication. All agents in the system interpret the content of received messages based on the ontology.

The implementation is also supported by JATLite. The kernel supporting part of the system is the planning agent and middle agent [41]. Figure 8.8 shows the internal structure of the planning agent. The KQML Message Interpreter (KMI) represents the interface between the KQML router and agents. Once an incoming KQML message is detected, it will be passed to the KMI. The KMI transfers incoming KQML messages into a form that agents can understand. The implementation of KMI is based on JATLite KQMLLayer Templates. The planning agent allows dynamic reorganization of connected agents in the system, while middle agent allows the agents to be connected or disconnected to the system dynamically. All of this facilitates flexibility and robustness.

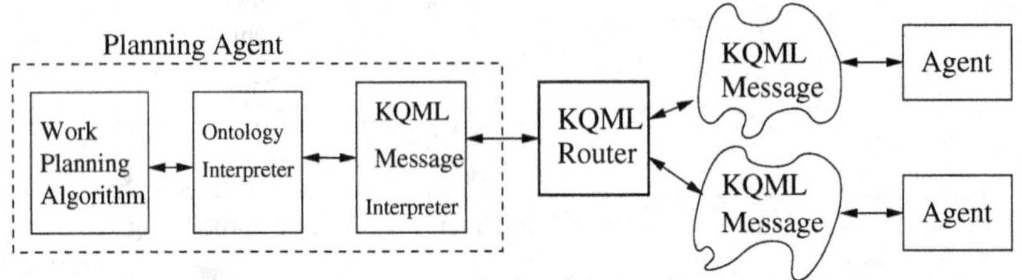

Fig. 8.8. Planning Agent Structure

Considering there are some legacy data mining (or machine learning) software packages available, approaches should be provided which integrate such software packages into the system when needed. This means that the software packages must somehow be converted into agents. As we did in the agent-based financial investment planning system, a wrapper is implemented to wrap the software packages by using the Java Native Interface [50] and JATLite KQML layer templates.

8.6 Case Study

The Weka system ([129] and *http://www.cs.waikato.ac.nz/ml/weka*) was re-implemented from agent perspectives based on the above discussion. The main focus of Weka is on classifier and filter algorithms. It also includes implementations of algorithms for learning association rules and for clustering data for which no class value is specified.

To re-implement the programs in Weka from agent perspectives, the programs in Weka (written in Java) were compiled into .DLLs (dynamic link library) first. The Java Native methods and JATLite KQML layer templates were then employed to wrap these programs in .DLL. In this way, all the programs in Weka were equipped with KQML communication capability and were ready to add to the agent system.

In this agent-based data mining experimental system, in addition to the supporting agents (interface agent, planning agent, middle agent, and so on) there are 7 attribute selection related agents, 25 classifier related agents, 9 filter related agents, and 2 cluster related agents.

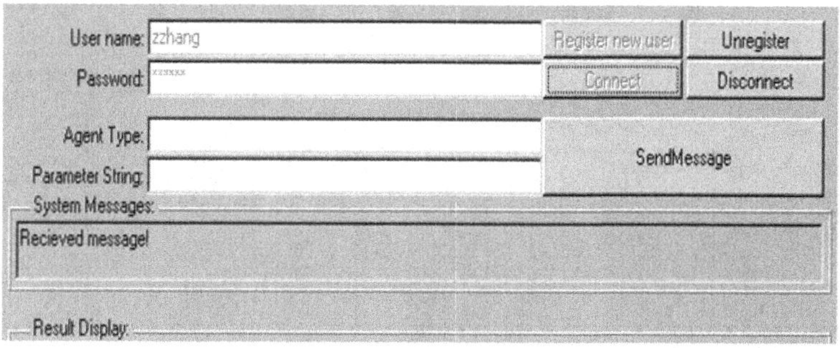

Fig. 8.9. User Interface of the System

Figure 8.9 shows the user interface of the system, which can start from any Internet Browser or appletviewer.

To use the system, the user needs to type the user name and preferred password in the corresponding fields and click 'register new user' to register for the first time. Thereafter, the registered user name and password are simply entyered and 'connect' clicked. If the user wants to leave the system, then click 'disconnect' and 'unregister'.

The system can work in two modes. In one mode, all the data mining related agents can run individually, which is similar to executing the original Weka program from the command line. In this mode, the user provides the system with the 'agent type' and corresponding 'parameter string' information in the corresponding input fields, and then clicks the 'SendMessage' button. The system will activate the given agent and display the results in the 'result display' window. For example, if we type in 'weka.classifiers.m5.M5Prime' in the 'agent type' field, and '-t data\cpu.arff' in the 'parameter string' field ('data\' was added before the data file as all data files in the system are in the 'data' subdirectory), the system will display the following results , which are the same as running this program from the command line in Weka. (See Fig. 8.10.)

Another mode is to provide the planning agent with a work plan. The system then activates different agents based on the work plan. The work plan can be generated automatically based on meta-knowledge of the task contained in the planning agent. A work plan can also be edited manually according to the work plan specification, and loaded into the planning agent. Here, only the latter is implemented in the experimental system.

It is worth pointing out that although agent-based implementation facilitates the integration of different techniques into a system in which different techniques can work cooperatively to solve complex problems, it does not directly contribute to the improvement of performance, or accuracy, of the original algorithms.

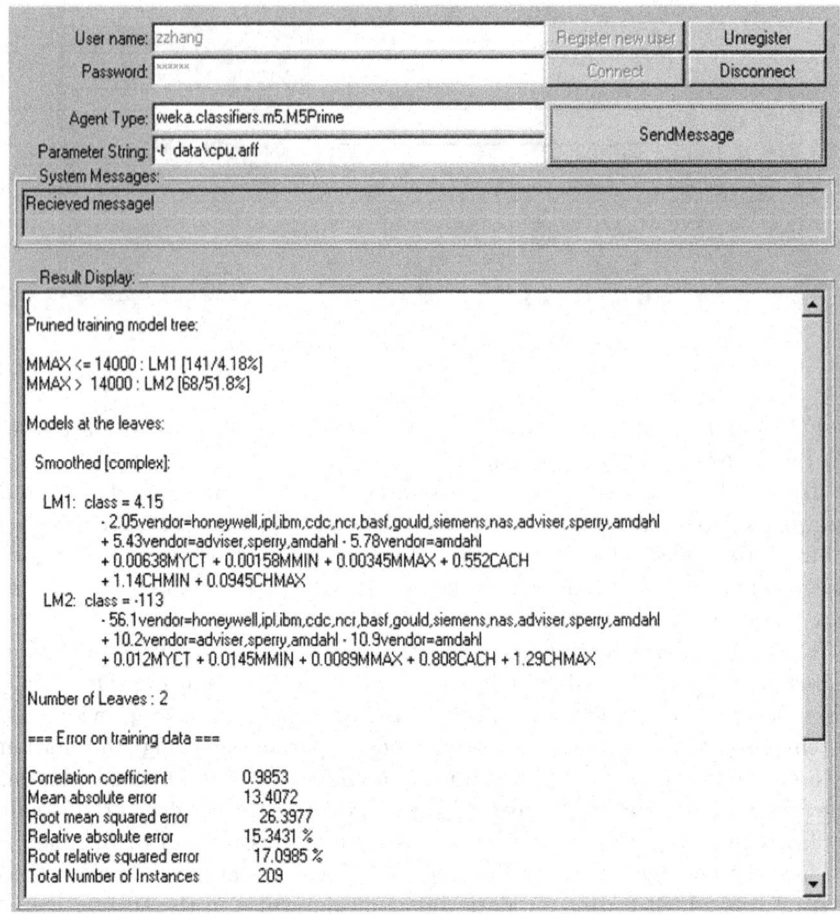


```
(
Pruned training model tree:

MMAX <= 14000 : LM1 [141/4.18%]
MMAX > 14000 : LM2 [68/51.8%]

Models at the leaves:

 Smoothed [complex]:

  LM1: class = 4.15
         - 2.05vendor=honeywell,ipl,ibm,cdc,ncr,basf,gould,siemens,nas,adviser,sperry,amdahl
         + 5.43vendor=adviser,sperry,amdahl - 5.78vendor=amdahl
         + 0.00638MYCT + 0.00158MMIN + 0.00345MMAX + 0.552CACH
         + 1.14CHMIN + 0.0945CHMAX
  LM2: class = -113
         - 56.1vendor=honeywell,ipl,ibm,cdc,ncr,basf,gould,siemens,nas,adviser,sperry,amdahl
         + 10.2vendor=adviser,sperry,amdahl - 10.9vendor=amdahl
         + 0.012MYCT + 0.0145MMIN + 0.0089MMAX + 0.808CACH + 1.29CHMAX

Number of Leaves : 2

=== Error on training data ===

Correlation coefficient          0.9853
Mean absolute error             13.4072
Root mean squared error          26.3977
Relative absolute error          15.3431 %
Root relative squared error      17.0985 %
Total Number of Instances        209
```

Fig. 8.10. Output from the M5 Agent for Numeric Prediction

9

The Less the More

The emphasis of this book is to promote the construction of hybrid intelligent systems that are essential for solving complex real-world problems. A variety of intelligent techniques can easily be integrated into one system under the proposed agent framework. Two agent-based hybrid intelligent systems were developed based on the framework. The systems built from agent perspectives are flexible, robust and interoperable. The success of these systems indicates that agent technologies can significantly facilitate the building of hybrid intelligent systems. As different complementary techniques can be easily integrated into one system under the unifying agent framework we proposed, many complex problems, such as financial investment planning, can be solved within a shorter time frame and also result in higher quality solutions.

In this last chapter, experiments on the flexibility and robustness testing are described briefly. The future work of agent-based hybrid intelligent systems is then outlined.

9.1 Flexibility and Robustness Testing

Our interest here does not reside in improving the performance of different models (techniques), but rather in how to integrate different models into one system under the unifying agent framework we proposed. Therefore, the experiments conducted are focused on integration, flexibility and robustness.

First, the functions of different agents were tested to see whether they could work properly after being integrated together. To do this, the same input data sets were used as those used in non-agent systems. The experimental results show that all agents in both systems behave correctly, as the two agent-based systems produce the same results as do non-agent systems.

The flexibility of the three systems was tested by launching them first, and then adding new agents to the systems as well as deleting running ones from them. These operations could be done on any host on the Internet. By

Z. Zhang, C. Zhang: Agent-Based Hybrid Intelligent Systems, LNAI 2938, pp. 145–147, 2004.

observing the performance of the systems, the prototypes demonstrated very high flexibility.

To test the robustness, a dedicated network was set up, and the agent system prototypes were run on this network environment. The network consisted of hosts running different operating systems including, Windows 2000, Windows XP, Linux (RedHat), and Unix (Sun Solaris). The agents were scattered among the hosts of the network and for some an 'out of order' was forced. In all situations, the systems still provide results. Thus, it was evident the systems were robust.

9.2 Future Work

As pointed out earlier, hybrid intelligent systems built on our framework have the following crucial characteristics that differentiate our framework from others.

- Each agent in the systems can easily access all the intelligent techniques, including fuzzy logic, neural networks and genetic algorithms, and also other techniques available in the system, whenever needed.
- The ability to add/delete service provider agents to/from the systems dynamically.
- The presence of middle agents in the systems allows adaptive system organization.
- Overall system robustness is facilitated through the use of middle agents. For example, if a particular service provider (e.g., an interest rate prediction agent) disappears, a requester agent (decision making agent) can find another one with the same, or similar, capabilities by interrogating the middle agent.
- The agent-based hybrid intelligent systems can make decisions about the nature and scope of interactions at run-time. They can be reorganized dynamically at running time based on the work plans generated by the planning agents.

To promote the use of our unifying agent framework for building hybrid intelligent systems, and pave the way for its introduction into industrial toolkits, the following two issues must be addressed.

There are many different varieties of intelligent techniques. Different intelligent technique agents can be built based on these diverse intelligent techniques, and can result in different internal structures for these agents. To avoid dealing with these intelligent technique agents case by case when integrating them into hybrid intelligent systems, a high level abstract model for all these intelligent technique agents is essential. This can provide transparency of the different internal structures of these agents for hybrid intelligent system developers. Then, it is unnecessary for developers to know the details of different intelligent techniques as well as the internal structures of the corresponding agents.

To reorganize an agent-based hybrid intelligent system dynamically at running time, the planning agents should have the capability to generate the work plans automatically, or at least semi-automatically, based on the tasks received. In the systems implemented, this was done by manually editing a work plan.

In [140], Hannebauer proposed the notion of *autonomous dynamic reconfiguration*. Two individual reconfiguration operations, called *agent melting* and *agent splitting* were introduced. Agent melting means unifying the problem solving knowledge, goals, resources and skills of two or more agents in a single agent. On the other hand, agent splitting denotes a process in which a single agent splits its problem solving knowledge, goals, resources and skills, and hands it over to one or more new or existing agents. In contrast to many other approaches, the approach proposed by Hannebauer resides mainly on the individual (micro-)level of behavior rather than on the social (macro-)level. To reconfigure an agent-based hybrid intelligent system dynamically, both the micro-level and macro-level operations are involved. Some solutions to this issue have yet to be explored.

Once these issues are solved, the way will be paved to the establishment of an industrial-strength toolkit that will revolutionize the construction of agent-based hybrid intelligent systems.

Appendix: Sample Source Codes of the Agent-Based Financial Planning System

In the agent-based financial investment planning systems implemented, there are 13 agents. The implementations are under the support of JATLite as well as the Native Method in Java. The system can run under Windows 95/98/NT/2000/XP with Java V1.4 and JATLite V0.4 Beta. Make sure that Java V1.4 and JATLite V0.4 can work properly and the home directory of the financial system is included in the *CLASSPATH* environment variable before starting the agent-based financial investment system. The source codes for nine of these agents are listed here.

- *StockData*: Data supply agent for other agents in the system;
- *Stock*: Planning agent for portfolio selection;
- *Moki*: Profolio selection agent based on Markowitz's model;
- *Fuzz*:Profolio selection agent based on fuzzy logic model;
- *Poss*:Profolio selection agent based on possibility distribution model;
- *Aggr*: Decision aggregation agent based on the ordered weighted averaging operators;
- *Invpolicy*:Planning agent for investment decision-making;
- *Invppt*: Investment decision making agent that determines the client's financial risk tolerance ability and the asset allocation;
- *Flga*: Interest rate prediction agent based on fuzzy logic and genetic algorithms;
- *Ffin*: Interest rate prediction agent based on neural networks.

The following parameters/data files are used by these agents:

- *stockdataaddressfile*: This file contains the information to configure JATLite Router, RouterRegister, and all other agents in the system. The configuration information for each agent consists of the following items: *agenttype, agentname, hostname, portnumber, description, registrequest, idletime, classfilename.*
- *stock.cfg*: This file contains the parameters to configure *StockData* and *Stock* agents.

Z. Zhang, C. Zhang: Agent-Based Hybrid Intelligent Systems, LNAI 2938, pp. 149–181, 2004.

- *flga.cfg*: This file contains the parameters used by *Flga* agent for training and predicting interest rate.
- *ffin.cfg*: This file contains the parameters used by *Ffin* agent for training and predicting interest rate.
- *stockdata file*: This file provides initial data for *moki*, *fuzz*, and *poss* agents.

A. Source Codes for Data Supply Agent (StockData)

```
import java.io.*;
import java.util.*;
import java.lang.*;
import java.awt.event.*;
import Abstract.*;
import KQMLLayer.*;
import RouterLayer.AgentClient.*;

public class StockData extends HHRouterClientAction {

  static String DataFile=null;
  String cfgfile="stock.cfg";
  public StockData()  {
    super();
    }
  public StockData(Address myaddress,
                   Address routeraddress,
                   Address registraraddress,
                   int durationtime,
                   boolean regrequest ){
  // use RouterLayer.AgentClient.RouterClientAction constructor
 super(myaddress,routeraddress,registraraddress,durationtime,regrequest);
    }
  public StockData(String cfgfname,String gname){
        super(cfgfname,gname);
    }
  public boolean Act(Object o)  {
    try {
     if(!superAct(o)) return false;
      if(perf.equals("task")){
       try {
        if(DataFile==null)getfilename(cfgfile);
         BufferedReader datain =
          new BufferedReader(new FileReader(new File(DataFile)));
         String datatype="";
         String sdata="",cdata="";
        while(true){
         String line = datain.readLine();
         if(line == null)  break;
         line=line.trim();
         if(line.equals("")) continue;

         if(line.startsWith(":STOCKDATA")){
```

```
      datatype=":STOCKDATA";
      continue;
      }
     if(line.startsWith(":END STOCKDATA")){
      datatype="";
      continue;
      }
     if(line.startsWith(":CHECKDATA")){
      datatype=":CHECKDATA";
      continue;
      }
     if(line.startsWith(":END CHECKDATA")){
      datatype="";
      continue;
      }
     if(datatype.equals(":STOCKDATA"))
      sdata+="("+line+") ";
     if(datatype.equals(":CHECKDATA"))
      cdata+="("+line+") ";
      }

    sdata="("+sdata+")";
    cdata="("+cdata+")";
    _returnString="("+sdata+" "+cdata+")";
    datain.close();
    } catch (Exception e)  {
      sendErrorMessage("error:"+e.toString());
      e.printStackTrace();
      }
// send result back to the receiver
sendResult();
}else if(perf.equals("data")){
      if(DataFile==null)getfilename(cfgfile);
       String datatype=kqml.getValue("datatype");
       String tmp=content.substring(1,content.length()-1);
       int rcode=0;
       if(datatype.equals("stockdata"))
        rcode=writetofile(DataFile,tmp);
       if(rcode==1)
        _returnString="(Write to file successfully.)";
       else if(rcode==-1)
             _returnString="(write to file failed!)";
           else
             _returnString="(bad datatype,data not write!)";
           sendResult();

       }else if(perf.equals("error")){
           System.out.println("receiever a error:"+content);

       }
       else{
           sendErrorMessage("invalid performtiv:"+perf);
           return false;
       }
```

```
        } catch (Exception e)  {
            sendErrorMessage("error:"+e.toString());
            e.printStackTrace();
            return false;
        }

        return true;
}
    protected int getfilename(String configfile){
        try{
            BufferedReader in = new BufferedReader(new FileReader
                (new File(configfile)));
            while(true)  {
                String line = in.readLine();
                if(line == null)  break;
                if(line.startsWith("stockdata")){
                    int tmp=line.indexOf("=");
                    DataFile=line.substring(tmp+1,line.length());
                }
            }
            in.close();
            return 1;
    }catch(Exception e){
    System.out.println("read stockdata filename from config file error:"
      +e.toString());
    e.printStackTrace();
      return -1;
        }
    }

    /* Main program */
    public static void main(String args[])  {
     try  {
      String addressfile="stockaddressfile";
      String groupname="stockdata";
      StockData server = new StockData(addressfile,groupname);
      server.startAgent();
      } catch (Exception e)  {
      System.out.println(e.toString());
      e.printStackTrace();
      System.exit(0);
        }
    }
}
```

B. Source Codes of Planning Agent for Portfolio Selection (Stock)

```
import java.io.*;
import java.util.*;
import java.lang.*;
import java.awt.event.*;
import Abstract.*;
import KQMLLayer.*;
import RouterLayer.AgentClient.*;


public class stock extends HHRouterClientAction {
    StockInfoList tasklist=new StockInfoList();
    String alf="0.7";
    String[][] data={
        {"alf","0.7"},
        {"starth","0.1"},
        {"steph","0.3"},
        {"up","0.75"},
        {"growth","1.17"}
    };
    int sorts=3;//moki,fuzz,poss
    String stockparmstr="";
    public stock()  {
        super();
    }

public stock(Address myaddress,
             Address routeraddress,
             Address registraraddress,
             int durationtime,
             boolean regrequest ){
 // use RouterLayer.AgentClient.RouterClientAction constructor
 super(myaddress,routeraddress,registraraddress,durationtime,regrequest);
    readparm("stock.cfg");
    }

public stock(String cfgfname,String gname){
        super(cfgfname,gname);
        readparm("stock.cfg");
    }

public boolean Act(Object o)  {
 try  {
  if(!superAct(o)) return false;
  if(content == null)  {
   sendErrorMessage("error:content is null!");
   return false;
   }else if(perf.equals("task")){
     if(msgstamp==null)
      msgstamp=""+mail.getTime();
```

```
Vector v=new takeOffList(content);
String risk,amount,invpolicy;
if(v.size() == 2)  {
  String tempstr=(String)v.elementAt(0);
  Vector v1=new takeOffList(tempstr);
  amount=(String)v1.elementAt(0);
  risk=(String)v1.elementAt(1);
  invpolicy=(String)v.elementAt(1);
  }else{
       amount="1";
       invpolicy="()";
       risk="()";
       }
if(tasklist.FindbyNo(msgstamp)==null){
  tasklist.Add(msgstamp);
  tasklist.setasker(msgstamp,tasksender);
  tasklist.setamount(msgstamp,amount);
  tasklist.setinvpolicy(msgstamp,invpolicy);
  tasklist.setrisk(msgstamp,risk);
  sendtask("stockdata");
  }
}else
 if(perf.equals("replytask")){
  String tempstr=content.substring(1,content.length()-1);
  String stockdata="";
  if(tasktype.equals("stockdata")){
    Vector vall=new takeOffList(content);
    if(vall.size() < 1)  {
     sendErrorMessage("Agent stock needs
                        more than 1 numbers in content!");
     return false;
     }
    stockdata=(String)vall.elementAt(0);
    String checkdata=(String)vall.elementAt(1);

    Vector v = new takeOffList(stockdata);
    Vector v1=new takeOffList((String)v.elementAt(0));
    int n=v1.size();
    int m=v.size();
    tasklist.setyears(msgstamp,""+(m-1));
    _returnString="";

    for(int i=1;i<m;i++){
     _returnString+=(String)v.elementAt(i)+" ";
     }
    _returnString="("+_returnString+") "+stockparmstr;
    sendtask("moki");
    sendtask("fuzz");
    sendtask("poss");
    tasklist.setStockData(msgstamp,stockdata);
    tasklist.setcheckdata(msgstamp,checkdata);
  }else
   if(tasktype.equals("moki")){
     tasklist.setmoki(msgstamp,tempstr);
```

```
    tempstr=tasklist.getResult(msgstamp);
    if(tempstr!=null){
      _returnString="("+alf+" "+tempstr+")";
      sendtask("aggr");
      }
}else
 if(tasktype.equals("fuzz")){
  tasklist.setfuzz(msgstamp,tempstr);
  tempstr=tasklist.getResult(msgstamp);
  if(tempstr!=null){
  _returnString="("+alf+" "+tempstr+")";
  sendtask("aggr");
  }
}else
 if(tasktype.equals("poss")){
  tasklist.setposs(msgstamp,tempstr);
  tempstr=tasklist.getResult(msgstamp);
  if(tempstr!=null){
  _returnString="("+alf+" "+tempstr+")";
  sendtask("aggr");
  }
}else
 if(tasktype.equals("aggr")){
  Vector vdata=new takeOffList
                    (tasklist.getstockdata(msgstamp));
  String stockname=(String)vdata.elementAt(0);
  Vector vstockname=new takeOffList(stockname);
  int m=vdata.size();
  int n=vstockname.size();
  double damount=
  (Double.valueOf(tasklist.getamount(msgstamp))).doubleValue();
  _returnString=tasklist.getyears(msgstamp)+" "
        +tasklist.getrisk(msgstamp)+" ";
  _returnString+="("+tasklist.getinvpolicy(msgstamp)+" (";
  Vector v2 = new takeOffList(content);
  double dt=0,maxdt=0;
  int maxdtxb=0;
  double[] pt=new double[n];
  for(int i=0;i<n;i++){
   String temp=(String)v2.elementAt(i);
   dt=Math.rint((Double.valueOf(temp)).doubleValue());
   pt[i]=dt;
   if(dt>maxdt){maxdt=dt;maxdtxb=i;}
   }
  int tempsum=0;
  for(int i=0;i<n;i++){
   if(i!=maxdtxb){tempsum+=pt[i];}
   }
  pt[maxdtxb]=100-tempsum;
  for(int i=0;i<n;i++){
   if(pt[i]>0){
     _returnString+="("+(String)vstockname.elementAt(i)+
                    " "+pt[i]*damount/100+" "+pt[i]+") ";
     }
```

```
    }
  _returnString+=")) ";
  String allresult=tasklist.getResult(msgstamp);
  String checkdata=tasklist.getcheckdata(msgstamp);

  _returnString+=" ("+stockname+" "+allresult+" "+content+") ";
  v2=new takeOffList("("+allresult+content+")");
  //System.out.println("Four Result:"+allresult+content);
  Vector v3=new takeOffList(checkdata);
  //System.out.println("checkdata:\n"+checkdata);
  int checkyears=v3.size();
  int cs=v2.size();

 double[][] dcheckdata=new double[checkyears][n];
 for(int i=0;i<checkyears;i++){
  Vector vv=new takeOffList((String)v3.elementAt(i));
  for(int j=0;j<vv.size();j++){
  dcheckdata[i][j]=
    (Double.valueOf((String)vv.elementAt(j))).doubleValue();
  }
  }

 double[][] dallresult=new double[n][cs];
 for(int i=0;i<cs;i++){
  Vector vv=new takeOffList((String)v2.elementAt(i));
  for(int j=0;j<vv.size() - 1;j++){
  dallresult[j][i]=
   (Double.valueOf((String)vv.elementAt(j))).doubleValue();
   }
   }

 for(int i=0;i<n;i++)
  dcheckdata[0][i]=dcheckdata[0][i]+1;
 for(int i=1;i<checkyears;i++){
  for(int j=0;j<n;j++){
   dcheckdata[i][j]=dcheckdata[i-1][j]*(1+dcheckdata[i][j]);
   }
   }
 for(int i=0;i<n;i++)
  dcheckdata[0][i]=dcheckdata[0][i]-1;

 for(int i=1;i<checkyears;i++){
  for(int j=0;j<n;j++){
   dcheckdata[i][j]=Math.pow(dcheckdata[i][j],(double)1/(i+1))-1;
   }
   }
 String checkresult="";
 double dtemp=0;
 for(int i=0;i<checkyears;i++){
   String temp="";
   for(int j=0;j<cs;j++){
    dtemp=0;
    for(int k=0;k<n;k++){
     dtemp+=dcheckdata[i][k]*dallresult[k][j];
```

```
          }

        temp+=Math.rint(dtemp*100)/100+" ";
        }
      checkresult+="("+temp+")";
      }
    checkresult=" ("+checkresult+") ";
    _returnString+=checkresult;
    _returnString="("+_returnString+")";
    tasktype="stock";
    sendResult();
    tasklist.DeletebyNo(msgstamp);
    }else{
      sendErrorMessage("invalid tasktype where replay!");
    }
    }else if(perf.equals("error")){
      sendErrorMessage(content);
    }else{
      sendErrorMessage("invalid performtiv:"+perf);
      return false;
       }
   } catch (Exception e)  {
       sendErrorMessage(e.toString());
       e.printStackTrace();
       return false;
   }
   return true;
}
private void readparm(String cfgfilename){
 try{
  BufferedReader in = new BufferedReader(new FileReader(
                      new File(cfgfilename)));
  while(true)  {
    String line = in.readLine();
    String tmpstr;
    if(line == null)  break;
    for(int i=0;i<data.length;i++){
    if(line.trim().startsWith((String)data[i][0])){
    int tmp=line.indexOf("=");
    tmpstr=line.substring(tmp+1,line.length());
    data[i][1]=tmpstr.trim();
    }
     }
      }
  in.close();
  alf=data[0][1];
  for(int i=1;i<data.length;i++){
    stockparmstr=stockparmstr+" :"+data[i][0]+" "+data[i][1]+" ";
    }
    System.out.println("stockparmstr: "+stockparmstr);
  }catch(Exception e){
   System.out.println("read flga filename from config file error:"
     +e.toString());
    }
```

```
    }

    /* Main program */

    public static void main(String args[])  {
        try  {
            String addressfile="stockaddressfile";
            String groupname="stock";
            stock server = new stock(addressfile,groupname);
            server.startAgent();
        } catch (Exception e)  {
            System.out.println(e.toString());
            System.exit(0);
        }
     }
}
```

C. Source Codes for Portfolio Selection Agent Based on Markowitz's Model (Moki)

```
import java.io.*;
import java.util.*;
import java.lang.*;
import java.awt.event.*;
import Abstract.*;
import KQMLLayer.*;
import RouterLayer.AgentClient.*;

public class moki extends HHRouterClientAction {

 public moki()  {
  super();
  }
 public moki(Address myaddress,
             Address routeraddress,
             Address registraraddress,
             int durationtime,
             boolean regrequest ){
 // use RouterLayer.AgentClient.RouterClientAction constructor
 super(myaddress,routeraddress,registraraddress,durationtime,regrequest);
    }
 public moki(String cfgfname,String gname){
  super(cfgfname,gname);
  }

 public boolean Act(Object o)  {
  try  {
   if(!superAct(o)) return false;
   if(content == null)  {
    sendErrorMessage("content is null");
    return false;
    }
   else
    if(perf.equals("task")){
     _returnString="";
     Vector v = new takeOffList(content);
     if(v.size() < 1)  {
      sendErrorMessage("parm less than 1!");
      return false;
      }
     int m=v.size();
     Vector v1=new takeOffList((String)v.elementAt(0));
     int n=v1.size();

     double arr[] = new double[n];
     double data[] = new double[m*n];
     String tmp;
     for(int i=0;i<m;i++){
      v1=new takeOffList((String)v.elementAt(i));
      for(int j=0;j<v1.size();j++){
```

```
        tmp=(String)v1.elementAt(j);
        data[i*n+j]=(Double.valueOf(tmp)).doubleValue();
       }
      }

      double starth=0.1,steph=0.3,up=0.75,growth=1.17;
      tmp=kqml.getValue("starth");
      if((tmp!=null)&&(!tmp.equals("null"))){
       starth=(Double.valueOf(tmp)).doubleValue();
       }
      tmp=kqml.getValue("steph");
      if((tmp!=null)&&(!tmp.equals("null"))){
       steph=(Double.valueOf(tmp)).doubleValue();
       }
      tmp=kqml.getValue("up");
      if((tmp!=null)&&(!tmp.equals("null"))){
       up=(Double.valueOf(tmp)).doubleValue();
       }
      tmp=kqml.getValue("growth");
      if((tmp!=null)&&(!tmp.equals("null"))){
       growth=(Double.valueOf(tmp)).doubleValue();
       }
      for (int i = 0; i < n-1; i++) {
       arr[i] = 0;
       }
      int risk=sovmoki.getportfilio(m,n,starth,steph,up,growth,data,arr);
      if(risk!=-1){
       for (int i = 0; i <= n-1; i++) {
         _returnString+=
           Double.toString(Math.rint(arr[i]*10000)/100)+" ";
           }
         _returnString+=risk;
         sendResult();
         }else
          sendErrorMessage("Error when call moki.dll");
         }else if(perf.equals("error")){
          sendErrorMessage(content);
         }
         else{
          sendErrorMessage("invalid performtiv:"+perf);
          return false;
             }
         } catch (Exception e)  {
            sendErrorMessage("error "+e.toString());
            return false;
         }

         return true;
}

    /* Main program */
    public static void main(String args[])  {
        try  {
            String addressfile="stockaddressfile";
```

```
            String groupname="moki";
            moki server = new moki(addressfile,groupname);
            server.startAgent();
        } catch (Exception e)  {
            System.out.println(e.toString());
            System.exit(0);
        }
    }
}
```

D. Source Codes for Portfolio Selection Agent Based on Fuzzy Logic Model (Fuzz)

```
import java.io.*;
import java.util.*;
import java.lang.*;
import java.awt.event.*;
import Abstract.*;
import KQMLLayer.*;
import RouterLayer.AgentClient.*;

public class fuzz extends HHRouterClientAction {

 public fuzz()  {
  super();
  }
 public fuzz(Address myaddress,
             Address routeraddress,
             Address registraraddress,
             int durationtime,
             boolean regrequest ){
 // use RouterLayer.AgentClient.RouterClientAction constructor
 super(myaddress,routeraddress,registraraddress,durationtime,regrequest);
 }
 public fuzz(String cfgfname,String gname){
   super(cfgfname,gname);
   }
 public boolean Act(Object o)  {
  try  {
   if(!superAct(o)) return false;

   if(content == null)  {
   //sendErrorMessage(kqml,receiver);
    sendErrorMessage("content is null");
    return false;
    }
    else
     if(perf.equals("task")){
  // send result back to the receiver
       _returnString="";
       Vector v = new takeOffList(content);
       if(v.size() < 1)  {
        sendErrorMessage("parm less than 1!");
        return false;
       }
       int m=v.size();
       Vector v1=new takeOffList((String)v.elementAt(0));
       int n=v1.size();

       double arr[] = new double[n];
       double data[] = new double[m*n];
       String tmp;
       for(int i=0;i<m;i++){
```

```
  v1=new takeOffList((String)v.elementAt(i));
  for(int j=0;j<v1.size();j++){
   tmp=(String)v1.elementAt(j);
   data[i*n+j]=(Double.valueOf(tmp)).doubleValue();
   }
  }
 double starth=0.1,steph=0.3,up=0.75,growth=1.17;
 tmp=kqml.getValue("starth");
 if((tmp!=null)&&(!tmp.equals("null"))){
  starth=(Double.valueOf(tmp)).doubleValue();
  }
 tmp=kqml.getValue("steph");
 if((tmp!=null)&&(!tmp.equals("null"))){
  steph=(Double.valueOf(tmp)).doubleValue();
  }
 tmp=kqml.getValue("up");
 if((tmp!=null)&&(!tmp.equals("null"))){
 up=(Double.valueOf(tmp)).doubleValue();
 }
 tmp=kqml.getValue("growth");
 if((tmp!=null)&&(!tmp.equals("null"))){
  growth=(Double.valueOf(tmp)).doubleValue();
  }
 for (int i = 0; i < n-1; i++) {
  arr[i] = 0;
  }
 int risk=
     sovfuzz.getportfilio(m,n,starth,steph,up,growth,data,arr);
 if(risk!=-1){
  for (int i = 0; i <= n-1; i++) {
   _returnString+=Double.toString(Math.rint(arr[i]*10000)/100)+" ";
   }
 _returnString+=risk;
 sendResult();
 }else
   sendErrorMessage("Error when call fuzz.dll");
 }else if(perf.equals("replyregister")){
   System.out.println(getName()+" register:"+content);
   if(!content.equals("success")){
    return false;
    }
 }else if(perf.equals("error")){
   sendErrorMessage(content);
   }
 else{
    sendErrorMessage("invalid performtiv:"+perf);
    return false;
    }
 } catch (Exception e)  {
    sendErrorMessage("error:"+e.toString());
    return false;
  }

 return true;
```

```
}

    /* Main program */

    public static void main(String args[])  {
        try  {
            String addressfile="stockaddressfile";
            String groupname="fuzz";
            fuzz server = new fuzz(addressfile,groupname);
            server.startAgent();
        } catch (Exception e)  {
            System.out.println(e.toString());
            System.exit(0);
        }
    }
}
```

E. Source Codes for Portfolio Selection Agent Based on Possibility Distribution Model (Poss)

```
import java.io.*;
import java.util.*;
import java.lang.*;
import java.awt.event.*;
import Abstract.*;
import KQMLLayer.*;
import RouterLayer.AgentClient.*;

public class poss extends HHRouterClientAction {

 public poss()  {
  super();
  }
 public poss(Address myaddress,
             Address routeraddress,
             Address registraraddress,
             int durationtime,
             boolean regrequest ){
 // use RouterLayer.AgentClient.RouterClientAction constructor
  super(myaddress,routeraddress,registraraddress,durationtime,regrequest);
  }
 public poss(String cfgfname,String gname){
  super(cfgfname,gname);
  }
 public boolean Act(Object o)  {
  try  {
   if(!superAct(o)) return false;
   if(content == null)  {
    sendErrorMessage("content is null");
    return false;
    }
   else
    if(perf.equals("task")){
// send result back to the receiver
      _returnString="";
      Vector v = new takeOffList(content);
      if(v.size() < 1)  {
       sendErrorMessage("parm less than 1!");
       return false;
       }
      int m=v.size();
      Vector v1=new takeOffList((String)v.elementAt(0));
      int n=v1.size();

      double arr[] = new double[n];
      double data[] = new double[m*n];
      String tmp;
      for(int i=0;i<m;i++){
       v1=new takeOffList((String)v.elementAt(i));
       for(int j=0;j<v1.size();j++){
```

```
      tmp=(String)v1.elementAt(j);
      data[i*n+j]=(Double.valueOf(tmp)).doubleValue();
      }
     }
    double starth=0.1,steph=0.3,up=0.75,growth=1.17;
     tmp=kqml.getValue("starth");
    if((tmp!=null)&&(!tmp.equals("null"))){
     starth=(Double.valueOf(tmp)).doubleValue();
     }
    tmp=kqml.getValue("steph");
    if((tmp!=null)&&(!tmp.equals("null"))){
     steph=(Double.valueOf(tmp)).doubleValue();
     }
    tmp=kqml.getValue("up");
    if((tmp!=null)&&(!tmp.equals("null"))){
     up=(Double.valueOf(tmp)).doubleValue();
     }
    tmp=kqml.getValue("growth");
    if((tmp!=null)&&(!tmp.equals("null"))){
     growth=(Double.valueOf(tmp)).doubleValue();
     }
    for (int i = 0; i < n-1; i++) {
     arr[i] = 0;
     }
    int risk=sovposs.getportfilio(m,n,starth,steph,up,growth,data,arr);
    if(risk!=-1){
     for (int i = 0; i <= n-1; i++) {
       _returnString+=
         Double.toString(Math.rint(arr[i]*10000)/100)+" ";
         }
     _returnString+=risk;
     sendResult();
     }else
       sendErrorMessage("Error when call poss.dll");
     }else if(perf.equals("replyregister")){
       System.out.println(getName()+" register:"+content);
        if(!content.equals("success")){
        return false;
        }
     }else if(perf.equals("error")){
       sendErrorMessage(content);
     }
     else{
     // error message
      sendErrorMessage("invalid performtiv:"+perf);
      System.out.println("invalid performtiv:"+perf);
      return false;
      }
     } catch (Exception e)  {
        sendErrorMessage("error:"+e.toString());
        return false;
     }
     return true;
}
```

```
    /* Main program */
    public static void main(String args[]) {
        try {
            String addressfile="stockaddressfile";
            String groupname="poss";
            poss server = new poss(addressfile,groupname);
            server.startAgent();
        } catch (Exception e) {
            System.out.println(e.toString());
            System.exit(0);
        }
    }
}
```

F. Source Codes for Decision Aggregation Agent Based on Ordered Weighted Averaging Operators (Aggr)

```
import java.io.*;
import java.util.*;
import java.lang.*;
import java.awt.event.*;
import Abstract.*;
import KQMLLayer.*;
import RouterLayer.AgentClient.*;
import javax.swing.*;

import java.awt.*;

public class aggr extends HHRouterClientAction {

 public aggr()  {
  super();
  }
 public aggr(Address myaddress,
             Address routeraddress,
             Address registraraddress,
             int durationtime,
             boolean regrequest ){
 // use RouterLayer.AgentClient.RouterClientAction constructor
    super(myaddress,routeraddress,registraraddress,durationtime,regrequest);
 }
 public aggr(String cfgfname,String gname){
  super(cfgfname,gname);
  }
 public boolean Act(Object o)  {
  try  {
   if(!superAct(o)) return false;

   if(content == null)  {
    sendErrorMessage("error:content is null!");
    return false;
    }
   else
    if(perf.equals("task")){
// send result back to the receiver
    _returnString="";
    Vector v = new takeOffList(content);

    if(v.size() < 2)  {
     sendErrorMessage("para numbers must be more than 2 parts!");
     return false;
     }
    String Salf=(String)v.elementAt(0);
    double alf=(Double.valueOf(Salf)).doubleValue();
    int kinds=v.size()-1;

    Vector v1=new takeOffList((String)v.elementAt(1));
```

```
    int n=v1.size();

    double arr[] = new double[n];
    double data[] = new double[kinds*n];
    String tmp;
    for(int k=1;k<=kinds;k++){
     v1=new takeOffList((String)v.elementAt(k));
     for(int i=0;i<v1.size();i++){
     tmp=(String)v1.elementAt(i);
     data[(k-1)*n+i]=(Double.valueOf(tmp)).doubleValue();
     }
    }
    for (int i = 0; i <n; i++) {
     arr[i] = 0;
    }
    int sum=sovaggr.getportfilio(kinds,n,alf,data,arr);
    if(sum!=-1){
     for (int i = 0; i < n; i++) {
      _returnString+=Double.toString(Math.rint(arr[i]*100)/100)+" ";
      }
     _returnString="("+_returnString+")";
     sendResult();
     }else
       sendErrorMessage("Error when call aggr.dll!");
     }else if(perf.equals("error")){
       sendErrorMessage(content);
       }
     else{
       sendErrorMessage("invalid performative:"+perf);
       return false;
       }
     } catch (Exception e)  {
        sendErrorMessage("error:"+e.toString());
        e.printStackTrace();
        return false;
     }

     return true;
    }

    /* Main program */

    public static void main(String args[])  {
        try  {
            String addressfile="stockaddressfile";
            String groupname="aggr";
            aggr server = new aggr(addressfile,groupname);
            server.startAgent();
        } catch (Exception e)  {
            System.out.println(e.toString());
            System.exit(0);
        }
    }
}
```

G. Source Codes for Planning Agent of Investment Decision-Making (Invpolicy)

```
import java.io.*;
import java.util.*;
import java.lang.*;
import java.awt.event.*;
import Abstract.*;
import KQMLLayer.*;
import RouterLayer.AgentClient.*;

public class invpolicy extends HHRouterClientAction {
 InvInfoList tasklist=new InvInfoList();

 public invpolicy()  {
  super();
  }
 public invpolicy(Address myaddress,
                  Address routeraddress,
                  Address registraraddress,
                  int durationtime,
                  boolean regrequest ){
 // use RouterLayer.AgentClient.RouterClientAction constructor
   super(myaddress,routeraddress,registraraddress,durationtime,regrequest);
   }
 public invpolicy(String cfgfname,String gname){
  super(cfgfname,gname);
  }
 public boolean Act(Object o)  {
  try  {
   if(!superAct(o)) return false;
   if(content == null)  {
    sendErrorMessage("error:content is null!");
    return false;
   }else if(perf.equals("task")){
     if(msgstamp==null)
     msgstamp=""+mail.getTime();

     if(tasklist.FindbyNo(msgstamp)==null){
      tasklist.Add(msgstamp);
      tasklist.setasker(msgstamp,tasksender);
      Vector v = new takeOffList(content);
      if(v.size() != 5)  {
       sendErrorMessage("agent invpolicy needs 5 numbers in content!");
       return false;
       }
      String n=(String)v.elementAt(0);
      tasklist.setcai(msgstamp,n);
      n=(String)v.elementAt(1);
      tasklist.setnetw(msgstamp,n);
      n=(String)v.elementAt(2);
      tasklist.setage(msgstamp,n);
      n=(String)v.elementAt(3);
```

```
   tasklist.setamount(msgstamp,n);
   n=(String)v.elementAt(4);
   tasklist.setautlevel(msgstamp,n);
   sendtask("flga");
   sendtask("ffin");
   }
  }else if(perf.equals("replytask")){
    String tempstr=content.substring(1,content.length()-1);
    _returnString=content;
    if(tasktype.equals("flga")){
     Vector v = new takeOffList(content);
     String n=(String)v.elementAt(0);
     tasklist.setirate(msgstamp,n);
     n=tasklist.getResult(msgstamp);
     if(n!=null){
       _returnString="("+n+")";
       sendtask("invppt");
       }
     else{
      System.out.println("result is null!");
      return false;
      }
     }else
       if(tasktype.equals("invppt")){
        sendtask("stock");
     }else
       if(tasktype.equals("stock")){
        tasktype="invpolicy";
        sendResult();
        tasklist.DeletebyNo(msgstamp);
       }else{
       //sender=tasklist.getasker(msgstamp);
       sendErrorMessage("invalid tasktype where replay!");
       }
     }else if(perf.equals("error")){
     //sender=tasklist.getasker(msgstamp);
       sendErrorMessage(content);
       }else{
        //sender=tasklist.getasker(msgstamp);
        sendErrorMessage("invalid performtiv:"+perf);
        return false;
        }
     } catch (Exception e)  {
         //sender=tasklist.getasker(msgstamp);
         sendErrorMessage(e.toString());
         return false;
     }
     return true;
}

/* Main program */

public static void main(String args[])  {
    try  {
```

```
            String addressfile="stockaddressfile";
            String groupname="invpolicy";
            invpolicy server = new invpolicy(addressfile,groupname);
            server.startAgent();
        } catch (Exception e)  {
            System.out.println(e.toString());
            System.exit(0);
        }
    }
}
```

H. Source Codes for Investment Decision-Making Agent (Invppt)

This agent takes client's tax status, annual income etc. as inputs, and determines the client's financial risk tolerance ability as well as the asset allocation percentage etc.

```
import java.io.*;
import java.util.*;
import java.lang.*;
import java.awt.event.*;
import Abstract.*;
import KQMLLayer.*;
import RouterLayer.AgentClient.*;

public class invppt extends HHRouterClientAction {
 public invppt()  {
  super();
  }
 public invppt(Address myaddress,
               Address routeraddress,
               Address registraraddress,
               int durationtime,
               boolean regrequest ){
  // use RouterLayer.AgentClient.RouterClientAction constructor
    super(myaddress,routeraddress,registraraddress,durationtime,regrequest);
    }
  public invppt(String cfgfname,String gname){
   super(cfgfname,gname);
   }
  public boolean Act(Object o)  {
   try  {
    if(!superAct(o)) return false;
    if(content == null)  {
     sendErrorMessage("content is null");
     return false;
     }
    else
     if(perf.equals("task")){
//   send result back to the receiver
     _returnString="";
     Vector v = new takeOffList(content);
     if(v.size() != 6)  {
      sendErrorMessage("Agent invppt need 6 numbers in content!");
      return false;
      }
     double cai=0,cnt=0,irate=0,amount=0,autlevel=0;
     int age=0;
     String Sm=(String)v.elementAt(0);
     cai=(Double.valueOf(Sm)).doubleValue();
     Sm=(String)v.elementAt(1);
     cnt=(Double.valueOf(Sm)).doubleValue();
     Sm=(String)v.elementAt(2);
```

```
 age=(Integer.valueOf(Sm)).intValue();
 Sm=(String)v.elementAt(3);
 irate=(Double.valueOf(Sm)).doubleValue();
 Sm=(String)v.elementAt(4);
 amount=(Double.valueOf(Sm)).doubleValue();
 Sm=(String)v.elementAt(5);
 autlevel=(Double.valueOf(Sm)).doubleValue();

 int invsorts=3;
 double risk[] = new double[3] ;
 double ret[] = new double[invsorts];
 double retcode=0;
 for (int i = 0; i < invsorts; i++) {
  ret[i] = 0;
  }
 for (int i = 0; i < 3; i++) {
  risk[i] = 0;
  }
 retcode=sovinvppt.getinvppt(cai,cnt,age,irate,autlevel,ret,risk);

 double maxpart=0,temp=0;
 int xb=0;
 for(int i=0;i<invsorts;i++){
  ret[i]=Math.rint(ret[i]);
  if(ret[i]>maxpart){
  maxpart=ret[i];
  xb=i;
  }
 }

for(int i=0;i<invsorts;i++){
 if(i!=xb){temp+=ret[i];}
 }
String riskstr="";
for(int i=0;i<3;i++){
 riskstr+=Math.rint(risk[i]*100)/100+" ";
 }
riskstr+=irate+" "+autlevel;
ret[xb]=100-temp;
_returnString="("+amount*ret[2]/100+" ("+riskstr+"))";
_returnString=" "+_returnString+"
     ((saving "+amount*ret[0]/100+" "+ret[0]+")";
_returnString=_returnString+"
     (income "+amount*ret[1]/100+" "+ret[1]+")";
_returnString=_returnString+"
     (growth "+amount*ret[2]/100+" "+ret[2]+"))";
_returnString="("+_returnString+")";
sendResult();
}else if(perf.equals("error")){
   sendErrorMessage(content);
   }
   else{
    sendErrorMessage("invalid performtiv:"+perf);
    return false;
```

```
        }
    } catch (Exception e) {
       sendErrorMessage("error:"+e.toString());
       return false;
    }

    return true;
 }

    /* Main program */
    public static void main(String args[]) {
        try {
            String addressfile="stockaddressfile";
            String groupname="invppt";
            invppt server = new invppt(addressfile,groupname);
            server.startAgent();
        } catch (Exception e) {
            System.out.println(e.toString());
            System.exit(0);
        }
    }
}
```

I. Source Codes for Interest Prediction Agent Based on Fuzzy Logic and Genetic Algorithms (Flga)

```
import java.io.*;
import java.util.*;
import java.lang.*;
importjava.awt.event.*;
import Abstract.*;
import KQMLLayer.*;
import RouterLayer.AgentClient.*;

public class flga extends HHRouterClientAction {

 String fuzzy_system_file_name,training_file_name,out_data_file_name;
 public flga()  {
  super();
  }
 public flga(Address myaddress,
             Address routeraddress,
             Address registraraddress,
             int durationtime,
             boolean regrequest ){

 // use RouterLayer.AgentClient.RouterClientAction constructor
  super(myaddress,routeraddress,registraraddress,durationtime,regrequest);
  }
 public flga(String cfgfname,String gname){
  super(cfgfname,gname);
  }
 public boolean Act(Object o)  {
  try  {
   if(!superAct(o)) return false;
   if(perf.equals("task")){
  // send results back to the receiver
     if(content.equals("(train)")){
     sovflga.train();
     _returnString="(train over!)";
     }
     else{
      double irate=sovflga.getirate();
      _returnString="("+irate+")";
       }
    sendResult();
    }else if(perf.equals("replyregister")){
      System.out.println(getName()+" register:"+content);
      if(!content.equals("success")){
       return false;
       }
      }else if(perf.equals("data")){
        if((fuzzy_system_file_name==null)||(training_file_name==null)
           ||(out_data_file_name==null)) getfilename("flga.cfg");
        String datatype=kqml.getValue("datatype");
        String tmp=content.substring(1,content.length()-1);
```

```
        int rcode=0;
         if(datatype.equals("fuzzy_system_file_name"))
          rcode=writetofile(fuzzy_system_file_name,tmp);
         else
          if(datatype.equals("training_file_name"))
           rcode=writetofile(training_file_name,tmp);
          else
           if(datatype.equals("out_data_file_name"))
            rcode=writetofile(out_data_file_name,tmp);
           if(rcode==1)
            _returnString="(Write to file successfully.)";
           else if(rcode==-1)
             _returnString="(write to file failed!)";
             else
              _returnString="(bad datatype,data not write!)";
             sendResult();

           }else if(perf.equals("error")){
            sendErrorMessage(content);
            System.out.println("receiever a error!");
           }
          else{
           sendErrorMessage("invalid performtiv:"+perf);
           return false;
           }
       } catch (Exception e)  {
           sendErrorMessage("error:"+e.toString());
           return false;
       }

       return true;
}
protected int getfilename(String configfile){
 try{
  BufferedReader in = new BufferedReader(
                      new FileReader(new File(configfile)));
  while(true)  {
   String line = in.readLine();
   if(line == null)  break;
   if(line.startsWith("fuzzy_system_file_name")){
    int tmp=line.indexOf("=");
    fuzzy_system_file_name=line.substring(tmp+1,line.length());
   }else
    if(line.startsWith("training_file_name")){
     int tmp=line.indexOf("=");
     training_file_name=line.substring(tmp+1,line.length());
    }else
      if(line.startsWith("out_data_file_name")){
       int tmp=line.indexOf("=");
       out_data_file_name=line.substring(tmp+1,line.length());
       }
      }
    in.close();
    return 1;
```

```
     }catch(Exception e){
     System.out.println("read flga filename from config file error:"
                                 +e.toString());
     return -1;
     }
   }

    /* Main program */

    public static void main(String args[])  {
        try  {
            String addressfile="stockaddressfile";
            String groupname="flga";
            flga server = new flga(addressfile,groupname);
            server.startAgent();
        } catch (Exception e)  {
            System.out.println(e.toString());
            System.exit(0);
        }
    }
}
```

J. Source Codes for Interest Prediction Agent Based on Neural Networks (Ffin)

```
import java.io.*;
import java.util.*;
import java.lang.*;
import java.awt.event.*;
import Abstract.*;
import KQMLLayer.*;
import RouterLayer.AgentClient.*;

public class ffin extends HHRouterClientAction {

 String in_wts_file_name,test_file_name;
 public ffin()  {
  super();
  }
 public ffin(Address myaddress,
             Address routeraddress,
             Address registraraddress,
             int durationtime,
             boolean regrequest ){
 // use RouterLayer.AgentClient.RouterClientAction constructor
   super(myaddress,routeraddress,registraraddress,durationtime,regrequest);
    }
 public ffin(String cfgfname,String gname){
  super(cfgfname,gname);
  }
 public boolean Act(Object o)  {
  try  {
   if(!superAct(o)) return false;
   if(perf.equals("task")){
    if(content.equals("train")){
     sovffin.train();
     _returnString="(train over)";
     }else
      if(content.equals("(createtrainfile)")){
       sovffin.createtrainfile();
       _returnString="(train file created!)";
       }else{
  //send result back to the receiver
  double irate=sovffin.getirate();
   _returnString="("+irate+")";
   }
   sendResult();
   }else if(perf.equals("replyregister")){
        System.out.println(getName()+" register:"+content);
        if(!content.equals("success")){
        return false;
        }
   }else if(perf.equals("data")){
     if((in_wts_file_name==null)||(test_file_name==null))
                    getfilename("ffin.cfg");
```

```
    String datatype=kqml.getValue("datatype");
    String tmp=content.substring(1,content.length()-1);
    int rcode=0;
    if(datatype.equals("in_wts_file_name"))
       rcode=writetofile(in_wts_file_name,tmp);
    else
     if(datatype.equals("test_file_name"))
       rcode=writetofile(test_file_name,tmp);
    if(rcode==1)
      _returnString="(Write to file successfully.)";
    else if(rcode==-1)
      _returnString="(write to file failed!)";
    else
      _returnString="(bad datatype,data not write!)";
      System.out.println("send result to :"+tasksender);
      sendResult();
    }else if(perf.equals("error")){
      sendErrorMessage(content);

    }
  else{
   sendErrorMessage("invalid performtiv:"+perf);
   return false;
   }
  } catch (Exception e)  {
     sendErrorMessage("error:"+e.toString());
     return false;
     }
     return true;
}
protected int getfilename(String configfile){
 try{
  BufferedReader in = new BufferedReader
                      (new FileReader(new File(configfile)));
  while(true)  {
   String line = in.readLine();
   if(line == null)  break;
   if(line.startsWith("in_wts_file_name")){
     int tmp=line.indexOf("=");
     in_wts_file_name=line.substring(tmp+1,line.length());
   }else
     if(line.startsWith("test_file_name")){
      int tmp=line.indexOf("=");
      test_file_name=line.substring(tmp+1,line.length());
       }
      }
     in.close();
     return 1;
    }catch(Exception e){
     System.out.println("read flga filename from config file error:"
              +e.toString());
     return -1;
       }
    }
```

```
    /*Main program*/
    public static void main(String args[])  {
        try  {
            String addressfile="stockaddressfile";
            String groupname="ffin";
            ffin server = new ffin(addressfile,groupname);
            server.startAgent();
        } catch (Exception e)  {
            System.out.println(e.toString());
            System.exit(0);
        }
    }
}
```

References

1. M. Wooldridge, Agent-Based Software Engineering, *IEE Proc. Software Engineering*, Vol. 144, No. 1, 1997, 26-37.
2. N. R. Jennings, On Agent-Based Software Engineering, *Artificial Intelligence*, Vol. 117, 2000, 277-296.
3. S. Russell and P. Norvig, *A Modern Approach to Artificial Intelligence*, Prentice-Hall, 1995.
4. M. Wooldridge, *An Introduction to Multiagent Systems*, John Wiley & Sons, Chichester, 2002.
5. K. Sycara, K. Decker and D. Zeng, Intelligent Agents in Portfolio Management, in: N. R. Jennings and M. J. Wooldridge (Eds.), *Agent Technology: Foundations, Applications, and Markets,* Springer, Berlin, 1998, 267-281.
6. S. Franklin and A. Graesser, Is It an Agent, or Just a Program? in: J. P. Mueller, M. Wooldridge, and N. R. Jennings (Eds.), *Intelligent Agents III*, Springer, Berlin, 1997, 21-36.
7. M. Wooldridge and N. R. Jennings, Intelligent Agents: Theory and Practice, *Knowledge Engineering Review*, Vol. 10, No. 2, 1995, 115-152.
8. N. R. Jennings, K. Sycara, and M. Wooldridge, A Roadmap of Agent Research and Development, *Autonomous Agents and Multi-Agent Systems*, Vol. 1, 1998, 7-38.
9. M. Luck, P. McBurney, and C. Preist, Agent Technology: Enabling Next Generation Computing–A Roadmap for Agent Based Computing, *AgentLink*, 2003.
10. G. Weiss (Ed.), *Multiagent Systems: A Modern Approach to Distributed Artificial Intelligence*, MIT Press, 1999.
11. N. R. Jennings and M. J. Wooldridge (Eds.), *Agent Technology: Foundations, Applications, and Markets,* Springer, Berlin, 1998.
12. L. A. Zadeh, The Roles of Fuzzy Logic and Soft Computing in the Conception, Design and Deployment of Intelligent Systems, in: H. S. Nwana and N. Azarmi (Eds.), *Software Agents and Soft Computing: Concepts and Applications*, LNAI 1198, Springer-Verlag, Berlin, 1997, 183-190.
13. L. A. Zadeh, Foreword, in:L. R. Medsker, *Hybrid Intelligent Systems*, Kluwer Academic Publisher, 1995.

Z. Zhang, C. Zhang: Agent-Based Hybrid Intelligent Systems, LNAI 2938, pp. 183–191, 2004.

14. K. Sycara, K. Decker, A. Pannu, M. Williamson, and D. Zeng, Distributed Intelligent Agents, *IEEE Expert*, Vol. 11, No. 6, 1996, 36-46.
15. K. Sycara and D. Zeng, Multi-Agent Integration of Information Gathering and Decision Support, *Proceedings of 12th European Conference on Artificial Intelligence*, John Wiley & Sons, 1996, 549-553.
16. E. H. Durfee and V. Lesser, Negotiating Task Decomposition and Allocation Using Partial Global Planning, in: L. Gasser and M. Huhns (Eds.), *Distributed Artificial Intelligence Volume II*, Pitman Publishing and Morgan Kaufmann, 1989, 229-244.
17. M. N. Huhns and M. P. Singh (Eds.), *Readings in Agents*, Morgan Kaufmann, CA, 1998.
18. K. Decker, K. Sycara, and D. Zeng, Designing a Multi-Agent Portfolio Management System, October 1995, *http://www.cs.cmu.edu/~softagents/publications.html.*
19. D. Martin, A. Cheyer, and D. Moran, The Open Agent Architecture: A Framework for Building Distributed Software Systems, *Applied Artificial Intelligence*, Vol. 13, Nos. 1-2, 1999, 92-128.
20. A. Cheyer and D. Martin, The Open Agent Architecture, *Autonomous Agents and Multi-Agent Systems*, Vol. 4, Nos. 1-2, 2001, 143-148.
21. V. Subrahmanian, P. Bonatti, J. Dix, et al., *Heterogeneous Agent Systems*, MIT Press, 2000.
22. R. J. Bayardo, W. Bohrer, R. Brice et al., InfoSleuth: Agent-Based Semantic Integration of Information in Open and Dynamic Environments, in: M. N. Huhns and M. P. Singh (Eds.), *Readings in Agents*, Morgan Kaufmann, CA, 1998, 205-216.
23. B. Perry, S. K. Chang et al., *Content-Based Access to Multimedia Information–From Technology Trends to State of the Art*, Kluwer Academic Publishers, 1999.
24. K. Krishna and V. C. Ramesh, From Wall Street to Main Street: Reaching out to Small Investors, *Proceedings of the 32nd Annual Hawaii International Conference on System Sciences*, IEEE Computer Society Press, 1999.
25. J. Yen, A. Chung, et al., Collaborative and Scalable Financial Analysis with Multi-Agent Technology, *Proceedings of the 32nd Annual Hawaii International Conference on System Sciences*, IEEE Computer Society Press, 1999.
26. C. Zhang, Z. Zhang and Y. Li, Multi-Agent Based Financial Investment Adviser: Design and Implementation, *Proceedings of International ICSC Symposium of Multi-Agents and Mobile Agents*, Wollongong, Australia, 2000, 33-43.
27. S. K. Chang and E. Jungert, *Symbolic Projection for Image Information Retrieval and Spatial Reasoning*, Academic Press, 1996.
28. C. Zhang, Z. Zhang and S. Ong, An Agent-Based Soft Computing Society, *Proceedings of 2nd International Conference on Rough Sets and Current Trends in Computing*, Banff, Canada, 2000, 621-628.
29. Z. Zhang and C. Zhang, Approaches to Incorporating Soft Computing Technologies into Software Agents, *Proceedings of 6th International Conference on Neural Information Processing*, IEEE Press, NJ, 1999, 952-957.

30. Z. Zhang, C. Zhang, and S. Ong, Building an Ontology for Financial Investment, *Proceedings of 2nd International Conference on Data Engineering and Automated Learning*, LNCS 1983, Springer, 2000, 308-313.
31. Z. Zhang and C. Zhang, Agent-Oriented Approaches to Constructing Hybrid Intelligent Systems, *Proceedings of 7th International Conference on Neural Information Processing*, Vol. 1, Taejon, Korea, 2000, 258-263.
32. Z. Zhang and C. Zhang, Decision Aggregation in Multi-Agent Systems, *Proceedings of International Conference on Advances in Intelligent Systems: Theory and Applications*, IOS Press, The Netherlands, 2000, 185-190.
33. Z. Zhang and C. Zhang, Result Fusion in Multi-Agent Systems Based on OWA Operator, *Proceedings of 23rd Australasian Computer Science Conference*, IEEE Computer Society Press, NJ, 2000, 234-240.
34. C. Zhang and Z. Zhang, Approaches to Implementing Decision Aggregation in Multi-Agent Systems, *Proceedings of ISCA 11th International Conference on Computers and Their Applications*, Seattle, USA, 2001, 314-317.
35. M. Knapik and J. Johnson, *Developing Intelligent Agents for Distributed Systems*, McGraw-Hill, New York, 1998.
36. M. V. Stuckelberg, Redesigning the MIX Multiagent Platform with Threads, *Technical Report UNIGE-AI-95-08*, CUI, University of Geneva, Switzerland, 1995.
37. M. Hilario, C. Pellegrini, and F. Alexandre, Modular Integration of Connectionist and Symbolic Processing in Knowledge-based Systems, in: *Int. Symposium on Integrating Knowledge and Neural Heuristics*, Pensacola, Florida, 1994, 123-132.
38. A. Scherer and G. Schlageter, A Multi-Agent Approach for the Integration of Neural Networks and Expert Systems, in: S. Goonatilake and S. Khebbal (Eds.), *Intelligent Hybrid Systems,* Wiley, 1995, 153-173.
39. R. Khosla and T. Dillon, *Engineering Intelligent Hybrid Multi-Agent Systems*, Kluwer Academic Publishers, Boston, 1997.
40. M. Delgado, A. F. Gómez-Skarmeta et al., A Multi-Agent Architecture for Fuzzy Modeling, *International Journal of Intelligent Systems*, Vol. 14, 1999, 305-329.
41. K. Decker, K. Sycara, and M. Williamson, Middle Agents for the Internet, *Proceedings of 15th International Joint Conference on Artificial Intelligence*, Nogoya, Japan, 1997, 578-583.
42. M. R. Genesereth and S. P. Ketchpel, Software Agents, *Communications of ACM*, Vol.37, No.7, 1994, 48-53.
43. K. Sycara, In-Context Information Management through Adaptive Collaboration of Intelligent Agents, in: M. Klusch (Ed.), *Intelligent Information Agents–Agent-Based Information Discovery and Management on the Internet*, Springer-Verlag, Berlin, 1999, 78-99.
44. Y. Labrou, T. Finin, and Y. Peng, Agent Communication Languages: The Current Landscape, *IEEE Intelligent Systems*, March/April 1999, 45-52.
45. FIPA, Agent Communication Language, *http://www.fipa.org/spec/f8a22.zip*.

46. T. Finin, Y. Labrou and J. Mayfield, KQML as an Agent Communication Language, in: J. M. Bradshaw (Ed.), *Software Agents*, AAAI Press/ The MIT Press, Menlo Park, CA, 1997, 291-316.
47. G. Bojadziev and M. Bojadziev, *Fuzzy Logic For Business, Finance, and Management*, World Scientific, Singapore, 1997.
48. L. A. Zadeh, A Theory of Approximate Reasoning, *Machine Intelligence 9*, Wiley, New York, 1979, 149-194.
49. Stephen T. Welstead, *Neural Network and Fuzzy Logic Applications in C/C++*, Wiley, New York, 1994, 395-421.
50. R. Gordon, *Essential JNI: Java Native Interface*, Prentice-Hall, New Jersey, 1998.
51. D. Beal, W. McKeown, *Personal Finance*, John Wiley & Sons Australia, 2000.
52. A. Newell, The Knowledge Level, *Artificial Intelligence*, Vol. 18, 1982, 87-127.
53. K. Arisha, F. Ozcan, R. Ross et al., Impact: A Platform for Collaborating Agents, *IEEE Intelligent Systems and Their Applications*, Vol. 14, No. 2, 1999, 64-72.
54. B. Chandrasekaran, J. R. Josephson, and V. R. Benjamins, What Are Ontologies, and Why Do We Need Them? *IEEE Intelligent Systems and Their Applications*, Vol. 14, No. 1, 1999, 20-26.
55. W. Swartout and A. Tate, Ontologies, *IEEE Intelligent Systems and Their Applications*, Vol. 14, No. 1, 1999, 18-19.
56. D. S. Weld (Ed.), The Role of Intelligent Systems in National Information Infrastructure, The American Association for Artificial Intelligence, *http://www.aaai.org/Resources/Policy/nii.html*, 47-50.
57. S. Trausan-Matu, Web Page Generation Facilitating Conceptualization and Immersion for Learning Finance Terminology, *http://rilw.emp.paed.uni-muenchen.de/99/papers/Trausan.html*, 1999.
58. D. Lenat and R. Guha, *Building Large Knowledge-Based Systems: Representation and Inference in the CYC Project*, Addison-Wesley, 1990.
59. C. Fellbaum, *WordNet: An Electronic Lexical Database*, MIT Press, 1998.
60. V. K. Chaudhri, A. Farquhar, R. Fikes, et al., OKBC: A Programmatic Foundation for Knowledge Base Interoperability, *Proc. 15th National Conference on Artificial Intelligence (AAAI'98)*, AAAI Press/MIT Press, 1998, 600-607.
61. R. Fikes and A. Farquhar, Distributed Repositories of Highly Expressive Reusable Ontologies, *IEEE Intelligent Systems and Their Applications*, Vol. 14, No. 2, 1999, 73-79.
62. R. S. Patil, R. E. Fikes, P. F. Patel-Schneider, et al., The DARPA Knowledge Sharing Effort: Progress Report. In: C. Rich, B. Nebel, and W. Swartout (Eds.), *Principles of Knowledge Representation and Reasoning: Proceedings of the Third International Conference*, Morgan Kaufmann, 1992. Also available online: *http://www-ksl.stanford.edu/knowledge-sharing/papers/index.html*.
63. D. W. Karolak, *Software Engineering Risk Management*, IEEE Computer Society Press, 1996, 43-51.

64. P. Dart, E. Kazmierczak, L. Sterling, et al., Combining Logical Agents with Rapid Prototyping for Engineering Distributed Applications, *Proc. Software Technology and Engineering Practice*, IEEE Computer Society Press, 1999, 40-49.

65. S. Goonatilake and S. Khebbal (Eds.), *Intelligent Hybrid Systems,* Wiley, 1995.

66. L. R. Medsker, *Hybrid Intelligent Systems*, Kluwer Academic Publisher, 1995.

67. L. C. Jain and R. K. Jain (Eds.), *Hybrid Intelligent Engineering Systems*, World Scientific, Singapore, 1997.

68. N. Lertpalangsunti and C. W. Chan, An Architecture Framework for the Construction of Hybrid Intelligent Forecasting Systems: Application for Electricity Demand Prediction, *Engineering Applications of Artificial Intelligence*, Vol. 11, No. 4, 1998, 549-565.

69. S. Li, The Development of a Hybrid Intelligent Systems for Developing Marketing Strategy, *Decision Support Systems*, Vol. 27, No. 4, 2000, 395-409.

70. N. Jennings and M. Wooldridge, Agent-Oriented Software Engineering, in: J. Bradshaw (Ed.), *Handbook of Agent Technology*, AAAI/MIT Press, 2001.

71. N. Jennings, An Agent-Based Approach for Building Complex Software Systems, *Communications of the ACM*, Vol. 44, No. 4, 2001, 35-41.

72. K. Sycara, M. Paolucci, M. van Velsen, and J. Giampapa, The RETSINA MAS Infrastructure, *Technical Report: CMU-RI-TR-01-05*, Robotics Institute, Carnegie Mellon University, March 2001.

73. N. Jennings, Agent-Based Computing: Promise and Perils, *Proceedings of 16th International Joint Conference on Artificial Intelligence*, AAAI Press, 1999, 1429-1436.

74. N. Jennings, Agent-Oriented Software Engineering, *Proceedings of 12th International Conference on Industrial and Engineering Applications of Artificial Intelligence*, Cairo, Egypt, 1999, 4-10.

75. F. Zambonelli, N. Jennings, A. Omicini, and M. Wooldridge, Agent-Oriented Software Engineering for Internet Applications, in: A. Omicini, F. Zambonelli, M. Klusch, and R. Tolksdorf (Eds.), *Coordination of Internet Agents: Models, Technologies and Applications*, Springer, 2001, 326-346.

76. C. Iglesias, M. Garijo, and J. Gonzales, A Survey of Agent-Oriented Methodologies, in: A. Rao, J. Muller, and M. Singh (Eds.), *Intelligent Agents IV (ATAL'98)*, LNAI, Springer, 1999, 317-330.

77. H. Parunak, Visualizing Agent Conversations: Using Enhanced Dooley Graphs for Agent Design and Analysis, *Proceedings of 2nd International Conference on Multi-Agent Systems (ICMAS'96)*, 1996, 275-282.

78. F. Brazier, B. Dunin-Keplicz, N. Jennings, and J. Treur, Formal Specifications of Multi-Agent Systems: a Real-World Case, *Proceedings of 1st International Conference on Multi-Agent Systems (ICMAS'95)*, 1995, 25-32.

79. M. Fox, An Organizational View of Distributed Systems, *IEEE Transactions on Systems, Man, and Cybernetics*, Vol. 11, No. 1, 1981, 70-80.

80. M. Wooldrige, N. Jennings, and D. Kinny, A Methodology for Agent-Oriented Analysis and Design, *Proceedings of 3rd International Conference on Autonomous Agents*, Seattle, WA, 1999, 69-76.

81. M. Wooldrige, N. Jennings, and D. Kinny, The Gaia Methodology for Agent-Oriented Analysis and Design, *Journal of Autonomous Agents and Multi-Agent Systems*, Vol. 3, No. 3, 2000, 285-312.
82. H. Simon, Decision Making and Problem Solving, in: *Research Briefings 1986: Report of the Research Briefing Panel on Decision Making and Problem Solving*, National Academy Press, 1986. Available online: *http://www.dieoff.org/page163.html.*
83. C. Iglesias, J. Gonzales, and J. Velasco, MIX: A General Purpose Multiagent Architecture, in: M. Wooldridge, J. Muller, and M. Tambe (Eds.), *Intelligent Agents II (ATAL'95)*, LNCS 1037, Springer, 1996, 251-266.
84. H. Simon, *The Sciences of the Artificial*, MIT Press, 1996.
85. G. Booch, *Object-Oriented Analysis and Design with Applications*, Addison Wesley, 1994.
86. M. Wooldridge and P. Ciancarini, Agent-Oriented Software Engineering: The State of the Art, in: P. Ciancarini and M. Wooldridge (Eds.), *Agent-Oriented Software Engineering*, Springer, LNAI 1957, January 2001. Available online: *http://www.csc.liv.ac.uk/~mjw/pubs/.*
87. F. Zambonelli, N. Jennings, and M. Wooldridge, Organizational Abstractions for the Analysis and Design of Multi-Agent Systems, in: P. Ciancarini and M. Wooldridge (Eds.), *Agent-Oriented Software Engineering*, Springer, LNAI 1957, January 2001. Available online: *http://www.csc.liv.ac.uk/~mjw/pubs/.*
88. A. Tveit, A Survey of Agent-Oriented Software Engineering, Available online: *http://www.jfipa.org/publications/AgentOrientedSoftware Engineering.*
89. S. DeLoach, Systems Engineering: A Methodology and Language for Designing Agent Systems, *Proceedings of Agent Oriented Information Systems*, 1999, 45-57.
90. D. Kinny and M. Georgeff, A Methodology and Modeling Technique for Systems of BDI Agents, *Workshop on Modeling Autonomous Agents in a Multi-Agent World, LNAI 1038*, Springer, 1996, 56-71.
91. J. Durkin, *Expert Systems: Design and Development*, Pretice-Hall, 1994.
92. J. P. Bigus and J. Bigus, *Constructing Intelligent Agents with Java – A Programmer's Guide to Smarter Applications*, John Wiley & Sons, 1998.
93. S. Goonatilake, J. Campbell, and N. Ahmad, Genetic-Fuzzy Systems for Financial Decision Making, in: T. Furuhashi (Ed.), *Advances in Fuzzy Logic, Neural Networks and Genetic Algorithms, LNAI 1011*, Springer, 1995, 202-223.
94. Z. Zhang and C. Zhang, Considering Agents' Track Records in Matchmaking of Middle Agents, *Proceedings of 4th Pacific Rim International Workshop on Multi-Agents*, Taipei, 2001, 281-292.
95. G. Klir and B. Yuan, *Fuzzy Sets and Fuzzy Logic: Theory and Applications*, Prentice-Hall, 1995.
96. B. Bouchon-Meunier (Ed.), *Aggregation and Fusion of Imperfect Information*, Studies in Fuzziness and Soft Computing, Vol. 12, Physical-Verlag, 1998.
97. R. Yager and D. Filev, *Essentials of Fuzzy Modeling and Control*, John Wiley & Sons, 1994.

98. B. B. Meunier, R. R. Yager, and L. A. Zadeh (Eds.), *Information, Uncertainty, and Fusion*, Kluwer Academic Publisher, 1999.

99. R. R. Yager, On Ordered Weighted Averaging Aggregation Operators in Multi-Criteria Decision Making, *IEEE Transactions on Systems, Man, Cybernetics*, Vol. 18, Jan/Feb, 1988, 183-190.

100. R. R. Yager, New Models of OWA Information Fusion, *Int. J. of Intelligent Systems*, Vol. 13, 1998, 661-681.

101. R. R. Yager and J. Kacprzyk (Eds.), *The Ordered Weighted Averaging Operators: Theory and Applications*, Kluwer Academic, 1997.

102. R. R. Yager and M. T. Lamata, Decision Making Under Uncertainty with Nonnumeric Payoffs, in: R. Ribeiro, H.-J. Zimmermann, R. R. Yager, and J. Kacprzyk (Eds.), *Soft Computing in Financial Engineering*, Physical-Verlag, 1999, 21-38.

103. M. Klusch (Ed.), *Intelligent Information Agents: Agent-Based Information Discovery and Management on the Internet*, Springer, Berlin, 1999, 351-445.

104. H. Markowitz, *Portfolio Selection: Efficient Diversification of Investments (2nd ed.)*, Blackwell, 1991.

105. H. Tanaka, P. Guo, and I. Turksen, Portfolio Selection Based on Fuzzy Probabilities and Possibility Distributions, *Fuzzy Sets and Systems*, Vol. 111, 2000, 387-397.

106. H. Tanaka and P. Guo, Portfolio Selection Based on Possibility Theory, in: R. A. Ribeiro, H. -J. Zimmermann, R. R. Yager, and J. Kacprzyk (Eds.), *Soft Computing in Financial Engineering*, Physical-Verlag, 1999, 159-185.

107. W. Brenner, R. Zarnekow, and H. Wittig, *Intelligent Software Agents: Foundations and Applications*, Springer, 1998.

108. R. G. Smith, The Contract Net Protocol: High-Level Communication and Control an a Distributed Problem Solver, *IEEE Transactions on Computers*, Vol. 29, No. 12 , 1980, 1104-1113.

109. H. C. Wong and K. Sycara, A Taxonomy of Middle Agents for the Internet, *Proceedings of 4th International Conference on MultiAgent Systems*, IEEE Computer Society Press, 2000, 465-466.

110. K. Sycara, M. Klusch, and S. Widoff, Dynamic Service Matchmaking Among Agents in Open Information Environments, *SIGMOD Record*, Vol. 28, No. 1, 1999, 47-53.

111. D. Kuokka and L. Harada, Matchmaking for Information Agents, *Proceedings of 14th International Joint Conference on Artificial Intelligence*, 1995, 672-678.

112. N. Singh, A Common Lisp API and Facilitator for ABSI: Version 2.0.3, *Technical Report Logic-93-4*, Logic Group, Computer Science Department, Stanford University, 1993.

113. M. Paolucci, Z. Niu, K. Sycara et al., Matchmaking to Support Intelligent Agents for Portfolio Management, *Proceedings of AAAI'2000* (Demo Session), *http://www.cs.cmu.edu/~softagents/publications.html.*

114. K. Sycara, J. Lu, M. Klusch, and S. Widoff, Matchmaking Among Heterogeneous Agents on the Internet, *Proceedings of AAAI Spring Symposium on Intelligent Agents in Cyberspace*, Stanford, USA, 1999, *http://www.cs.cmu.edu/~softagents/publications.html.*

115. G. J. Wickler, *Using Expressive and Flexible Action Representations to Reason about Capabilities for Intelligent Agent Cooperation*, PhD thesis, University of Edinburgh, 1999.

116. M. Klusch and K. Sycara, Brokering and Matchmaking for Coordination of Agent Societies: A Survey, in: A. Omicini, F. Zambonelli, M. Klusch, and R. Tolksdorf (Eds.), *Coordination of Internet Agents: Models, Technologies and Applications*, Springer, 2001, Chap. 8.

117. E. Peter, *Chaos and Order in the Capital Markets*, John Wiley & Sons, Inc., 1991.

118. F. Hoppner, F. Klawonn, R. Kruse, and T. Runkler, *Fuzzy Cluster Analysis*, John Wiley & Sons, 1999.

119. F. Hoppner, Fuzzy Clustering Algorithms – A Tool Library, Open Source Project, *http://www.fuzzy-clustering.de.*

120. C. Larman, *Applying UML and Patterns – An Introduction to Object-Oriented Analysis and Design*, Prentice Hall, Inc., 1998.

121. H.-A. Jacobsen, A Generic Architecture for Hybrid Intelligent Systems, in: T. Furuhashi et al. (Eds.), *Deep Fusion of Computational and Symbolic Processing*, Physica-Verlag, 2001, 145-173.

122. S. Goonatilake, Intelligent Hybrid Systems for Financial Decision Making, *Proceedings of ACM Symposium on Applied Computing*, Nashville, TN, USA, 1995, 471-476.

123. V. Pandey, W. Ng, and E. Lim, Financial Advisor Agent in a Multi-Agent Financial Trading System, *Proceedings of 11th International Workshop on Database and Expert System Applications*, 2000, 482-486.

124. Australian Stock Exchange, *Stock Exchange Financial and Profitability Study*, Sydney Stock Exchange, 1986-1996.

125. BRW Business Library, *The Share Investor's Handbook*, Information Australia, 1998 and 1999.

126. Z. Zhang, *An Agent-Based Hybrid Framework for Decision-Making on Complex Problems*, PhD Thesis, Deakin University, Australia, 2001.

127. N. R. Jennings et al., Using ARCHON to Develop Real-World DAI Applications for Electricity Transportation Management and Particle Acceleration Control, *IEEE Expert*, Vol. 11, No. 6, 60-88, 1996.

128. K. Cios, W. Pedrycz, and R. Swiniarski, *Data Mining Methods for Knowledge Discovery*, Kluwer Academic Publishers, 1998.

129. I. Witten and E. Frank, *Data Mining: Practical Machine Learning Tools and Techniques with Java Implementations*, Morgan Kaufmann, 2000.

130. H. Kargupta, B. Stafford, and I. Hamzaoglu, Web Based Parallel/Distributed Medical Data Mining Using Software Agents, *Proceedings of 1997 Fall Symposium*, American Informatics Association, 1997. Available online *http://www.eecs.wsu.edu/~hillol/pubs.html.*

131. H. Kargupta, I. Hamzaoglu, and B. Stafford, Scalable, Distributed Data Mining Using an Agent Based Architecture, *Proceedings of Knowledge Discovery and Data Mining*, AAAI Press, 1997, 211-214.

132. A. Prodromidis, P. Chan, and S. Stolfo, Meta-learning in Distributed Data Mining Systems: Issues and Approaches, in: H. Kargupta and P.Chan (Eds.), *Advances in Distributed and Parallel Knowledge Discovery*, AAAI/MIT Press, 1999.

133. U. Fayyad, G. Piatetsky-Shapiro, and P. Smyth, From Data Mining to Knowledge Discovery: An Overview, in: U. Fayyad, G. Piatetsky-Shapiro, P. Smyth, and R. Uthurusamy (Eds.), *Advances in Knowledge Discovery and Data Mining*, MIT Press, Cambridge, MA, 1996, 1-34.

134. S. Dzeroski, Data Mining in a Nutshell, in: S. Dzeroski and N. Lavrac (Eds.), *Relational Data Mining*, Springer, 2001, 3-27.

135. U. Fayyad, Knowledge Discovery in Databases: An Overview, in: S. Dzeroski and N. Lavrac (Eds.), *Relational Data Mining*, Springer, 2001, 28-47.

136. R. Kerber, B. Livezey, and E. Simoudis, A Hybrid System for Data Mining, in: S. Goonatilake and S. Khebbal (Eds.), *Intelligent Hybrid Systems*, John Wiley & Sons, 1995, 121-142.

137. L. R. Medsker and D. L. Bailey, Models and Guidelines for Integrating Expert Systems and Neural Networks, in: A. Kandel and G. Langholz (Eds.), *Hybrid Architectures for Intelligent Systems*, CRC Press, Boca Raton, 1992, 154-171.

138. M. Hilario, An Overview of Strategies for Neurosymbolic Integration,Chapter 2 of R. Sun and F. Alexandre, Connectionist-Symbolic Integration: From Unified to Hybrid Approaches. Hillsdale, NJ: Lawrence Erlbaum Associates, 1997.

139. L. Padgham and M. Winikoff, Prometheus: A Methodology for Developing Intelligent Agents, in: F. Giunchiglia, J. odell, and G. Weiβ (Eds.), Agent-Oriented Software Engineering III, LNCS 2585, Springer, Berlin, 2003,174-193.

140. M. Hannebauer, *Autonomous Dynamic Reconfiguration in Multi-Agent Systems – Improving the Quality and Efficiency of Collaborative Problem Solving*, Springer, Berlin, 2002.

141. M. Larrain, Testing Chaos and Nonlinearities in T-Bill Rates, *Financial Analysts Journal*, 1991, 51-62.

142. E. Feigenbaum, P. McCorduck, and H. P. Nii, *The Rise of the Expert Company: How Visionary Companies Are Using Artificial Intelligence to Achieve Higher Productivity and Profits*, Times Books, New York, 1988.

143. N. Nilsson, Artificial Intelligence: A New Synthesis, Morgan Kaufmann, San Francisco, 1998.

144. D. Goldberg, *Genetic Algorithms in Search, Optimization, and Machine Learning*, Reading, Mass., Addison-Wesley, 1989.

145. M. H. Dunham, *Data Mining: Introductory and Advanced Topics*, Pearson Education, New Jersey, 2003.

Index

A-Match 68
ABSI 67
abstract model 146
ACL 34
acquaintance model 47
activation function 18
agent 94, 127
agent capability description language 68
agent communication language 34
agent instances 53
agent melting 147
agent model 47, 53, 108
agent splitting 147
agent technology 23, 28, 29
agent type tree 53
agent types 53
Agent-Based Software Interoperability 67
agent-based system 115
agent-based systems 3, 9, 11, 43, 45, 47, 145
agent-oriented approach 8–10
agent-oriented methodologies 43, 46, 55
agent-oriented systems 11
agents 3–5, 7–9, 29–31, 57, 58
alternating optimization 81
ambient Intelligence 30
appletviewer 115
approximate reasoning 16, 22, 95
artificial neural networks 16
asset allocation model 93, 95
autonomous dynamic reconfiguration 147
average vector 97

backward chaining 14
Bayesian classification 129
benchmark problems 74, 75, 79, 83
benchmark results 74, 85
benchmark values 74–76, 80
bioinformatics 30
blackboard 36, 67
broker 65, 67

C4.5 129
C5.0 129
capability description 65
capability description language 68
capability retrieval 65, 66
capability subsumption 68
CART 129
case-based reasoning 13, 22
CDL 68
characteristic function 16
chromosome 19, 20
chromosomes 19
classification problem 128
classifier systems 22
client/server architecture 127
cluster analysis 81
clustering problem 130
clusters 130
COINS 67
common-sense reasoning 16
complex problem

decision making 3
problem solving 3
complex problems 3, 5, 11
computational biology 30
contract net 66
coordination model 47
coordination-oriented methodology 45, 46
covariance matrix 97
crossover 19, 20
CYC 60

data mining 93, 127
association rules 128, 131
classification 128
clustering 128
decision aggregation agent 111
decision making agent 59, 60, 111
decision making agents 101
defuzzification 103
degree of satisfaction 73
DT 129

electronic business 30
entropy 102
Euclidean distance 75, 85
evolutionary computing 19
expert system 93
expert systems 3, 13, 14, 21–23, 33
ARCHON 33
MYCIN 33

facilitator 38, 67
FAM 16
federated systems 67
financial investment planning 3, 60, 93, 94, 100, 104, 145
financial risk tolerance model 93, 95
find_nn 69, 70, 75, 85
fitness function 20
forward chaining 14
frequent itemset 132
function-replacing hybrids 26
fuzzy associative memory 16
fuzzy average vector 98
fuzzy cluster analysis 81
fuzzy clustering algorithm 130
fuzzy clustering algorithms 81
fuzzy logic 3–5, 13, 14, 16, 21, 22, 35, 93, 99, 146
fuzzy set 16
fuzzy sets 16, 22
fuzzy systems 13

Gaia 44, 45, 49
Gaia methodology 44, 46, 47, 55
genes 19
genetic algorithms 3–5, 13, 14, 19–22, 35, 99, 146
grid computing 30

hard computing 14, 21
Horn clauses 67
hybrid intelligent system 104
hybrid intelligent systems 3–7, 9–11, 13, 14, 23, 27–30, 33–35, 38, 43, 46, 47, 55, 57, 58, 60, 64, 145, 146
loosely-coupled model 25
stand-alone model 24
tightly-coupled model 25
transformational model 24

I3 61
ID3 129
IMAHDA 37
IMPACT 69
inference engine 14
information gathering agents 100
InfoSleuth 67
initial value generation 74, 75
intelligent agents 8, 29, 30, 37
intelligent technique agents 112, 146
intelligent techniques 3–6, 35, 38, 39, 146
inter-communicating hybrids 26
interaction model 47, 51
interest rate prediction 77
interest rates 94
interface agent 111, 138
Internet Browser 115
investment policy 94
itemset 132

JAM 127
JAT 69
JATLite 69, 112, 115, 139
Java 69
Java Native Interface 34, 115, 140

KIF 67
KMI 113, 139
knowledge acquisition 15, 21, 62
knowledge base 14, 15, 37
knowledge discovery 127
knowledge engineer 14, 15
knowledge engineering 44
Knowledge Interchange Format 67
knowledge model 54, 64
knowledge query and manipulation language 34
knowledge-based systems 14, 44
KQML 34, 67, 74, 112, 113, 115, 139

Larflast project 61
LARKS 68
legacy programs 33, 34
LINDO 94
linguistic variables 16, 95
Linux 146
  RedHat 146
Lisp 63
Loom 61

machine intelligence quotient 5
MASE 45
matchmaker 65, 67
matchmaking 57, 65, 67, 73, 90, 115
matchmaking algorithm 57, 61, 64–67, 69, 73, 85
matchmaking algorithms 69
MatrixLib 94
MAX 67
mean of maximum method 104
membership function 16
meta knowledge 37, 54
middle agent 57–60, 63–66, 74, 90, 111, 115, 139
mining agent 139
MIQ 5
MIX 35
MIX multi-agent platform 35
multi-agent system 74
multi-agent systems 3, 7, 8, 11, 29, 31, 38, 39, 43–45, 47, 54, 55, 60, 64, 66, 100
mutation algorithm 20

native method 34
Nearest Neighbor 61
nearest neighbor 68
nearest neighbors 129
neural networks 3–5, 13, 14, 16, 17, 21–24, 35, 99, 146
  feedback 17
  feedforward 17, 18, 99
non-agent systems 145

object-oriented languages 31
  C++ 31
  Java 31
  Smalltalk 31
OKBC 63
Ontolingua 61–63
ontologies 60, 64, 68, 139
ontology 54, 59, 61, 70, 112, 139
Open Agent Architecture 67
Open Knowledge Base Connectivity 63
ordered weighted averaging 93
organization abstraction 46, 47
organization-oriented methodologies 45
organizational abstractions 45, 55
organizational model 49
  organizational patterns 49
  organizational rules 49
  organizational structure 49
OWA 93, 97, 101, 121

PADMA 127
planning agent 111, 138
polymorphic hybrids 26
population 19, 20, 22
portfolio management 93
portfolio selection 93, 96
  fuzzy probability model 93, 97, 120
  Markowitz's model 93, 97, 120
  possibility distribution model 93, 120
  possibility portfolio selection model 97
post-processing agent 139
PREDICTOR system 36
preprocessing agent 139
Prolog 67
Prometheus methodology 45
protocols 47, 49

QP 98, 99
quadratic programming 98

rand() 88
random variables 97, 98
range search algorithm 72
Recon 127
Retsina 67
risk tolerance 94
role model 47, 49
roles 47

SC agent 119
SC agents 77
SDL 68
self-interested agents 45, 46
Service Description Language 68
service model 47
service provider agent 59, 64, 65, 69, 111
service provider agents 146
service requester agent 59
serving agent 111–113
SHADE 67
share market 60
skill model 53, 95, 108
  services 53
soft computing 3, 5, 14, 21
soft computing agent 59, 60
software agents 8, 43
software risk analysis 75
software risk factors 75, 83
stock market 60, 94

T-bill rates 77
Term Frequency-Inverse Document Frequency 67
TF-IDF 67
track record 65, 73, 90, 130
transducer 33, 34, 58

ubiquitous computing 30
UML 44
Unified Modeling Language 44
Unix 146
  Sun Solaris 146
user agent 111

visualization agent 139

Weka system 140
Windows 2000 146
Windows XP 146
WordNet 59
Wordnet 60
wrapper 33, 34, 58

Yellow Page 38
yellow page 67